Joseph Rawson Lumby, Abraham Cowley

Prose Works

With an Introduction

Joseph Rawson Lumby, Abraham Cowley

Prose Works
With an Introduction

ISBN/EAN: 9783744685733

Printed in Europe, USA, Canada, Australia, Japan

Cover: Foto ©Thomas Meinert / pixelio.de

More available books at **www.hansebooks.com**

𝔓𝔦𝔱𝔱 𝔓𝔯𝔢𝔰𝔰 𝔖𝔢𝔯𝔦𝔢𝔰.

COWLEY'S PROSE WORKS

WITH INTRODUCTION AND NOTES,

BY

THE REV. J. RAWSON LUMBY, D.D.

FELLOW OF ST CATHARINE'S COLLEGE AND
NORRISIAN PROFESSOR OF DIVINITY.

EDITED FOR THE SYNDICS OF THE UNIVERSITY PRESS.

CONTENTS.

BIOGRAPHICAL SKETCH OF COWLEY.

ABRAHAM COWLEY, the son of Thomas Cowley[1], a citizen of London, was born in 1618. The father died before his boy's birth, so that he was brought up by a widowed mother. Of her character he speaks most affectionately in his Essays[2]. He appears to have been tenderly cared for also by his godfather; to whom in the *Sylva*, a collection of the poems of his early years, he writes:

'I'm glad that city to whom I ow'd before
(But ah me! Fate hath crost that willing score:)
A father, gave me a godfather too,
And I'm more glad because it gave me you,
    Whom I may rightly think and term to be
    Of the whole city an epitome[3].'

Cowley's was no eventful life, and it is possible from his writings to make such a notice of him as it is proposed to give largely autobiographical.

He describes in the essay already quoted his shy and retiring manner which led him to steal away from his school-fellows into the fields, with a book for his company. The books of his choice however were not dry schoolbooks, for

---

[1] Dr Johnson, following Wood, says the father was a grocer and that the omission of his name in the register of St Dunstan's parish gives reason to suspect that he was a sectary.

[2] See p. 170.

[3] *Sylva*, p. 46. For convenience of reference all the quotations are made from the collected edition of Cowley's works 1684.

by no persuasions (he says) or encouragements could he be induced to commit to memory the common rules of grammar. Reading and observation however gave him the power of doing the requisite school-exercises to the satisfaction of his teachers. He ascribes his first attraction to poetry to the study of a copy of Spenser's poems which lay in his mother's parlour, unused by her, but a treasure of interest for her young son, who was charmed with the tales of knights and giants and monsters and brave houses scattered all through the *Fairy Queen.*

The study of such literature led to early attempts at verse-writing, and *Piramus and Thisbe*, followed by *Constantia and Philetus*, attest the mental food on which Cowley had been reared. The latter of these youthful productions was dedicated to the Dean of Westminster, to whom he says 'I hope your nobleness will rather smile at the faults committed by a child than censure them.' The *Piramus and Thisbe* had been inscribed to Mr Lambert Osbolston, then Headmaster of Westminster, where Cowley was being educated, as 'the earliest offering of his grateful pen.'

Cowley retained much regard and many pleasant memories of his school-life, as we can see from a poem on the death of Mr Jordan, who was second Master at Westminster. Of him he says, 'And though he taught but boys, he made them men.' And again,

> 'So true, so faithful and so just as he
> Was nought on earth, but his own memorie.'

During these school-days Cowley produced an English play, with the title 'Love's Riddle, a Pastoral Comedy.' This, on its publication at a later time (1638) he dedicated (for nothing passed in those days without a dedication) 'to the truly worthy and noble, Sir Kenelm Digby, Knight,' and makes allusion in so doing to the learned as well as to the martial fame of Sir Kenelm :

> 'Learning by right of conquest is your own,
> And every liberal art your captive grown.'

At a later period these boyish productions were reprinted,

and in his address 'To the reader' Cowley then says 'I
'should not be angry to see any one burn my Piramus and
'Thisbe, nay I would do it myself, but that I hope a pardon
'may easily be gotten for the errors of ten years of age. My
'Constantia and Philetus confesseth me two years older
'when I writ it.'

In the 3rd edition there were added to the above-named
longer poems a collection of shorter pieces under the title of
Sylva. Among these one is addressed to a former school-
fellow, named Nichols, who had preceded Cowley to the
University, and had sent him an invitation to visit him in
Cambridge. Cowley's reply looks forward to a time when he
would himself come into residence:

> ''Tis my chief wish to live with thee,
> But not till I deserve thy company:
> Till then we'll scorn to let that toy,
> Some forty miles, divide our hearts:
> Write to me and I shall enjoy
> Friendship and wit, thy better parts.'

But in the few notices which we have of Cowley's college
life we find no further mention of Nichols.

It was in 1637 that Cowley entered Trinity College, Cambridge, as a Westminster scholar. He took the oath and was
admitted on the 14th of June in that year. In due course he
became a Fellow of the College, and his admission to a
Minor fellowship is dated Oct. 30th, 1640. There is no
record of his admission as a major Fellow, and it is probable
that in those troublous times he was obliged to leave Cambridge without proceeding to a full degree. In the list of
major Fellows where his name should have appeared, as it
had stood before in the other lists between those of Humphry
Babington and William Croyden, it is absent. Cowley
alludes to the public troubles as the reason why he left Cambridge, in the dedicatory Latin elegy prefixed to his collected works. Addressing his Alma Mater, he writes

> 'Scis bene, scis quae me tempestas publica mundi
> Raptatrix vestro sustulit e gremio.'

And testifies to the love which he had for Cambridge thus :

    ' O mihi jucundum Grantae super omnia nomen !
      O penitus toto corde receptus amor ! '

We have not to wait long after the commencement of his residence before we come upon signs of the poet's literary activity.

On the 2nd of February, 1638, there was performed in Trinity College a Latin Comedy written by Cowley, entitled *Naufragium Joculare*, the scene of which is laid at Dunkirk. Dr Comber, Dean of Carlisle, was then Master of Trinity, and to him the play was dedicated, and in the closing lines of the Latin verses in which it is presented, the writer allows himself to look forward to a fellowship in the future and promises by that time to produce something better.

    ' Collegii nam qui nostri dedit ista scholaris,   .
      Si socius tandem sit, meliora dabit.'

On another occasion also during his residence at Cambridge Cowley's dramatic power was exhibited, but this time in English. In March 164½, Charles Prince of Wales (afterwards Charles II.), being then somewhat less than 12 years of age, visited the University, the king his father also passing through on his way to Huntingdon. For the entertainment of the young prince a play was hastily arranged[1]. This was *The Guardian*, which Cowley afterwards remodelled and published as *Cutter of Coleman Street*. In the prologue, addressed to the prince, the author alludes to the hurried way in which it had been produced.

    ' Accept our hasty zeal; a thing that's play'd
      Ere 'tis a play, and acted ere 'tis made.'

---

[1] In the books of Trinity College among the 'Extraordinaries' for 1642 is the entry 'To Mr Willis for Dr Cooley's Comœdy £65. 16s.' The spelling 'Cooley' occurs more than once in the College books. Cf. 'Cooper' and 'Cowper.' For the particulars in this sketch which are derived from the Trinity College records I am indebted to the kindness of Mr W. Aldis Wright, Fellow and Senior Bursar of the College.

And in the Epilogue, expressing a doubt whether the 'Great Sir' (of eleven years) before whom it had been presented would approve, he says :

'Though it should fall beneath your mortal scorn,
Scarce could it die more quickly than 'twas born.'

A letter is preserved[1] which gives us some notice of this royal entertainment. The writer was Joseph Beaumont, afterwards Master of Peterhouse, and of the play he tells us : 'From the Regenthouse his Highness (Prince Charles) 'went to Trinity College, where after dinner he saw a 'Comedy in English and gave all signs of great acceptance 'which he could, and more than the University dared expect.' The later history of this play is given in the preface which is here reprinted[2] after the Essays.

Of the friends whom Cowley made in Cambridge we do not know much, and perhaps the retiring manner of his boyhood did not leave him when he entered the University. Yet over the death of one Mr William Harvey he has left us a lamentation which, if it be marked by some of those conceits which were deemed essential to poetry in his day, is yet very full of feeling.

'He was my friend, the truest friend on earth,'

he wrote; and again

'Ye fields of Cambridge, our dear Cambridge, say,
Have ye not seen us walking every day?
Was there a tree about which did not know
    The love betwixt us two.
Henceforth, ye gentle trees, for ever fade
    Or your sad branches thicker join
    And into darksome shades combine;
Dark as the grave wherein my friend is laid.'

It was by Mr John Harvey, the brother of this friend, that Cowley was subsequently introduced[3] to Henry Jermyn,

[1] See Cooper's *Annals of Cambridge*, Vol. III. 321.
[2] See pp. 178 seqq.
[3] Wood (*Athen. Oxon.*) says it was Dr Stephen Goffe, a brother of the Oratory, who commended Cowley to Jermyn.

afterwards Baron Jermyn, and subsequently Earl of St Alban's, an introduction which affected the whole future course of Cowley's life.

Another friend made in Cowley's university life was Richard Crashaw, the poet. He was a little senior to Cowley, having been elected from Pembroke Hall to a fellowship at Peterhouse in the year in which Cowley came up. Crashaw during the troublous times was, like Cowley, ejected from his fellowship and subsequently joined the Church of Rome. For some time he lived in Italy as secretary to Cardinal Palotta and was eventually made Canon of the church at Loretto, but soon after died of a fever. Cowley wrote a poem on his death which testifies to the warm attachment that existed between the two and deserves to be ranked among the best of Cowley's verses. In one passage he compares himself to Elisha and his friend to Elijah, and continues,

> 'Lo here I beg (I whom thou once didst prove
> So humble to esteem, so good to love,)
> Not that thy spirit might on me doubled be,
> I ask but half thy mighty spirit for me;
> And when my muse soars with so strong a wing,
> 'Twill learn of things divine, and first of thee to sing.'

The allusion to Crashaw's change of religion is extremely tender and full of charity:

> 'Pardon, my mother Church, if I consent
> That angels led him when from thee he went;
> For even in error sure no danger is
> When joined with so much piety as his.
> His faith perhaps in some nice tenents might
> Be wrong: his life, I'm sure, was in the right,
> And I myself a Catholick will be,
> So far at least, great saint, to pray to thee.'

Concerning other Cambridge friends of Cowley's we have no record. The books of Trinity College shew that he was admitted and sworn as a minor Fellow on the 30th of October, 1640. But though admitted there cannot have been a fellowship vacant for him[1], since in 1642 his name appears still among the Scholars, and similarly in 1643, though in that year he stands first in the list. Early in the next year (Feb. 5, 164¾) came the commission of the Earl of Manchester 'to take special care that the solemn League and Covenant be tendered and taken in the University of Cambridge,' which resulted in almost universal ejection of Masters and Fellows. Cowley, and with him Humphry Babington, was among the ejected members of Trinity College, and if Dr Sprat's statement be correct[2] that he 'was absent from his native country above 12 years,' he must have gone from Cambridge to Oxford at once and begun that attendance on Baron Jermyn[3] which lasted till 1656. It was in 1644 that, after the birth of a daughter at Exeter, queen Henrietta Maria was helped by the vessels of the Prince of Orange to cross from Falmouth into France, and Cowley's service appears to have kept him constantly with the queen, on whom Jermyn was perpetually attendant. In 1648 Clarendon (x. 175) describes the position of Jermyn as her Majesty's chief officer, and it was in this period that Cowley was so largely employed in cyphering and decyphering[4] with his own hand

---

[1] It was allowed at that time, as it now is under the new Statutes, to elect to fellowships even when there was no vacancy, the elected persons undertaking to make no claim till the number of fellows was sufficiently reduced to admit them to a dividend. Thus Babington, Travis, Campian, Culverwell and Burton signed an engagement on March 21, 1641 not to 'claim any profitts of our fellowships till places fall that we come into numbers.'

[2] Wood says about 10 years. He also tells us that on going from Cambridge Cowley settled in St John's College, Oxford. During the year 1643, while resident in Oxford, he published under the name of 'an Oxford Scholar' a satire called 'the Puritan and the Papist,' but this he never included among his acknowledged writings.

[3] Mr Jermyn was made a Baron in 1643. See Clarendon vii. 242.

[4] Clarendon (x. 22) speaks of a letter from the king which was decyphered by the Lord Jermyn, a task probably performed by the poet, who then (1646) had been about two years in Paris.

the letters which passed between their Majesties that for some years together the labour of this correspondence took up all his days and two or three nights every week. These duties continued after the execution of Charles I., and were only brought to an end when Charles II. left the queen in France and departed to the Low Countries. Then apparently in 1656 Cowley returned to England and was presently arrested in mistake for some other person, and only released from custody on the security of Dr Scarborough[1] who was his bail for £1000.

It was during his residence in France that most of those Poems which he entitles 'The Mistress' must have been written, for they were separately published in 1647 and included in the collected poems which he put forth soon after his return to England.

The occasion of that collection is best told in his own words, 'At my return lately into England I met by great 'accident (for such I account it to be that any copy of it 'should be extant anywhere so long, unless at his house 'who printed it) a book intituled 'The Iron Age' and published 'under my name during the time of my absence. I wondered 'very much how one who could be so foolish to write so 'ill verses should yet be so wise to set them forth as another 'man's rather than his own: though perhaps he might 'have made a better choice, and not fathered the bastard 'upon such a person whose stock of reputation is, I fear, 'little enough for maintenance of his own numerous legiti- 'mate offspring of that kind.'

In the preface from which the above is an extract Cowley complains of 'the publication of some things of his without 'his consent or knowledge, and those so mangled and im- 'perfect that he could neither with honour acknowledge nor 'with honesty quite disavow them.' To such treatment his Comedy *The Guardian* had been subjected, and the conduct of others towards his writings is pleaded as the reason for the

---

[1] To the celebration of Dr Scarborough's skill in medicine Cowley devotes one of his 'Pindarique Odes' (p. 35).

appearance of the volume. In this Preface the poet states
that his desire has been for some years past, and does still
vehemently continue, to retire himself to some of the American
plantations, and to bury himself there in some obscure
retreat.

The contents of the volume, in the preface to which
Cowley thus relates a part of his history and intentions, are
(1) 'The Miscellanies,' some of which he says were 'made
'when I was very young, which it is perhaps superfluous to
'tell the reader.' (2) 'The Mistress' or 'Love Verses,' written
because 'so it is that poets are scarce thought free-men of
'their company, without paying some duties, and obliging
'themselves to be true to Love.' Most assuredly, however, it
would be difficult to point to any other verses on the same
subject, with less fire in them. (3) Next follow the 'Pindarique Odes,' of whose versification the poet tells us 'the
'numbers are various and irregular, and sometimes seem
'harsh and uncouth if the just measures and cadencies be
'not observed in the pronunciation. So that almost all their
'sweetness...lies wholly at the mercy of the reader.' In
one of these Odes, Cowley describes the style thus[1] :

   ' 'Tis an unruly and a hard-mouth'd horse,
      Fierce and unbroken yet,
      Impatient of the spur or bit.
   Now praunces stately, and anon flies o'er the place,
   Disdains the servile law of any settled pace,
   Conscious and proud of his own natural force,
      'Twill no unskilful touch endure,
   But flings writer and reader too that sits not sure.'

of which last remark any one will surely find the truth who
tries to read them. The last portion of the volume was
(4) 'The Davideis,' or an heroical poem of the troubles of
David, of which only 4 books, out of 12 which Cowley
designed to write, are completed in English and Latin. The
history is carried down only to 1 Sam. xv. 3. Dr Sprat says

<hr>

[1] 'Pindarique Odes,' p. 22.

that Cowley had finished the greatest part of this poem while he was yet a young student at Cambridge.

Besides the Essays and other Prose pieces here printed, Cowley published (1) a Collection of Verses written on several occasions, which are interesting as throwing light upon his life, and which will be alluded to hereafter, and (2) in Latin, Six Books of Plants. The last-named work was the result of his application to the study of physic, to which he turned his attention when he had come back to England, in order to dissemble the main intention of his coming, which was, as it seems, to be at hand to give notice to the Queen mother and Charles II. of the condition of matters in this country. Accordingly we find Cowley incorporated in the University of Oxford (Dec. 2, 1657) as Doctor of Physic[1]. In that year he had acted as best man to George Villiers, duke of Buckingham, when he was married to the daughter of General Fairfax, and the duke proved himself to the end of Cowley's life to be a firm friend.

After the death of Cromwell[2] Cowley went over to France once more and remained there almost till the Restoration. In 1660 he wrote his 'Ode upon His Majesty's Restauration and Return,' in which he proceeds to most astounding lengths in his flattery of the Royal family. This is the fashion of his strain :

'He who had seen how by the power divine
All the young branches of this royal line
Did in their fire without consuming shine:
How through a rough Red sea they had been led,
By wonders guarded and by wonders fed;
How many years of trouble and distress
They'd wander'd in their fatal wilderness,
And yet did never murmur or repine,

[1] See Wood, *Fasti Oxonienses.* It is said that this degree was granted him because he complied with some of the men in power, and that this submission was much taken notice of by the royal party.

[2] He is said by Wood to have made a copy of verses on Oliver's death, but these are not among his published works.

Might (methinks) plainly understand,
That after all these conquered trials past
The almighty Mercy would at last
Conduct them with a strong unerring hand
To their own promised land.'

Charles and his brothers he compares to the three youths in the furnace of Nebuchadnezzar, and their two sisters to angels who bear them company, and adds, with what sounds to modern ears like gross profanity :

'Less favour to those three of old was shewn,
To solace with their company
The fiery trials of adversity,
Two angels join with these, the others had but one.'

And in like manner addressing the restored king, he says

'Come mighty Charles, desire of nations, come.'

And of the Queen mother :

'Where's now the royal mother, where,
To take her mighty share
In this so ravishing sight
And with the part she takes to add to the delight?
Ah! why art thou not here,
Thou always best and now the happiest queen,
To see our joy and with new joy be seen?'

In this same year, steps had been taken for restoring Cowley to his fellowship at Trinity. In the Admission Book under the date of Febr. 11, 1660, it is entered : "Whereas we received a Letter from his Ma^ty dated the last of January in the behalfe of Mr Abraham Cowley Fellow of Trinity Colledge, for the continuance of his seven years before taking holy Orders, in regard of his being eiected immediately after his taking degree of Master of Ars, in those troublesome Times, we have thought it good to record this in our conclusion book, that it may be considered as a special case, and so his Ma^ty makes it expressly in his Lettres, and not to be drawn hereafter into example.

H. FERNE."

And so Cowley was restored as Dr Cowley, and not required to take orders, though for 1660 he received no dividend. His payments commence in 1661, and for that year and the next he is described as Mr Cowley, afterwards from 1663 to the third quarter of 1667 he is entered as Dr Cowley.   Thus he held his fellowship up to the time of his death.

After his long services to the Royal family Cowley was not unlikely to expect some recognition of a larger kind than the royal letters that he should be restored to his fellowship. The Mastership of the Savoy was said to have been promised to him both by Charles I. and Charles II., but the promise, like so many others from the same lips, was never fulfilled. Cowley felt this neglect, and gave utterance to it in 'The Complaint,' where he pictures himself 'the melancholy Cowley' lying in the shade 'where reverend Cam cuts out his famous way.' Here the muse appears to him and rebukes him for deserting her[1]:

> 'Thou changeling, thou, bewitched with noise and show,
>   Would'st into courts and cities from me go.'

And after further reproaches she taunts him with the foolish gains which are all he has come to for quitting her :

> 'The sovereign is tost at sea no more
>   And thou with all the noble company
>   Art got at last to shore.
>   But whilst thy fellow-voyagers I see
>   All march'd up to possess the promised land,
>   Thou still alone (alas) dost gaping stand
>   Upon the naked beach, upon the barren sand.'

And she compares his case to one of Gideon's miracles, where all around 'with pearly dew was crowned, and nothing but the Muses' fleece was dry.'   His expectations are likened to Rachel, served for with faith and labour for twice seven years and more, but at last given to another.   And the Muse concludes her speech with,

> 'Thou, to whose share so little bread did fall,
>   In the miraculous year when manna rained on all.'

[1] See 'Verses written on several occasions,' p. 28.

Cowley in his reply confesses that he has been wrong in acting only as a demi-votary, and not giving himself wholly to poetry. And then with his usual fondness for Biblical language and similes he adds,

> 'Thus with Sapphira and her husband's fate,
> (A fault which I like them am taught too late,)
> For all that I gave up I nothing gain,
> And perish for the part that I retain.' .

But clearly at this time he had not lost all hope of recompense, for he adds that he ought to be accurst if he were not content to wait on the king's will, when Charles had so cheerfully depended on that of his great Sovereign. And he closes,

> 'Kings have long hands (they say), and though I be
> So distant, they may reach at length to me.'

A hope doomed to disappointment. For Charles was content to discharge his debt by saying after the poet's death, 'Mr Cowley has not left behind him a better man in England.'

It is said that the royal displeasure had been incurred by Cowley's poem on 'Brutus[1].' An attempt had also been made, as will be seen from the preface to *Cutter of Coleman Street*, to turn that comedy into a ground of disfavour, though as the author well observes it would have been the height of folly in one who had clung to the Royal house in adversity to write anything to their offence after the Restoration.

Through the friendship of Lord Jermyn (created by Chas. II. in 1660 Earl of St Alban's) and of the Duke of Buckingham Cowley obtained a favourable lease of some of the queen's lands, and thus was raised above want, and left at liberty to follow his poetic and scientific tastes. To science he gave up much of his time and thought, as will be seen from his Proposal for a College of Natural Philo-

---

[1] See 'Pindarique Odes,' p. 33. The poem begins : 'Excellent Brutus, of all humane race the best,' and such praise of such a character was said to be distasteful to Royalty.

sophy. In 1663, when the Royal Society, founded a few years before, was by charter constituted a body political and corporate under the title of the 'President, Council and Fellows of the Royal Society of London for improving Natural Knowledge,' Dr Cowley appears among its first list of members. At the close of the fifth year of the Society's existence he sings its praises in verse, and compares its early progress to that of the infant Hercules:

> 'None e'er but Hercules and you would be
> At five years age worthy a historie[1].'

In these years of expectation and disappointment Cowley wrote his Essays, in which he displays a naturalness and purity of style far beyond what is found in his poetry. Had his life been spared it is said that he intended to have added to their number, and to have dedicated his work to the Earl of St Alban's. He died, however, in his forty-ninth year, July 28, 1667. After his retirement from public life he had made his home on the banks of the Thames, first at Barn-Elms and afterwards at Chertsey, where the Porch-house, though enlarged and changed in character, is marked with an inscription as Cowley's former home.

He was buried 3rd Aug. 1667 in Westminster Abbey, near Chaucer and Spenser, to whom he attributes his first inspiration. His body had been brought to Wallingford House, near Whitehall, the London residence of the Duke of Buckingham, who in 1675 at his own charges erected and monument to Cowley in Westminster Abbey. An entry in the books of Trinity College, two years after his death, among the 'Extraordinaries,' shews that the poet had retained to the last his affection for his college, though it is not easy to understand why the payment recorded had to be made:

'To Mr Alestry for books given by Dr Cowley to Library, £51.'

[1] 'Verses written on several occasions,' p. 42.

admirable wit and worthy labours of many of the ancients, much less of Aristotle, the most eminent among them; but it were madness to imagine that the cisterns of men should afford us as much, and as wholesome waters, as the fountains of nature. As we under- 5 stand the manners of men by conversation among them, and not by reading romances, the same is our case in the true apprehension and judgement of things. And no man can hope to make himself as rich by stealing out of others trunks, as he might by opening and digging of 10 new mines. If he conceive that all are already exhausted, let him consider that many lazily thought so hundred years ago, and yet nevertheless since that time whole regions of art have been discovered, which the ancients as little dreamt of as they did of America. There is yet 15 many a *terra incognita* behind to exercise our diligence, and let us exercise it never so much, we shall leave work enough too for our posterity.

This therefore being laid down as a certain foundation, that we must not content ourselves with that inheritance 20 of knowledge which is left us by the labour and bounty of our ancestors, but seek to improve those very grounds and adde to them new and greater purchases; it remains to be considered by what means we are most likely to attain the ends of this vertuous covetousness. 25

And certainly the solitary and unactive contemplation of nature, by the most ingenious persons living, in their own private studies, can never effect it. Our reasoning faculty as well as fancy does but dream, when it is not guided by sensible objects. We shall compound where 30 nature has divided, and divide where nature has compounded, and create nothing but either deformed monsters, or at best pretty but impossible mermaids. 'Tis like painting by memory and imagination which can

never produce a picture to the life. Many persons of admirable abilities (if they had been wisely managed and profitably employed) have spent their whole time and diligence in commentating upon Aristotle's philosophy,
5 who could never go beyond him, because their design was only to follow, not grasp, or lay hold on, or so much as touch nature, because they catcht only at the shadow of her in their own brains. And therefore we see that for above a thousand years together nothing almost of
10 ornament or advantage was added to the uses of humane society, except only guns and printing, whereas since the industry of men has ventured to go abroad, out of books and out of themselves, and to work among God's creatures, instead of playing among their own, every age
15 has abounded with excellent inventions, and every year perhaps might do so, if a considerable number of select persons were set apart, and well directed, and plentifully provided for the search of them. But our Universities having been founded in those former times that I com-
20 plain of, it is no wonder if they be defective in their constitution as to this way of learning, which was not then thought on.

For the supplying of which defect it is humbly pro-posed to his sacred Majesty, his most honourable par-
25 liament, and Privy Council, and to all such of his subjects as are willing and able to contribute any thing towards the advancement of real and useful learning, that by their authority, encouragement, patronage and bounty, a philosophical Colledge may be erected, after this ensuing,
30 or some such like model.

The Colledge.

THAT the philosophical colledge be situated within one, two or (at farthest) three miles of London; and, if it be possible to find that convenience, upon the side of the river, or very near it.

That the revenue of this colledge amount to four thou- 5 sand a year. That the company received into it be as follows :

1. Twenty philosophers or professors. 2. Sixteen young scholars, servants to the professors. 3. A chaplain. 4. A baily for the revenue. 5. A manciple or 10 purveyor for the provisions of the house. 6. Two gardeners. 7. A master-cook. 8. An under-cook. 9. A butler. 10. An under-butler. 11. A chirurgeon. 12. Two lungs, or chymical servants. 13. A library-keeper, who is likewise to be apothecary, druggest, and keeper of 15 instruments, engines, &c. 14. An officer, to feed and take care of all beast, fowl, &c. kept by the colledge. 15. A groom of the stable. 16. A messenger, to send up and down for all uses of the colledge. 17. Four old women, to tend the chambers, keep the house clean, and 20 such like services.

That the annual allowance for this company be as follows :

1. To every professor, and to the chaplain, one hundred and twenty pounds. 2. To the sixteen scholars 25 twenty pounds apiece, ten pounds for their diet, and ten pounds for their entertainment. 3. To the baily, thirty pounds, besides allowance for his journeys. 4. To the purveyor, or manciple, thirty pounds. 5. To each of the gardeners, twenty pounds. 6. To the master-cook, twenty 30

pounds. 7. To the under-cook, four pounds. 8. To the butler, ten pounds. 9. To the under-butler, four pounds. 10. To the chirurgeon, thirty pounds. 11. To the library-keeper, thirty pounds. 12. To each of the lungs, 5 twelve pounds. 13. To the keeper of the beasts, six pounds. 14. To the groom, five pounds. 15. To the messenger, twelve pounds. 16. To the four necessary women, ten pounds. For the manciples table at which all the servants of the house are to eat, except the 10 scholars, one hundred sixty pounds. For three horses for the service of the colledge, thirty pounds.

All which amounts to three thousand two hundred eighty-five pounds. So that there remains for keeping of the house and gardens, and operatories, and instru-15 ments and animals, and experiments of all sorts, and all other expençes, seven hundred and fifteen pounds.

Which were a very inconsiderable sum for the great uses to which it is designed, but that I conceive the industry of the colledge will, in a short time, so enrich 20 itself, as to get a far better stock for the advance and inlargement of the work when it is once begun: neither is the continuance of particular men's liberality to be despaired of, when it shall be encouraged by the sight of that publick benefit which will accrue to all mankind, 25 and chiefly to our nation, by this foundation. Something likewise will arise from leases and other casualties; that nothing of which may be diverted to the private gain of the professors, or any other use besides that of the search of nature, and by it the general good of the 30 world, and that care may be taken for the certain performance of all things ordained by the institution, as likewise for the protection and encouragement of the company, it is proposed:

That some person of eminent quality, a lover of solid

learning, and no stranger in it, be chosen chancellor or
president of the colledge; and that eight governors more,
men qualified in the like manner, be joyned with him,
two of which shall yearly be appointed visitors of the
colledge, and receive an exact account of all expences 5
even to the smallest, and of the true estate of their
publick treasure, under the hands and oaths of the professors resident.

That the choice of the professors in any vacancy
belong to the chancellor and the governours; but that the 10
professors (who are likeliest to know what men of the
nation are most proper for the duties of their society)
direct their choice by recommending two or three persons
to them at every election. And 'that, if any learned
person within his majesties dominions discover, or 15
eminently improve, any useful kind of knowledge, he
may upon that ground, for his reward and the encouragement of others, be preferr'd, if he pretend to the place,
before any body else.

That the governours have power to turn out any pro- 20
fessor, who shall be proved to be either scandalous or
unprofitable to the society.

That the colledge be built after this, or some such
manner: That it consist of three fair quadrangular
courts, and three large grounds, inclosed with good walls 25
behind them. That the first court be built with a fair
cloyster: and the professors' lodgings, or rather little
houses, four on each side, at some distance from one
another, and with little gardens behind them, just after
the manner of the Chartreux beyond sea. That the in- 30
side of the cloyster be lined with a gravel-walk, and that
walk with a row of trees; and that in the middle there
be a parterre of flowers, and a fountain.

That the second quadrangle, just behind the first, be

so contrived, as to contain these parts. 1. A chappel. 2.
A hall with two long tables on each side for the scholars
and officers of the house to eat at, and with a pulpit and
forms at the end for the publick lectures. 3. A large
5 and pleasant dining-room within the hall, for the professors to eat in, and to hold their assemblies and conferences. 4. A publick school-house. 5. A library. 6.
A gallery to walk in, adorned with the pictures or statues
of all the inventors of any thing useful to human life;
10 as, printing, guns, America, &c. and of late in anatomy,
the circulation of the blood, the milky veins, and such
like discoveries in any art, with short elogies under the
portraictures: as likewise the figures of all sorts of creatures, and the stuft skins of as many strange animals as
15 can be gotten. 7. An anatomy-chamber, adorned with
skeletons and anatomical pictures, and prepared with
all conveniences for dissection. 8. A chamber for all
manner of druggs, and apothecaries' materials. 9. A
mathematical chamber, furnisht with all sorts of mathe-
20 matical instruments, being an appendix to the library.
10. Lodgings for the chaplain, chirurgeon, library-keeper,
and purveyor, near the chappel, anatomy-chamber,
library, and hall.

That the third court be on one side of these, very
25 large, but meanly built, being designed only for use
and not for beauty too, as the others. That it contain
the kitchin, butteries, brew-house, bake-house, dairy,
lardry, stables, &c. and especially great laboratories
for chymical operations, and lodgings for the under-
30 servants.

That behind the second court be placed the garden,
containing all sorts of plants that our soil will bear; and
at the end a little house of pleasure, a lodge for the
gardiner, and a grove of trees cut into walks.

That the second enclosed ground be a garden, destined only to the trial of all manner of experiments concerning plants, as their melioration, acceleration, retardation, conservation, composition, transmutation, coloration, or whatsoever else can be produced by art 5 either for use or curiosity, with a lodge in it for the gardiner.

That the third ground be employed in convenient receptacles for all sorts of creatures which the professors shall judge necessary, for their more exact search into 10 the nature of animals, and the improvement of their uses to us.

That there be likewise built, in some place of the colledge where it may serve most for ornament of the whole, a very high tower for observation of 15 celestial bodies, adorned with all sorts of dyals and such like curiosities; and that there be very deep vaults made under ground, for experiments most proper to such places, which will be undoubtedly very many. 20

Much might be added; but truly I am afraid this is too much already for the charity or generosity of this age to extend to; and we do not design this after the model of Solomon's house in my Lord Bacon (which is a project for experiments that can never be experi- 25 mented), but propose it within such bounds of expence as have often been exceeded by the buildings of private citizens.

OF THE PROFESSORS, SCHOLARS, CHAPLAIN, AND OTHER OFFICERS.

THAT of the twenty professors, four be always travelling beyond the seas, and sixteen always resident, unless by 30 permission upon extraordinary occasions; and every one so absent, leaving a deputy behind him to supply his duties.

That the four professors itinerate be assigned to the
5 four parts of the world, Europe, Asia, Africa, and America, there to reside three years at least; and to give a constant account of all things that belong to the learning, and especially natural experimental philosophy, of those parts

10   That the expense of all dispatches, and all books, simples, animals, stones, metals, minerals, &c. and all curiosities whatsoever, natural or artificial, sent by them to the colledge, shall be defrayed out of the treasury, and an additional allowance (above the £120.)
15 made to them as soon as the colledges revenue shall be improved.

That, at their going abroad, they shall take a solemn oath, never to write any thing to the colledge, but what, after very diligent examination, they shall fully believe
20 to be true, and to confess and recant it as soon as they find themselves in an errour.

That the sixteen professors resident shall be bound to study and teach all sorts of natural experimental philosophy, to consist of the mathematicks, mechanicks,
25 medicine, anatomy, chymistry, the history of animals, plants, minerals, elements, &c. ; agriculture, architecture, art military, navigation, gardening; the mysteries of all trades, and improvement of them; the facture of all merchandises, all natural magick or divination; and
30 briefly all things contained in the catalogue of natural histories annexed to my Lord Bacon's Organon.

That once a day from Easter till Michaelmas, and twice a week from Michaelmas to Easter, in the hours in the afternoon most convenient for auditors from

London, according to the time of the year, there shall be
a lecture read in the hall, upon such parts of natural
experimental philosophy, as the professors shall agree on
among themselves, and as each of them shall be able to
perform usefully and honourably.   5

That two of the professors, by daily, weekly, or
monthly turns, shall teach the publick schools according
to the rules hereafter prescribed.

That all the professors shall be equal in all respects
(except precedency, choice of lodging, and such like 10
priviledges, which shall belong to seniority in the colledge); and that all shall be masters and treasurers by
annual turns, which two officers for the time being shall
take place of all the rest, and shall be *arbitri duarum
mensarum.*   15

That the master shall command all the officers of the
colledge, appoint assemblies or conferences upon occasion, and preside in them with a double voice; and in
his absence, the treasurer, whose business is to receive
and disburss all moneys by the master's order in writing 20
(if it be an extraordinary), after consent of the other
professors.

That all the professors shall sup together in the
parlour within the hall every night, and shall dine there
twice a week (to wit, Sundays and Thursdays) at two 25
round tables, for the convenience of discourse, which
shall be, for the most part, of such matters as may improve their studies and professions; and to keep them
from falling into loose or unprofitable talk, shall be the
duty of the two *arbitri mensarum*, who may likewise 30
command any of the servant-scholars to read to them
what they shall think fit, whilst they are at table: that it
shall belong likewise to the said *arbitri mensarum* only to
invite strangers; which they shall rarely do, unless they

be men of learning or great parts, and shall not invite
above two at a time to one table, nothing being more
vain and unfruitful than numerous meetings of acquaintance.

5   That the professors resident shall allow the colledge
twenty pounds a year for their diet, whether they continue there all the time or not.

That they shall have once a week an assembly, or
conference, concerning the affairs of the colledge and
10 the progress of their experimental philosophy.

That if any one find out any thing which he conceives
to be of consequence, he shall communicate it to the
assembly to be examined, experimented, approved, or
rejected.

15   That, if any one be author of an invention that may
bring in profit, the third part of it shall belong to the
inventor, and the two other to the society; and besides,
if the thing be very considerable, his statue or picture,
with an elogy under it, shall be placed in the gallery,
20 and made a denison of that corporation of famous
men.

That all the professors shall be always assigned to
some particular inquisition (besides the ordinary course
of their studies), of which they shall give an account to
25 the assembly; so that by this means there may be every
day some operation or other made in all the arts,
as chymistry, anatomy, mechanicks, and the like; and
that the colledge shall furnish for the charge of the
operation.

30   That there shall be kept a register under lock and
key, and not to be seen but by the professors, of all the
experiments that succeed, signed by the persons who
made the tryal.

That the popular and received errors in experimental

philosophy (with which, like weeds in a neglected garden,
it is now almost all over-grown) shall be evinced by tryal,
and taken notice of in the publick lectures, that they
may no longer abuse the credulous, and beget new ones
by consequence or similitude.   5

That every third year (after the full settlement of the
foundation) the colledge shall give an account in print, in
proper and ancient Latine, of the fruits of their triennial
industry.

That every professor resident shall have his scholar 10
to wait upon him in his chamber and at table; whom he
shall be obliged to breed up in natural philosophy, and
render an account of his progress to the assembly, from
whose election he received him, and therefore is re-
sponsible to it, both for the care of his education and 15
the just and civil usage of him.

That the scholar shall understand Latine very well,
and be moderately initiated in the Greek, before he be
capable of being chosen into the service; and that he
shall not remain in it above seven years.   20

That his lodging shall be with the professor whom he
serves.

That no professor shall be a married man, or a divine,
or lawyer in practice; only physick he may be allowed to
prescribe, because the study of that art is a great part of 25
the duty of his place, and the duty of that is so great that
it will not suffer him to lose much time in mercenary
practice.

That the professors shall, in the colledge, wear the
habit of ordinary masters of art in the universities, or of 30
doctors, if any of them be so.

That they shall all keep an inviolable and exemplary
friendship with one another; and that the assembly shall
lay a considerable pecuniary mulct upon any one who

shall be proved to have entered so far into a quarrel as
to give uncivil language to his brother-professor; and
that the perseverance in any enmity shall be punish'd by
the governors with expulsion.

5   That the chaplain shall eat at the master's table (paying his twenty pounds a year as the others do); and that
he shall read prayers once a day at least, a little before
supper-time; that he shall preach in the chappel every
Sunday morning, and catechize in the afternoon the
10 scholars and the school-boys; that he shall every month
administer the holy sacrament; that he shall not trouble
himself and his auditors with the controversies of divinity,
but only teach God in his just commandments, and in
his wonderful works.

The School.

15 THAT the school may be built so as to contain about an
hundred boys.

That it be divided into four classes, not as others are
ordinarily into six or seven; because we suppose that
the children sent hither, to be initiated in things as well
20 as words, ought to have past the two or three first, and
to have attained the age of about thirteen years, being
already well advanced in the Latine grammar, and some
authors.

That none, though never so rich, shall pay any thing
25 for their teaching; and that, if any professor shall be
convicted to have taken any money in consideration of
his pains in the school, he shall be expelled with ignominy by the governours; but if any persons of great
estate and quality, finding their sons much better pro-
30 ficients in learning here, than boys of the same age

commonly are at other schools, shall not think fit to
receive an obligation of so near concernment without
returning some marks of acknowledgment, they may, if
they please, (for nothing is to be demanded) bestow
some little rarity or curiosity upon the society, in recom- 5
pense of their trouble.

And because it is deplorable to consider the loss
which children make of their time at most schools, em-
ploying, or rather casting away, six or seven years in
the learning of words only, and that too very imper- 10
fectly :

That a method be here established, for the infusing
knowledge and language at the same time into them;
and that this may be their apprenticeship in natural philosophy. This, we conceive, may be done, by breeding 15
them in authors, or pieces of authors, who treat of some
parts of nature, and who may be understood with as
much ease and pleasure, as those which are commonly
taught; such are, in Latine, Varro, Cato, Columella,
Pliny, part of Celsus and of Seneca, Cicero de Divina- 20
tione, de Natura Deorum, and several scattered pieces,
Virgil's Georgicks, Grotius, Nemetianus, Manilius : And
because the truth is, we want good poets (I mean we
have but few), who have purposely treated of solid and
learned, that is, natural matters (the most part indulg- 25
ing to the weakness of the world, and feeding it either
with the follies of love, or with the fables of gods and
heroes), we conceive that one book ought to be compiled
of all the scattered little parcels among the antient poets
that might serve for the advancement of natural sciences 30
and which would make no small and unuseful or unpleasant volume. To this we would have added the
morals and rhetoricks of Cicero, and the institutions of
Quintilian ; and for the comedians, from whom almost

all that necessary part of common discourse, and all the most intimate proprieties of the language, are drawn, we conceive the boys may be made masters of them, as a part of their recreation, and not of their task, if once a 5 month, or at least once in two, they act one of Terence's Comedies, and afterwards (the most advanced) some of Plautus his; and this is for many reasons one of the best exercises they can be enjoyned, and most innocent pleasures they can be allowed. As for the Greek authors, 10 they may study Nicander, Oppianus (whom Scaliger does not doubt to prefer above Homer himself, and place next to his adored Virgil), Aristotle's history of animals and other parts, Theophrastus and Dioscorides of plants, and a collection made out of several both poets 15 and other Grecian writers. For the morals and rhetorick, Aristotle may suffice, or Hermogenes and Longinus be added for the latter. With the history of animals they should be shewed anatomy as a divertisement, and made to know the figures and natures of those creatures 20 which are not common among us, disabusing them at the same time of those errors which are universally admitted concerning many. The same method should be used to make them acquainted with all plants; and to this must be added a little of the antient and modern 25 geography, the understanding of the globes, and the principles of geometry and astronomy. They should likewise use to declaim in Latine and English, as the Romans did in Greek and Latine; and in all this travel be rather led on by familiarity, encouragement, and 30 emulation, than driven by severity, punishment, and terror. Upon festivals and play-times, they should exercise themselves in the fields, by riding, leaping, fencing, mustering and training after the manner of soldiers, &c. And, to prevent all dangers and all disorder, there should

always be two of the scholars with them, to be as wit-
nesses and directors of their actions; in foul weather, it
would not be amiss for them to learn to dance, that is,
to learn just so much (for all beyond is superfluous, if
not worse) as may give them a graceful comportment of 5
their bodies.

Upon Sundays, and all days of devotion, they are to
be a part of the chaplain's province.

That, for all these ends, the colledge so order it, as
that there may be some convenient and pleasant houses 10
thereabouts, kept by religious, discreet, and careful persons, for the lodging and boarding of young scholars;
that they have a constant eye over them, to see
that they be bred up there piously, cleanly, and plentifully, according to the proportion of the parents' 15
expences.

And that the colledge, when it shall please God, either
by their own industry and success, or by the benevo-
lence of patrons, to enrich them so far, as that it may
come to their turn and duty to be charitable to others, 20
shall, at their own charges, erect and maintain some
house or houses for the entertainment of such poor men's
sons, whose good natural parts may promise either use
or ornament to the commonwealth, during the time of
their abode at school; and shall take care that it shall 25
be done with the same conveniences as are enjoyed even
by rich men's children (though they maintain the fewer
for that cause), there being nothing of eminent and
illustrious to be expected from a low, sordid, and hospital-like education. 30

CONCLUSION.

IF I be not much abused by a natural fondness to my own conceptions (that στοργὴ of the Greeks, which no other language has a proper word for), there was never any project thought upon, which deserves to meet with
5 so few adversaries as this; for who can without impudent folly oppose the establishment of twenty well-selected persons in such a condition of life, that their whole business and sole profession may be to study the improvement and advantage of all other professions,
10 from that of the highest general even to the lowest artisan? Who shall be obliged to employ their whole time, wit, learning, and industry, to these four, the most useful that can be imagined, and to no other ends; first, to weigh, examine, and prove all things of nature deli-
15 vered to us by former ages; to detect, explode, and strike a censure through all false moneys with which the world has been paid and cheated so long; and (as I may say) to set the mark of the colledge upon all true coins, that they may pass hereafter without any farther tryal:
20 secondly, to recover the lost inventions, and, as it were, drown'd lands of the antients: thirdly, to improve all arts which we now have; and lastly, to discover others which we yet have not. And who shall besides all this (as a benefit by the by), give the best education in the
25 world (purely *gratis*) to as many men's children as shall think fit to make use of the obligation? Neither does it at all check or interfere with any parties in state or religion, but is indifferently to be embraced by all differences in opinion, and can hardly be conceived
30 capable (as many good institutions have done) even of degeneration into any thing harmful. So that, all things

considered, I will suppose this proposition will encounter
with no enemies: the only question is, whether it will
find friends enough to carry it on from discourse and
design to reality and effect; the necessary expences of
the beginning (for it will maintain itself well enough 5
afterwards) being so great (though I have set them as
low as is possible in order to so vast a work), that it
may seem hopeless to raise such a sum out of those few
dead reliques of human charity and publick generosity
which are yet remaining in the world. 10

A DISCOURSE BY WAY OF VISION CONCERNING THE GOVERNMENT OF OLIVER CROMWEL.

T was the funeral day of the late man who made himself to be called protector. And though I bore but little affection, either to the memory of him, or to the trouble and
5 folly of all publick pageantry, yet I was forced by the importunity of my company, to go along with them, and be a spectator of that solemnity, the expectation of which had been so great, that it was said to have brought some very curious persons (and no doubt singular
10 virtuosos) as far as from the Mount in Cornwal, and from the Orcades. I found there had been much more cost bestowed than either the dead man or indeed death itself could deserve. There was a mighty train of black assistants, among which, too, divers princes in the
15 persons of their ambassadors (being infinitely afflicted for the loss of their brother) were pleased to attend; the herse was magnificent, the idol crowned, and (not to mention all other ceremonies which are practised at royal interments, and therefore by no means could be omitted
20 here) the vast multitude of spectators made up, as it uses

to do, no small part of the spectacle itself. But yet, I
know not how, the whole was so managed, that, methoughts, it somewhat represented the life of him for
whom it was made; much noise, much tumult, much
expence, much magnificence, much vain-glory; briefly 5
a great show; and yet, after all this, but an ill sight.
At last (for it seemed long to me, and, like his short
reign too, very tedious) the whole scene past by; and
I retired back to my chamber, weary, and I think more
melancholy than any of the mourners. Where I began 10
to reflect on the whole life of this prodigious man : and
sometimes I was filled with horrour and detestation of
his actions, and sometimes I inclined a little to reverence
and admiration of his courage, conduct, and success; till,
by these different motions and agitations of mind, rocked, 15
as it were, asleep, I fell at last into this vision ; or if you
please to call it but a dream, I shall not take it ill,
because the father of poets tells us, even dreams, too,
are from God.

   But sure it was no dream; for I was suddainly trans- 20
ported afar off (whether in the body, or out of the body,
like St Paul, I know not) and found myself on the top of
that famous hill in the island Mona, which has the
prospect of three great, and not long since most happy,
kingdoms. As soon as ever I look'd on them, the *not-* 25
long-since struck upon my memory, and called forth the
sad representation of all the sins, and all the miseries,
that had overwhelmed them these twenty years. And I
wept bitterly for two or three hours; and, when my
present stock of moisture was all wasted, I fell a sighing 30
for an hour more; and, as soon as I recovered from my
passion the use of speech and reason, I broke forth,
as I remember (looking upon England), into this complaint :

1.

Ah, happy isle, how art thou chang'd and curst,
 Since I was born, and knew thee first!
When peace, which had forsook the world around,
(Frighted with noise, and the shrill trumpet's sound)
5 Thee, for a private place of rest,
  And a secure retirement, chose
  Wherein to build her halcyon nest;
No wind durst stir abroad the air to discompose.

2.

When all the riches of the globe beside
10 Flow'd in to thee with every tide:
When all, that nature did thy soil deny,
The growth was of thy fruitful industry;
  When all the proud and dreadful sea
  And all his tributary streams,
15 A constant tribute paid to thee,
When all the liquid world was one extended Thames;

3.

When plenty in each village did appear,
  And bounty was it's steward there;
When gold walk'd free about in open view,
20 E'er it one conquering party's prisoner grew;
  When the religion of our state
  Had face and substance with her voice,
  E'er she, by her foolish loves of late,
Like echo (once a nymph) turn'd only into noise.

4.

When men to men respect and friendship bore,
   And God with reverence did adore;
When upon earth no kingdom could have shown
A happier monarch to us than our own;
   And yet his subjects by him were   5
   (Which is a truth will hardly be
   Receiv'd by any vulgar ear,
A secret known to few) made happier ev'n than he.

5.

Thou dost a chaos, and confusion now,
   A Babel, and a Bedlam, grow,   10
   And, like a frantick person, thou dost tear
The ornaments and cloaths, which thou should'st wear,
   And cut thy limbs; and, if we see
   (Just as thy barbarous Britons did)
   Thy body with hypocrisie   15
Painted all o'er, thou think'st thy naked shame is hid.

6.

The nations, which envied thee erewhile,
   Now laugh (too little 'tis to smile):
They laugh, and would have pitied thee (alas!)
But that thy faults all pity do surpass.   20
   Art thou the countrey, which didst hate
   And mock the French inconstancie?
   And have we, have we seen of late
Less change of habits there, than governments in thee?

7.

Unhappy Islè! no ship of thine at sea,
  Was ever tost and torn like thee.
Thy naked hulk loose on the waves does beat,
The rocks and banks around her ruine threat;
5   What did thy foolish pilots ail,
  To lay the compass quite aside?
  Without a law or rule to sail,
And rather take the winds, than heavens, to be their guide?

8.

Yet, mighty God, yet, yet, we humbly crave,
10   This floating isle from shipwrack save;
And though, to wash that bloud which does it stain,
It well deserve to sink into the main;
  Yet, for the royal martyr's prayer,
  (The royal martyr prays, we know)
15   This guilty, perishing vessel spare;
Hear but his soul above, and not his bloud below.

I think, I should have gone [on,] but that I was
interrupted by a strange and terrible apparition; for
there appeared to me (arising out of the earth, as I
20 conceived) the figure of a man, taller than a gyant, or
indeed the shadow of any gyant in the evening. His
body was naked; but that nakedness adorn'd, or rather
deform'd all over, with several figures, after the manner
of the antient Britons, painted upon it: and I perceived
25 that most of them were the representation of the battels
in our civil wars, and (if I be not much mistaken) it was
the battel of Naseby that was drawn upon his breast.
His eyes were like burning brass; and there were three
crowns of the same metal (as I guest), and that look'd as
30 red-hot too, upon his head. He held in his right hand

a sword, that was yet bloody, and nevertheless the motto of it was, *Pax quæritur bello;* and in his left hand a thick book, upon the back of which was written in letters of gold, Acts, Ordinances, Protestations, Covenants, Engagements, Declarations, Remonstrances, &c.   5

Though this sudden, unusual, and dreadful object might have quelled a greater courage than mine, yet so it pleased God (for there is nothing bolder than a man in a vision) that I was not at all daunted, but ask'd him resolutely and briefly, "What art thou?" And he 10 said, "I am called the north-west principality, his highness the protector of the commonwealth of England, Scotland, and Ireland, and the dominions belonging thereunto; for I am that angel, to whom the Almighty has committed the government of those three kingdoms, which thou 15 seest from this place." And I answered and said, "If it be so, Sir, it seems to me that for almost these twenty years past, your highness has been absent from your charge: for not only if any angel, but if any wise and honest man had since that time been our governor, we 20 should not have wandred thus long in these laborious and endless labyrinths of confusion, but either not have entred at all into them, or at least have returned back e'r we had absolutely lost our way; but, instead of your highness, we have had since such a protector as was his 25 predecessor Richard the Third to the king his nephew; for he presently slew the commonwealth, which he pretended to protect, and set up himself in the place of it: a little less guilty, indeed, in one respect, because the other slew an innocent, and this man did but murder a 30 murderer. Such a protector we have had, as we would have been glad to have changed for an enemy, and rather receive a constant Turk, than this every month's apostate; such a protector, as man is to his flocks, which

he shears, and sells, or devours himself; and I would fain know, what the wolf, which he protects them from, could do more? Such a protector—" and as I was proceeding, methought his highness began to put on a
5 displeased and threatning countenance, as men use to do when their dearest friends happen to be traduced in their company; which gave me the first rise of jealousie against him, for I did not believe that Cromwel, among all his forreign correspondences, had ever held any with
10 angels. However, I was not hardn'd enough to venture a quarrel with him then; and therefore (as if I had spoken to the protector himself in Whitehal) I desired him "that his highness would please to pardon me, if I had unwittingly spoken any thing to the disparagement of
15 a person, whose relations to his highness I had not the honour to know."

At which he told me, "that he had no other concernment for his late highness, than as he took him to be the greatest man that ever was of the English nation,
20 if not (said he) of the whole world; which gives me a just title to the defence of his reputation, since I now account myself, as it were, a naturalized English angel, by having had so long the management of the affairs of that countrey. And pray, countreyman (said he, very
25 kindly and very flatteringly) for I would not have you fall into the general error of the world, that detests and decries so extraordinary a virtue, what can be more extraordinary, than that a person of mean birth, no fortune, no eminent qualities of body, which have sometimes, or
30 of mind, which have often, raised men to the highest dignities, should have the courage to attempt, and the happiness to succeed in, so improbable a design, as the destruction of one of the most antient and most solidly founded monarchies upon the earth? That he should have

the power or boldness to put his prince and master to an open and infamous death; to banish that numerous and strongly-allied family; to do all this under the name and wages of a parliament; to trample upon them too as he pleased, and spurn them out of doors, when he grew 5 weary of them; to raise up a new and unheard of monster out of their ashes; to stifle that in the very infancy, and set up himself above all things that ever were called soveraign in England; to oppress all his enemies by arms, and all his friends afterwards by artifice; to serve 10 all parties patiently for a while, and to command them victoriously at last; to over-run each corner of the three nations, and overcome with equal felicity both the riches of the south, and the poverty of the north; to be feared and courted by all forreign princes, and adopted a brother 15 to the gods of the earth; to call together parliaments with a word of his pen, and scatter them again with the breath of his mouth; to be humbly and daily petitioned that he would please to be hired, at the rate of two millions a year, to be master of those who had hired 20 him before to be their servant; to have the estates and lives of three kingdoms as much at his disposal, as was the little inheritance of his father, and to be as noble and liberal in the spending of them; and lastly (for there is no end of all the particulars of his glory) to bequeath all 25 this with one word to his posterity; to dye with peace at home, and triumph abroad; to be buried among kings, and with more than regal solemnity; and to leave a name behind him, not to be extinguished but with the whole world; which, as it is now too little for his praises, 30 so might have been too for his conquests, if the short line of his humane life could have been stretcht out to the extent of his immortal designs?"

By this speech, I began to understand perfectly well

what kind of angel his pretended highness was; and having fortified myself privately with a short mental prayer, and with the sign of the cross (not out of any superstition to the sign, but as a recognition of my
5 baptism in Christ,) I grew a little bolder, and replyed in this manner; "I should not venture to oppose what you are pleased to say in commendation of the late great, and (I confess) extraordinary person, but that I remember Christ forbids us to give assent to any other doctrine
10 but what himself has taught us, even though it should be delivered by an angel; and if such you be, Sir, it may be you have spoken all this rather to try than to tempt my frailty, for sure I am, that we must renounce or forget all the laws of the New and Old Testament, and those
15 which are the foundation of both, even the laws of moral and natural honesty, if we approve of the actions of that man whom I suppose you commend by irony.

"There would be no end to instance in the particulars of all his wickedness: but to sum up a part of it
20 briefly: What can be more extraordinarily wicked, than for a person, such as yourself qualifie him rightly, to endeavour not only to exalt himself above, but to trample upon, all his equals and betters? To pretend freedom for all men, and under the help of that pretence to make all
25 men his servants? To take arms against taxes of scarce two hundred thousand pounds a year, and to raise them himself to above two millions? To quarrel for the loss of three or four ears, and strike off three or four hundred heads? To fight against an imaginary suspicion of I know
30 not what two thousand guards to be fetcht for the king, I know not from whence, and to keep up for himself no less than forty thousand? To pretend the defence of parliaments, and violently to dissolve all even of his own calling, and almost choosing? To undertake the reform-

ation of religion, to rob it even to the very skin, and then
to expose it naked to the rage of all sects and heresies?
To set up councils of rapine, and courts of murder? To
fight against the king under a commission for him? To
take him forcibly out of the hands of those for whom 5
he had conquer'd him? To draw him into his net, with
protestations and vows of fidelity, and when he had
caught him in it, to butcher him, with as little shame as
conscience or humanity, in the open face of the whole
world? To receive a commission for king and parliament, 10
to murder (as I said) the one, and destroy no less impudently the other? To fight against monarchy when he
declared for it, and declare against it when he contrived
for it in his own person? To abuse perfidiously and sup-
plant ingratefully his own general first, and afterwards 15
most of those officers, who, with the loss of their honour,
and hazard of their souls, had lifted him up to the top of
his unreasonable ambitions? To break his faith with all
enemies and with all friends equally, and to make no
less frequent use of the most solemn perjuries, than the 20
looser sort of people do of customary oaths? To usurp
three kingdoms without any shadow of the least pre-
tensions, and to govern them as unjustly as he got them?
To set himself up as an idol (which we know, as St Paul
says, in itself is nothing), and make the very streets of 25
London like the valley of Hinnom, by burning the
bowels of men as a sacrifice to his Molochship? To seek
to entail this usurpation upon his posterity, and with it
an endless war upon the nation? And lastly, by the
severest judgment of Almighty God, to die hardned, and 30
mad, and unrepentant, with the curses of the present
age, and the detestation of all to succeed?"

    Though I had much more to say (for the life of man
is so short, that it allows not time enough to speak
against a tyrant) yet because I had a mind to hear how 35

my strange adversary would behave himself upon this subject, and to give even the devil (as they say) his right, and fair play in disputation, I stopt here, and expected (not without the frailty of a little fear) that he should V 5 have broke into a violent passion in behalf of his favourite: but he on the contrary very calmly, and with the dove-like innocency of a serpent that was not yet warm'd enough to sting, thus reply'd to me:

"It is not so much out of my affection to that person 10 whom we discourse of (whose greatness is too solid to be shaken by the breath of any oratory), as for your own sake (honest countryman,) whom I conceive to err rather by mistake than out of malice, that I shall endeavour to reform your uncharitable and unjust opinion. And, in 15 the first place, I must needs put you in mind of a sentence of the most antient of the heathen divines, that you men are acquainted withal,

Οὐχ ὅσιον κταμένοισιν ἐπ᾽ ἀνδράσιν εὐχετάασθαι.

'Tis wicked with insulting feet to tread
20   Upon the monuments of the dead.

And the intention of the reproof there is no less proper for this subject; for it is spoken to a person who was proud and insolent against those dead men, to whom he had been humble and obedient whilst they lived."

25   "Your highness may please (said I) to add the verse that follows, as no less proper for this subject:

Whom God's just doom and their own sins have sent
Already to their punishment.

"But I take this to be the rule in the case, that, when 30 we fix any infamy upon deceased persons, it should not be done out of hatred to the dead, but out of love and charity to the living: that the curses, which only remain in men's thoughts, and dare not come forth against tyrants (because they are tyrants) whilst they are so, may

at least be for ever setled and engraven upon their
memories, to deter all others from the like wickedness;
which else, in the time of their foolish prosperity, the
flattery of their own hearts and of other men's tongues
would not suffer them to perceive. Ambition is so subtil 5
a tempter, and the corruption of humane nature so
susceptible of the temptation, that a man can hardly
resist it, be he never so much forewarn'd of the evil
consequences; much less if he find not only the con-
currence of the present, but the approbation too of 10
following ages, which have the liberty to judge more
freely. The mischief of tyranny is too great, even in
the shortest time that it can continue; it is endless and
insupportable, if the example be to reign too, and if a
Lambert must be invited to follow the steps of a Cromwel, 15
as well by the voice of honour, as by the sight of power
and riches. Though it may seem to some fantastically,
yet was it wisely done of the Syracusians, to implead
with the forms of their ordinary justice, to condemn and
destroy even the statutes of all their tyrants: if it were 20
possible to cut them out of all history, and to extinguish
their very names, I am of opinion that it ought to be
done; but, since they have left behind them too deep
wounds to be ever closed up without a scar, at least let
us set such a mark upon their memory, that men of the 25
same wicked inclinations may be no less affrighted with
their lasting ignominy, than enticed by their momentany
glories. And that your highness may perceive, that I
speak not all this out of any private animosity against
the person of that late protector, I assure you upon my 30
faith, that I bear no more hatred to his name, than I do
to that of Marius or Sylla, who never did me, or any
friend of mine, the least injury; and with that, transported
by a holy fury, I fell into this sudden rapture:

1.

CURST be the man (what do I wish? as though
The wretch already were not so ;
But curst on let him be) who thinks it brave
And great, his country to enslave,
5   Who seeks to overpoise alone
The balance of a nation,
Against the whole but naked state,
Who in his own light scale makes up with arms the
weight.

2.

Who of his nation loves to be the first,
10   Though at the rate of being worst.
Who would be rather a great monster, than
A well-proportion'd man.
The son of earth with hundred hands
Upon his three-pil'd mountain stands,
15   Till thunder strikes him from the skie ;
The son of earth again in his earth's womb does lie.

3.

What blood, confusion, ruine, to obtain
A short and miserable reign !
In what oblique and humble creeping wise
20   Does the mischievous serpent rise !
But ev'n his forked tongue strikes dead :
When he's rear'd up his wicked head,
He murders with his mortal frown ;
A basilisk he grows, if once he gets a crown.

4.

But no guards can oppose assaulting fears,
 Or undermining tears,
No more than doors or close-drawn curtains keep
 The swarming dreams out, when we sleep.
 That bloody conscience, too, of his   5
 (For, oh, a rebel red-coat 'tis)
 Does here his early hell begin,
He sees his slaves without, his tyrant feels within.

5.

Let, gracious God, let never more thine hand
 Lift up this rod against our land.   10
A tyrant is a rod and serpent too,
 And brings worse plagues than Egypt knew.
 What rivers stain'd with blood have been !
 What storm and hail-shot have we seen !
 What sores deform'd the ulcerous state !   15
What darkness to be felt has buried us of late !

6.

How has it snatcht our flocks and herds away !
 And made ev'n of our sons a prey !
What croaking sects and vermin has it sent,
 The restles nation to torment !   20
 What greedy troops, what armed power
 Of flies and locusts, to devour
 The land, which every where they fill !
Nor fly they, Lord, away; no, they devour it still.

L. C.   3

7.

Come the eleventh plague, rather than this should be;
    Come sink us rather in the sea.
Come rather pestilence and reap us down;
    Come God's sword rather than our own,
5   Let rather Roman come again,
    Or Saxon, Norman, or the Dane:
    In all the bonds we ever bore,
We griev'd, we sigh'd, we wept; we never blusht before.

8.

If by our sins the divine justice be
10   Call'd to this last extremitie,
Let some denouncing Jonas first be sent,
    To try if England can repent.
    Methinks, at least, some prodigy,
    Some dreadful comet from on high,
15   Should terribly forewarn the earth,
As of good princes' deaths, so of a tyrant's birth."

Here, the spirit of verse beginning a little to fail, I stopt: and his highness, smiling, said, "I was glad to see you engaged in the enclosures of metre; for, if 20 you had staid in the open plain of declaiming against the word Tyrant, I must have had patience for half a dozen hours, till you had tired yourself as well as me. But pray, countryman, to avoid this sciomachy, or imaginary combat with words, let me know, Sir, what 25 you mean by the name tyrant, for I remember that, among your antient authors, not only all kings, but even Jupiter himself (your *juvans pater*) is so termed; and perhaps, as it was used formerly in a good sense, so we shall find it, upon better consideration, to be still a good thing for the benefit and peace of mankind; at least, it will appear whether your interpretation of it may be justly applyed to the person who is now the subject of our discourse."

"I call him (said I) a tyrant, who either intrudes 5 himself forcibly into the government of his fellow citizens without any legal authority over them; or who, having a just title to the government of a people, abuses it to the destruction, or tormenting, of them. So that all tyrants are at the same time usurpers, either of the whole, 10 or at least of a part, of that power which they assume to themselves: and no less are they to be accounted rebels, since no man can usurp authority over others, but by rebelling against them who had it before, or at least against those laws which were his superiors: and 15 in all these senses, no history can afford us a more evident example of tyranny, or more out of all possibility of excuse, or palliation, than that of the person whom you are pleased to defend; whether we consider his reiterated rebellions against all his superiors, or his 20 usurpation of the supreme power to himself, or his tyranny in the exercise of it: and, if lawful princes have been esteemed tyrants, by not containing themselves within the bounds of those laws which have been left them as the sphere of their authority by their 25 forefathers, what shall we say of that man, who, having by right no power at all in this nation, could not content himself with that which had satisfied the most ambitious of our princes? nay, not with those vastly extended limits of soveraignty, which he (disdaining all that had 30 been prescribed and observed before) was pleased (out of great modesty) to set to himself; not abstaining from rebellion and usurpation even against his own laws, as well as those of the nation?"

"Hold, friend, said his highness, pulling me by my arm, for I see your zeal is transporting you again; whether the protector were a tyrant in the exorbitant exercise of his power, we shall see anon; it is requisite
5 to examine, first, whether he were so in the usurpation of it. And I say, that not only he, but no man else, ever was, or can be so; and that for these reasons. First, because all power belongs only to God, who is the source and fountain of it, as kings are of all honours
10 in their dominions. Princes are but his viceroys in the little provinces of this world; and to some he gives their places for a few years, to some for their lives, and to others (upon ends or deserts best known to himself, or meerly for his indisputable good pleasure) he bestows,
15 as it were, leases upon them and their posterity, for such a date of time as is prefixt in that <u>patent of their destiny</u>, which is not legible to you men below. Neither is it more unlawful for Oliver to succeed Charles in the kingdom of England, when God so disposes of it, than
20 it had been for him to have succeeded the Lord Strafford in his lieutenancy of Ireland, if he had been appointed to it by the king then reigning. Men are in both the cases obliged to obey him, whom they see actually invested with the authority by that sovereign from whom
25 he ought to derive it, without disputing or examining the causes, either of the removal of the one, or the preferment of the other. Secondly, because all power is attained, either by the election and consent of the people, and that takes away your objection of forcible
30 intrusion; or else, by a conquest of them, and that gives such a legal authority as you mention to be wanting in the usurpation of a tyrant; so that either this title is right, and then there are no usurpers, or else it is a wrong one, and then there are none else but usurpers,

if you examine the original pretences of the princes of
the world. Thirdly, (which, quitting the dispute in
general, is a particular justification of his highness) the
government of England was totally broken and dissolved, and extinguisht by the confusions of a civil 5
war; so that his highness could not be accused to have
possest himself violently of the antient building of the
commonwealth, but to have prudently and peaceably
built up a new one out of the ruines and ashes of the
former; and he who, after a deplorable shipwrack, can 10
with extraordinary industry gather together the disperst
and broken planks and pieces of it, and with no less
wonderful art and felicity so rejoyn them as to make a
new vessel more tight and beautiful than the old one,
deserves, no doubt, to have the command of her (even 15
as his highness had by the desire of the seamen and
passengers themselves). And do but consider, lastly, (for
I omit a multitude of weighty things, that might be
spoken upon this noble argument) do but consider .
seriously and impartially with yourself, what admirable 20
parts of wit and prudence, what indefatigable diligence
and invincible courage, must of necessity have con-
curred in the person of that man, who from so contemptible beginnings (as I observed before) and through
so many thousand difficulties, was able not only to make 25
himself the greatest and most absolute monarch of this
nation; but to add to it the entire conquest of Ireland
and Scotland (which the whole force of the world, joyned
with the Roman virtue, could never attain to), and to
crown all this with illustrious and heroical undertakings 30
and success upon all our forreign enemies: do but (I
say again) consider this, and you will confess, that his
prodigious merits were a better title to imperial dignity,
than the blood of an hundred royal progenitors; and

will rather lament that he had lived not to overcome more nations, than envy him the conquest and dominion of these."

"Whoever you are (said I, my indignation making me somewhat bolder), your discourse (methinks) becomes as little the person of a tutelar angel, as Cromwel's actions did that of a protector. It is upon these principles, that all the great crimes of the world have been committed, and most particularly those which I have had the misfortune to see in my own time, and in my own country. If these be to be allowed, we must break up human society, retire into the woods, and equally there stand upon our guards against our brethren mankind, and our rebels the wild beasts. For if there can be no usurpation upon the rights of a whole nation, there can be none most certainly upon those of a private person; and, if the robbers of countries be God's vicegerents, there is no doubt but the thieves and banditos, and murderers, are his under officers. It is true which you say, that God is the source and fountain of all power; and it is no less true, that he is the creator of serpents as well as angels; nor does his goodness fail of its ends, even in the malice of his own creatures. What power he suffers the devil to exercise in this world is too apparent by our daily experience; and by nothing more than the late monstrous iniquities which you dispute for, and patronize in England: but would you inferr from thence, that the power of the devil is a just and lawful one; and that all men ought, as well as most men do, obey him? God is the fountain of all powers; but some flow from the right hand (as it were) of his goodness, and others from the left hand of his justice; and the world, like an island between these two rivers, is sometimes refresht and nourisht by the

one, and sometimes over-run and ruin'd by the other;
and (to continue a little farther the allegory) we are never
overwhelm'd with the latter, till, either by our malice
or negligence, we have stopt and damm'd up the former.

But to come up a little closer to your argument, or 5
rather the image of an argument, your similitude. If
Cromwel had come to command in Ireland in the place
of the late Lord Strafford, I should have yielded
obedience, not for the equipage, and the strength, and
the guards which he brought with him, but for the com- 10
mission which he should first have shewed me from our
common sovereign which sent him; and, if he could have
done that from God Almighty, I would have obeyed
him too in England; but that he was so far from being
able to do, that, on the contrary, I read nothing but 15
commands, and even public proclamations, from God
Almighty, not to admit him.

Your second argument is, that he had the same right
for his authority, that is the foundation of all others,
even the right of conquest. Are we then so unhappy 20
as to be conquer'd by the person, whom we hired at a
daily rate, like a labourer, to conquer others for us?
Did we furnish him with arms, only to draw and try upon
our enemies (as we, it seems, falsly thought them), and
keep them for ever sheath'd in the bowels of his friends? 25
Did we fight for liberty against our prince, that we might
become slaves to our servant? This is such an impudent
pretence, as neither he nor any of his flatterers for him
had ever the face to mention. Though it can hardly be
spoken or thought of without passion, yet I shall, if you 30
please, argue it more calmly than the case deserves.

The right, certainly, of conquest can only be exercised
upon those, against whom the war is declared, and the
victory obtained. So that no whole nation can be said

to be conquered, but by foreign force. In all civil
wars, men are so far from stating the quarrel against
their country, that they do it only against a person, or
party, which they really believe, or at least pretend, to
5 be pernicious to it; neither can there be any just cause
for the destruction of a part of the body, but when it is
done for the preservation and safety of the whole. 'Tis
our country that raises men in the quarrel, our country
that arms, our country that pays them, our country that
10 authorises the undertaking, and, by that, distinguishes it
from rapine and murder; lastly, 'tis our country that
directs and commands the army, and is indeed their
general. So that to say, in civil wars, that the prevailing
party conquers their country, is to say, the country-
15 conquers itself. And if the general only of that party be
conqueror, the army by which he is made so is no less
conquered than the army which is beaten, and have as
little reason to triumph in that victory, by which they
lose both their honour and liberty. So that if Cromwel
20 conquer'd any party, it was only that against which he
was sent; and what that was must appear by his commission. It was (says that) against a company of evil
counsellors and disaffected persons, who kept the king
from a good intelligence and conjunction with his people.
25 It was not then against the people. It is so far from
being so, that even of that party which was beaten, the
conquest did not belong to Cromwel, but to the parliament
which employed him in their service, or rather, indeed,
to the king and parliament, for whose service (if there
30 had been any faith in men's vows and protestations) the
wars were undertaken. Merciful God! did the right of
this miserable conquest remain then in his majesty; and
didst thou suffer him to be destroyed with more barbarity
than if he had been conquered even by savages and

cannibals? Was it for king and parliament that we fought; and has it fared with them just as with the army which we fought against, the one part being slain, and the other fled? It appears therefore plainly, that Cromwel was not a conqueror, but a thief and a robber 5 of the rights of the king and parliament, and an usurper upon those of the people. I do not here deny conquest to be sometimes (though it be very rarely) a true title; but I deny this to be a true conquest. Sure I am, that the race of our princes came not in by such a one. One 10 nation may conquer another, sometimes, justly; and if it be unjustly, yet still it is a true conquest, and they are to answer for the injustice only to God Almighty (having nothing else in authority above them,) and not as particular rebels to their country, which is, and ought 15 always to be, their superior and their lord. If, perhaps, we find usurpation instead of conquest in the original titles of some royal families abroad (as, no doubt, there have been many usurpers before ours, though none in so impudent and execrable a manner;) all I can say for 20 them is, that their title was very weak, till, by length of time, and the death of all juster pretenders, it became to be the true, because it was the only one.

Your third defence of his highness (as your highness pleases to call him) enters in most seasonably after his 25 pretence of conquest; for then a man may say any thing. The government was broken; who broke it? It was dissolved; who dissolved it? It was extinguisht; who was it, but Cromwel, who not only put out the light, but cast away even the very snuff of it? As if a man 30 should murder a whole family, and then possess himself of the house, because 'tis better that he, than that only rats should live there. Jesus God! (said I, and at that word I perceived my pretended angel to give a start and

trembled, but I took no notice of it, and went on) this
were a wicked pretension, even though the whole family
were destroyed; but the heirs (blessed be God) are yet
surviving, and likely to outlive all heirs of their dispos-
5 sessors, besides their infamy. "Rode caper vitem," &c.
There will be yet wine enough left for the sacrifice of
those wild beasts, that have made so much spoil in the
vineyard. But did Cromwel think, like Nero, to set
the city on fire, only that he might have the honour of
10 being founder of a new and more beautiful one? He
could not have such a shadow of virtue in his wickedness;
he meant only to rob more securely and more richly in
midst of the combustion; he little thought then that he
should ever have been able to make himself master of
15 the palace, as well as plunder the goods of the commonwealth. He was glad to see the publick vessel (the
sovereign of the seas) in as desperate a condition as his
own little canow, and thought only, with some scattered
planks of that great shipwrack, to make a better fisher-
20 boat for himself. But when he saw that, by the drowning
of the master (whom he himself treacherously knockt on
the head, as he was swimming for his life), by the flight
and dispersion of others, and cowardly patience of the
remaining company, that all was abandoned to his
25 pleasure; with the old hulk and new misshapen and
disagreeing pieces of his own, he made up, with much
ado, that piratical vessel which we have seen him command, and which, how tight indeed it was, may best be
judged by its perpetual leaking.
30 First then (much more wicked than those foolish
daughters in the fable, who cut their old father into
pieces, in hope, by charms and witchcraft, to make him
young and lusty again), this man endeavoured to destroy
the building, before he could imagine in what manner,

with what materials, by what workmen, or what architect, it was to be rebuilt. Secondly, if he had dreamt himself to be able to revive that body which he had killed, yet it had been but the insupportable insolence of an ignorant mountebank; and, thirdly, (which concerns us nearest,) that very new thing which he made out of the ruines of the old, is no more like the original, either for beauty, use, or duration, than an artificial plant, raised by the fire of a chymist, is comparable to the true and natural one which he first burnt, that out of the ashes of it he might produce an imperfect similitude of his own making.

Your last argument is such (when reduced to syllogism), that the major proposition of it would make strange work in the world, if it were received for truth ; to wit, that he who has the best parts in a nation, has the right of being king over it. We had enough to do here of old with the contention between two branches of the same family : what would become of us, when every man in England should lay his claim to the government? And truly, if Cromwel should have commenced his plea, when he seems to have begun his ambition, there were few persons besides, that might not at the same time have put in theirs too. But his deserts, I suppose, you will date from the same term that I do his great demerits, that is, from the beginning of our late calamities (for, as for his private faults before, I can only wish, and that with as much charity to him as to the publick, that he had continued in them till his death, rather than changed them for those of his later days); and, therefore, we must begin the consideration of his greatness from the unlucky æra of our own misfortunes, which puts me in mind of what was said less truly of Pompey the Great, "Nostrâ miseriâ magnus es." But, because the general ground of your argumentation con-

44 *A DISCOURSE CONCERNING THE*

sists in this, that all men who are the effectors of extraordinary mutations in the world, must needs have
extraordinary forces of nature by which they are enabled
to turn about, as they please, so great a wheel; I shall
5 speak first a few words upon this universal proposition,
which seems so reasonable, and is so popular, before I
descend to the particular examination of the eminencies
of that person which is in question.

I have often observed (with all submission and resig-
10 nation of spirit to the inscrutable mysteries of Eternal
Providence), that, when the fulness and maturity of time
is come, that produces the great confusions and changes
in the world, it usually pleases God to make it appear
by the manner of them, that they are not the effects of
15 humane force or policy, but of the divine justice and
predestination; and, though we see a man, like that
which we call Jack of the clock-house, striking, as it
were, the hour of that fulness of time, yet our reason
must needs be convinced, that his hand is moved by
20 some secret, and, to us that stand without, invisible
direction. And the stream of the current is then so
violent, that the strongest men in the world cannot draw
up against it; and none are so weak, but they may sail
down with it. These are the spring-tides of publick
25 affairs, which we see often happen, but seek in vain to
discover any certain causes:

—Omnia fluminis
Ritu feruntur, nunc medio alveo
Cum pace delabentis Etruscum
30 In mare, nunc lapides adesos,
Stirpesque raptas, & pecus, & domos
Volventis una, non sine montium
Clamore, vicinæque sylvæ;
Cum fera diluvies quietos
35 Irritat amnes.

And one man then, by maliciously opening all the
sluyces that he can come at, can never be the sole author
of all this (though he may be as guilty as if really he
were, by intending and imagining to be so); but it is
God that breaks up the flood-gates of so general a deluge, 5
and all the art then, and industry of mankind, is not
sufficient to raise up dikes and ramparts against it. In
such a time it was as this, that not all the wisdom and
power of the Roman senate, nor the wit and eloquence
of Cicero, nor the courage and virtue of Brutus, was 10
able to defend their country or themselves, against the
unexperienced rashness of a beardless boy, and the loose
rage of a voluptuous madman. The valour, and prudent
counsels, on the one side, are made fruitless, and the
errors, and cowardise, on the other, harmless, by unex- 15
pected accidents. The one general saves his life, and
gains the whole world, by a very dream; and the other
loses both at once, by a little mistake of the shortness
of his sight. And though this be not always so, for we
see that, in the translation of the great monarchies from 20
one to another, it pleased God to make choice of the
most eminent men in nature, as Cyrus, Alexander,
Scipio and his contemporaries, for his chief instruments,
and actors, in so admirable a work (the end of this
being, not only to destroy or punish one nation, which 25
may be done by the worst of mankind, but to exalt and
bless another, which is only to be effected by great and
virtuous persons); yet, when God only intends the temporary chastisement of a people, he does not raise up
his servant Cyrus (as he himself pleased to call him), 30
or an Alexander (who had as many virtues to do good,
as vices to do harm); but he makes the Massenellos,
and the Johns of Leyden, the instruments of his vengeance, that the power of the Almighty might be more

evident by the weakness of the means which he chooses
to demonstrate it. He did not assemble the serpents,
and the monsters of Africk, to correct the pride of the
Egyptians; but called for his army of locusts out of
5 Æthiopia, and formed new ones of vermin out of the
very dust; and, because you see a whole country destroyed by these, will you argue from thence they must
needs have had both the craft of foxes, and the courage
of lions?

10 It is easie to apply this general observation to the
particular case of our troubles in England: and that
they seem only to be meant for a temporary chastisement of our sins, and not for a total abolishment of the
old, and introduction of a new government, appears
15 probable to me from these considerations, as far as we
may be bold to make a judgment of the will of God in
future events. First, because he has suffered nothing
to settle, or take root, in the place of that which hath
been so unwisely and unjustly removed, that none of
20 these untempered mortars can hold out against the next
blast of wind, nor any stone stick to a stone, till that
which these ioolish builders have refused be made again
the head of the corner. For, when the indisposed and
long-tormented commonwealth hath wearied and spent
25 itself almost to nothing, with the chargeable, various,
and dangerous experiments of several mountebanks, it
is to be supposed, it will have the wit at last to send for
a true physician, especially when it sees (which is the
second consideration) most evidently (as it now begins
30 to do, and will do every day more and more, and might
have done perfectly long since) that no usurpation
(under what name or pretext soever) can be kept up
without open force, nor force without the continuance
of those oppressions upon the people, which will at last

tire out their patience, though it be great even tò stupidity. They cannot be so dull (when poverty and hunger begin to whet their understanding) as not to find out this no extraordinary mystery, that it is madness in a nation to pay three millions a year for the 5 maintaining of their servitude under tyrants, when they might live free for nothing under their princes. This, I say, will not always lye hid, even to the slowest capacities; and the next truth they will discover afterwards is, that a whole people can never have the will, 10 without having, at the same time, the power to redeem themselves. Thirdly, it does not look (methinks) as if God had forsaken the family of that man, from whom he hath raised up five children, of as eminent virtue, and all other commendable qualities, as ever lived perhaps (for 15 so many together, and so young) in any other family in the whole world. Especially, if we add hereto this consideration, that, by protecting and preserving some of them already through as great dangers as ever were past with safety, either by prince or private person, he 20 hath given them already (as we may reasonably hope to be meant) a promise and earnest of his future favours. And, lastly, (to return closely to the discourse from which I have a little digress'd) because I see nothing of those excellent parts of nature, and mixture of merit 25 with their vices, in the late disturbers of our peace and happiness, that uses to be found in the persons of those who are born for the erection of new empires.

And, I confess, I find nothing of that kind, no nor any shadow (taking away the false light of some pros- 30 perity) in the man whom you extol for the first example of it. And, certainly, all virtues being rightly divided into moral and intellectual, I· know not how we can better judge of the former, than by men's actions; or of

the latter, than by their writings, or speeches. As for
these latter (which are least in merit, or, rather, which
are only the instruments of mischief, where the other
are wanting,) I think you can hardly pick out the name
5 of a man who ever was called great, besides him we are
now speaking of, who never left the memory behind him
of one wise or witty apothegm even amongst his
domestic servants or greatest flatterers. That little in
print, which remains upon a sad record for him, is
10 such, as a satyre against him would· not have made him
say, for fear of transgressing too much the rules of probability. I know not what you can produce for the
justification of his parts in this kind, but his having been
able to deceive so many particular persons, and so many
15 whole parties; which, if you please to take notice of for
the advantage of his intellectuals, I desire you to allow
me the liberty to do so too when I am to speak of his
morals. / The truth of the thing is this, that if craft be
wisdom, and dissimulation wit (assisted both and im-
20 proved with hypocrisies and perjuries), I must not deny
him to have been singular in both; but so gross was the
manner in which he made use of them, that, as wise men
ought not to have believed him at first, so no man was
fool enough to believe him at last: neither did any man
25 seem to do it, but those who thought they gained as much
by that dissembling, as he did by his. His very actings
of godliness grew at last as ridiculous, as if a player, by
putting on a gown, should think he represented excellently a woman, though his beard, at the same time,
30 were seen by all the spectators. If you ask me, why
they did not hiss, and explode him off the stage; I can
only answer, that they durst not do so, because the
actors and the door-keepers were too strong for the
company. I must confess that by these arts (how

grossly soever managed, as by hypocritical praying and
silly preaching, by unmanly tears and whinings, by false-
hoods and perjuries even diabolical) he had at first the
good-fortune (as men call it that is the ill-fortune) to
attain his ends; but it was because his ends were so un- 5
reasonable, that no human reason could foresee them;
which made them who had to do with him believe, that
he was rather a well-meaning and deluded bigot, than a
crafty and malicious impostor: that these arts were
helpt by an indefatigable industry (as you term it), I 10
am so far from doubting, that I intended to object that
diligence as the worst of his crimes. It makes me
almost mad, when I hear a man commended for his
diligence in wickedness. If I were his son, I should
wish to God he had been a more lazy person, and that 15
we might have found him sleeping at the hours when
other men are ordinarily waking, rather than waking
for those ends of his when other men were ordinarily
asleep. How diligent the wicked are, the Scripture
often tells us; *Their feet run to evil, and they make haste* 20
to shed innocent blood, Isai. lix. 7. *He travails with*
iniquity, Psal. vii. 14. *He deviseth mischief upon his bed,*
Psal. xxxiv. 4. *They search out iniquity, they accomplish*
a diligent search, Psal. lxiv. 6; and in a multitude of
other places. And would it not seem ridiculous to 25
praise a wolf for his watchfulness, and for his indefatigable industry in ranging all night about the countrey,
whilst the sheep, and perhaps the shepherd, and perhaps
the very dogs too, are asleep?

> The Chartreux wants the warning of a bell 30
> To call him to the duties of his cell;
> There needs no noise at all t'awaken sin,
> Th' adulterer and the thief his 'larum has within.

And if the diligence of wicked persons be so much

to be blamed, as that it is only an emphasis and ex‑
aggeration of their wickedness, I see not
courage can avoid the same censure. If t
taking bold and vast and unreasonable design
5 serve that honourable name, I am sure, Faux, and his
fellow gun-powder fiends, will have cause to pretend,
though not an equal, yet at least the next place of
honour; neither can I doubt but, if they too had suc‑
ceeded, they would have found their applauders and
10 admirers. It was bold, unquestionably, for a man, in
defiance of all humane and divine laws, (and with so little
probability of a long impunity,) so publickly and so out‑
ragiously to murder his master; it was bold, with so
much insolence and affront, to expel and disperse all
15 the chief partners of his guilt, and creators of his
power; it was bold, to violate, so openly and so scorn‑
fully, all acts and constitutions of a nation, and after‑
wards even of his own making; it was bold, to assume
the authority of calling, and bolder yet of breaking, so
20 many parliaments; it was bold, to trample upon the
patience of his own, and provoke that of all neighbour‑
ing countries; it was bold, I say, above all boldnesses,
to usurp the tyranny to himself; and impudent above
all impudences, to endeavour to transmit it to his pos‑
25 terity. But all this boldness is so far from being a design
of manly courage, which dares not transgress the rules
of any other virtue, that it is only a demonstration of
brutish madness or diabolical passion. In both which
last cases there use frequent examples to appear, of such
30 extraordinary force as may justly seem more wonderful
and astonishing than the actions of Cromwe
it stranger to believe that a whole nation s
able to govern him and a mad army, thar
six men should not be strong enough to bind a distracted

girl. There is no man ever succeeds in one wickedness,
but ▮▮▮▮▮▮▮▮▮▮▮▮ ▮ness to attempt a greater. 'Twas
▮▮▮▮▮▮▮▮▮▮▮ to kill his mother, and all the
▮▮▮▮▮▮▮▮▮ empire; 'twas boldly done, to
set the metropolis of the whole world on fire, and un- 5
dauntedly play upon his harp, whilst he saw it burning;
I could reckon up five hundred boldnesses of that great
person, (for why should not he too be called so?) who
wanted, when he was to dyė, that courage which could
hardly have failed any woman in the like necessity. 10

It would look (I must confess,) like envy, or too
much partiality, if I should say that personal kind of
courage had been deficient in the man we speak of; I
am confident it was not: and yet I may venture, I
think, to affirm, that no man ever bore the honour of so 15
many victories, at the rate of fewer wounds or dangers
of his own body; and though his valour might perhaps
have given him a just pretension to one of the first
charges in an army, it could not certainly be a sufficient
ground for a title to the command of three nations. 20
What then shall we say, that he did all this by
witchcraft? He did so, indeed, in a great measure, by
a sin that is called like it in the Scriptures. But, truly
and unpassionately reflecting upon the advantages of
his person, which might be thought to have produced 25
those of his fortune, I can espy no other but extraordinary diligence, and infinite dissimulation; and believe he was exalted above his nation, partly by his own
faults, but chiefly for ours.

▮▮▮▮▮▮▮rought him thus briefly (not through all 30
▮▮▮▮▮ to the supream usurpt authority; and,
▮▮▮▮y it was great pity he did not live to
▮▮▮▮and more kingdoms, be pleased to let me represent
to you, in a few words, how well I conceive he governed

these. And we will divide the consideration into that
of his foreign and domestique actions. The first of his
foreign was a peace with our brethren of Holland (who
were the first of our neighbours that God chastised for
5 having had so great a hand in the encouraging and
abetting our troubles at home): who would not imagine,
at first glympse, that this had been the most virtuous
and laudable deed, that his whole life could have made
any parade of? But no man can look upon all the cir-
10 cumstances, without perceiving, that it was purely the
sale and sacrificing of the greatest advantages that this
countrey could ever hope, and was ready to reap, from
a foreign war, to the private interests of his covetousness and ambition, and the security of his new and un-
15 setled usurpation. No sooner is that danger past, but
this Beatus Pacificus is kindling a fire in the northern
world, and carrying a war two thousand miles off, westwards. Two millions a year (besides all the vails of
his protectorship) is as little capable to suffice now
20 either his avarice or prodigality, as the two hundred
pounds were, that he was born to. He must have his
prey of the whole Indies, both by sea and land, this
great aligator. To satisfy our Anti-Solomon (who has
made silver almost as rare as gold, and gold as precious
25 stones in his new Jerusalem) we must go, ten thousand
of his slaves, to fetch him riches from his fantastical
Ophir. And, because his flatterers brag of him as the
most fortunate prince (the Faustus as well as Sylla of
our nation, whom God never forsook in any of his un-
30 dertakings), I desire them to consider, how, since the
English name was ever heard of, it never received so
great and so infamous a blow as under the imprudent
conduct of this unlucky Faustus; and herein let me
admire the justice of God, in this circumstance, that

they who had enslaved their country, though a great army, (which I wish, may be observed by ours with trembling), should be so shamefully defeated, by the hands of forty slaves. It was very ridiculous to see how prettily they endeavoured to hide this ignominy, 5 under the great name of the conquest of Jamaica; as if a defeated army should have the impudence to brag afterwards of the victory, because, though they had fled out of the field of battel, yet they quartered that night in a village of the enemies. The war with Spain was 10 a necessary consequence of this folly; and how much we have gotten by it, let the custom-house and exchange inform you; and, if he please to boast of the taking a part of the silver fleet, (which indeed nobody else but he, who was the sole gainer, has cause to do), at least, 15 let him give leave to the rest of the nation (which is the only loser), to complain of the loss of twelve hundred of her ships.

But, because it may here, perhaps, be answered, that his successes nearer home have extinguisht the dis- 20 grace of so remote miscarriages, and that Dunkirk ought more to be remembered for his glory, than S. Domingo for his disadvantage; I must confess, as to the honour of the English courage, that they were not wanting upon that occasion (excepting only the fault of serving at 25 least indirectly against their master), to the upholding of the renown of their war-like ancestors. But, for his particular share of it, who sate still at home, and exposed them so frankly abroad, I can only say, that for less money than he in the short time of his reign 30 exacted from his fellow-subjects, some of our former princes (with the daily hazard of their own persons) have added to the dominion of England, not only one town, but even a greater kingdom than itself. And, this being all considerable as concerning his enterprises abroad, let us examine, in the next place, how much we owe him for his justice and good government at home.

5   And, first, he found the commonwealth (as then they called it) in ready stock of about 800,000 pounds; he left the commonwealth (as he had the impudent raillery still to call it) some two millions and a half in debt. He found our trade very much decayed indeed, in com-
10 parison of the golden times of our late princes; he left it, as much again more decayed than he found it: and yet, not only no prince in England, but no tyrant in the world, ever sought out more base or infamous means to raise moneys. I shall only instance in one that he put
15 in practice, and another that he attempted, but was frighted from the execution (even he) by the infamy of it. That which he put in practice, was decimation; which was the most impudent breach of a public faith that the whole nation had given, and all private capitu-
20 lations which himself had made, as the nation's general and servant, that can be found out (I believe) in all history, from any of the most barbarous generals of the most barbarous people. Which, because it has been most excellently, and most largely, laid open by a whole
25 book written upon that subject, I shall only desire you here to remember the thing in general, and to be pleased to look upon that author, when you would recollect all the particulars and circumstances of the iniquity. The other design, of raising a present sum of money, which
30 he violently pursued, but durst not put in execution, was by the calling in and establishment of the Jews at London; from which he was rebuked by the universal outcry of the divines, and even of the citizens too, who took it ill, that a considerable number, at least amongst

themselves, were not thought Jews enough by their own Herod. And for this design, they say, he invented (O Antichrist ! Πονηρòν and Πονηρòς) to sell S. Paul's to them for a synagogue, if their purses and devotions could have reacht to the purchase. And this, indeed, 5 if he had done only to reward that nation, which had given the first noble example of crucifying their king, it might have had some appearance of gratitude : but he did it only for love of their mammon ; and would have sold afterwards, for as much more, S. Peter's (even at his 10 own Westminster) to the Turks for a *mosquito.* Such was his extraordinary piety to God, that he desired he might be worshiped in all manners, excepting only that heathenish way of the Common-prayer-book. But what do I speak of his wicked inventions for getting money ; 15 when every peny, that for almost five years he took every day from every man living in England, Scotland, and Ireland, was as much robbery, as if it had been taken by a thief upon the highways? Was it not so ? or can any man think that Cromwel, with the assistance of 20 his forces and moss-troopers, had more right to the command of all men's purses, than he might have had to any one's, whom he had met, and been too strong for, upon a road? And yet, when this came, in the case of Mr Coney, to be disputed by a legal tryal, he (which was 25 the highest act of tyranny that ever was seen in England) not only discouraged and threatned, but violently imprisoned the council of the plaintiff; that is, he shut up the law itself close prisoner, that no man might have relief from, or access to it. And it ought to be re- 30 membred, that this was done by those men, who, a few years before, had so bitterly decried, and openly opposed, the king's regular and formal way of proceeding in the trial of a little ship-money.

But, though we lost the benefit of our old courts of justice, it cannot be denied that he set up and such they were that, as no virtuous prince before would, so no ill one durst erect. What, have we lived
5 so many hundred years under such a form of justice as has been able regularly to punish all men that offend against it; and is it so deficient just now, that we must seek out new ways how to proceed against offenders? The reason which can only be given in nature for a
10 necessity of this is, because those things are now made crimes, which were never esteemed so in former ages; and there must needs be a new court set up to punish that, which all the old ones were bound to protect and reward. But I am so far from declaiming (as you call
15 it) against these wickednesses, (which, if I should undertake to do, I should never get to the peroration), that you see I only give a hint of some few, and pass over the rest, as things that are too many to be numbred, and must only be weighed in gross. Let any man shew me,
20 (for, though I pretend not to much reading, I will defie him in all history), let any man shew me (I say) an example of any nation in the world, (though much greater than ours), where there have, in the space of four years, been so many prisoners, only out of the endless
25 jealousies of one tyrant's guilty imagination. I grant you that Marius and Sylla, and the cursed triumvirate after them, put more people to death; but the reason, I think, partly was, because in those times, that had a mixture of some honour with their madness, they thought
30 it a more civil revenge against a Roman, to take away his life, than to take away his liberty. But tru point of murder too we have little reason to our late tyranny has been deficient to the exam have ever been set it, in other countries. Our judges

of justice have not been idle: and, to
reign of our late king (till the beginning
of the war), in which no drop of blood was ever drawn
but from two or three ears, I think the longest time of
our worst princes scarce saw many more executions, 5
than the short one of our blest reformer. And we saw,
and smelt in our open streets, (as I markt to you at
first), the broyling of human bowels as a burnt-offering
of a sweet savour to our idol; but all murdering, and all
torturing (though after the subtilest invention of his 10
predecessors of Sicilie), is more humane and more sup-
portable, than his selling of Christians, Englishmen,
gentlemen; his selling of them (oh monstrous! oh in-
credible!) to be slaves in America. If his whole life
could be reproacht with no other action, yet this alone 15
would weigh down all the multiplicity of crimes in any
one of our tyrants; and I dare only touch, without
stopping or insisting upon so insolent and so execrable
a cruelty, for fear of falling into so violent (though a
just) passion, as would make me exceed that temper and 20
moderation, which I resolve to observe in this discourse
with you.

These are great calamities; but even these are not
the most insupportable that we have indured; for so it
is, that the scorn, and mockery, and insultings of an 25
enemy are more painful than the deepest wounds of his
serious fury. This man was wanton and merry (unwittily
and ungracefully merry) with our sufferings: he loved to
say and do senseless and fantastical things, only to shew
his power of doing or saying anything. It would ill 30
or any civil mouth, to repeat those words
poke concerning the most sacred of our
laws, the Petition of Right, and Magna Charta.
To-day you should see him ranting so wildly, that no-

body durst come near him; the morrow flinging of
cushions, and playing at snow-balls with his servants.

This month he assembles a parliament, and professes
himself, with humble tears, to be only their servant and
5 their minister; the next month he swears by the living
God, that he will turn them out of doors, and he does
so, in his princely way of threatning, bidding them, turn
the buckles of their girdles behind them. The representative of a whole, nay of three whole nations,
10 was, in his esteem, so contemptible a meeting, that he
thought the affronting and expelling of them to be a
thing of so little consequence, as not to deserve that he
should advise with any mortal man about it. What shall
we call this? boldness, or brutishness? rashness, or
15 phrensie? There is no name can come up to it; and
therefore we must leave it without one. Now a parliament must be chosen in the new manner, next time in
the old form, but all cashiered still after the newest
mode. Now he will govern by major-generals, now by
20 one house, now by another house, now by no house;
now the freak takes him, and he makes seventy peers of
the land at one clap (*ex tempore*, and *stans pede in uno*);
and to manifest the absolute power of the potter, he
chooses not only the worst clay he could find, but picks
25 up even the dirt and mire, to form out of it his vessels
of honour. It was antiently said of Fortune, that, when
she had a mind to be merry, and to divert herself, she
was wont to raise up such kind of people to the highest
dignities. This son of Fortune, Cromwel (who was
30 himself one of the primest of her jests), found out the
true *haut-goust* of this pleasure, and rejoyced in the ex-
travagance of his ways, as the fullest demonstration of
his uncontroulable soveraignty. Good God! What have
we seen? and what have we suffered? what do all these

actions signifie? what do they say aloud to the whole
nation, but this, (even as plainly as if it were proclaimed
by heralds through the streets of London), "You are
slaves and fools, and so I'll use you!"

These are briefly a part of those merits which you 5
lament to have wanted the reward of more kingdoms,
and suppose that, if he had lived longer, he might have
had them : which I am so far from concurring to, that I
believe his seasonable dying to have been a greater good
fortune to him, than all the victories and prosperities of 10
his life. For he seemed evidently (methinks) to be near
the end of his deceitful glories; his own army grew at
last as weary of him, as the rest of the people; and I
never pass'd of late before his palace (his, do I call it?
I ask God and the king pardon), but I never passt of 15
late before Whitehal, without reading upon the gate of
it, *Mene Mene, Tekel, Upharsin.* But it pleascd God to
take him from the ordinary courts of men, and juries of
his peers, to his own high court of justice; which being
more merciful than ours below, there is a little room yet 20
left for the hope of his friends, if he have any; though
the outward unrepentance of his death afford but small
materials for the work of charity, especially if he designed
even then to entail his own injustice upon his children,
and, by it, inextricable confusions and civil wars upon 25
the nation. But here's at least an end of him. And
where's now the fruit of all that blood and calamity,
which his ambition has cost the world? Where is it?
Why, his son (you'l say) has the whole crop; I doubt he
will find it quickly blasted; I have nothing to say 30
against the gentleman, or any living of his family; on
the contrary, I wish him better fortune, than to have a
long and unquiet possession of his master's inheritance.
Whatsoever I have spoken against his father, is that

which I should have thought (though decency, perhaps, might have hindered me from saying it) even against mine own, if I had been so unhappy, as that mine, by the same ways should have left me three kingdoms.

5   Here I stopt; and my pretended protector, who, I expected, should have been very angry, fell a laughing; it seems at the simplicity of my discourse, for thus he replyed: "You seem to pretend extreamly to the old obsolete rules of virtue and conscience, which makes me 10 doubt very much, whether, from the vast prospect of three kingdoms, you can shew me any acres of your own. But these are so far from making you a prince, that I am afraid your friends will never have the contentment to see you so much as a justice of peace in 15 your own country. For this I perceive which you call virtue, is nothing else but either the frowardness of a Cynick, or the laziness of an Epicurean. I am glad you allow me at least artful dissimulation, and unwearied diligence in my heroe; and I assure you, that he, whose 20 life is constantly drawn by those two, shall never be misled out of the way of greatness. But I see you are a pedant, and Platonical statesman, a theoretical commonwealth's-man, an Utopian dreamer. Was ever riches gotten by your golden mediocrities? or the supream 25 place attained to by virtues that must not stir out of the middle? Do you study Aristotle's politicks, and write, if you please, comments upon them; and let another but practise Machiaval: and let us see, then, which of you two will come to the greatest preferments. If the desire 30 of rule and superiority be a virtue, (as sure I am it is more imprinted in human nature than any of your lethargical morals;) and what is the virtue of any creature, but the exercise of those powers and inclinations which God hath infused into it? If that (I say) be

virtue, we ought not to esteem any thing vice, which is
the most proper, if not the only, means of attaining of it.

IT is a truth so certain, and so clear,
That to the first-born man it did appear;
Did not the mighty heir, the noble Cain,   5
By the fresh laws of nature taught, disdain
That (though a brother) any one should be
A greater favourite to God than he?
He struck him down; and, so (said he) so fell
The sheep, which thou didst sacrifice so well.   10
Since all the fullest sheaves which I could bring,
Since all were blasted in the offering,
Lest God should my next victim too despise,
The acceptable priest I'll sacrifice.
Hence, coward fears; for the first blood so spilt,   15
As a reward, he the first city built.
'Twas a beginning generous and high,
Fit for a grand-child of the Deity.
So well advanc'd, 'twas pity there he staid;
One step of glory more he should have made,   20
And to the utmost bounds of greatness gone;
Had Adam too been kill'd, he might have reign'd alone.
One brother's death, what do I mean to name,
A small oblation to revenge and fame?
The mighty-soul'd Abimelech, to shew   25
What for a high place a higher spirit can do,
A hecatomb almost of brethren slew,
And seventy times in nearest blood he dy'd
(To make it hold) his royal purple pride.
Why do I name the lordly creature man?   30
The weak, the mild, the coward woman, can,
When to a crown she cuts her sacred way,
All that oppose, with manlike courage, slay.

So Athaliah, when she saw her son,
And with his life her dearer greatness gone,
With a majestick fury slaughter'd all
Whom high birth might to high pretences call:
5 Since he was dead who all her power sustain'd,
  Resolv'd to reign alone; resolv'd and reign'd.
  In vain her sex, in vain the laws withstood,
  In vain the sacred plea of David's blood;
  A noble, and a bold contention, she
10 (One woman) undertook with destinie.
  She to pluck down, destiny to uphold
  (Oblig'd by holy oracles of old)
  The great Jessæan race on Judah's throne;
  Till 'twas at last an equal wager grown,
15 Scarce fate, with much ado, the better got by one.
  Tell me not, she herself at last was slain;
  Did she not, first, seven years (a life-time) reign?
  Seven royal years to a public spirit will seem
  More than the private life of a Mathusalem.
20 'Tis godlike to be great; and, as they say,
  A thousand years to God are but a day;
  So to a man, when once a crown he wears,
  The coronation day's more than a thousand years."

He would have gone on, I perceive, in his blasphe-
25 mies, but that, by God's grace, I became so bold as
thus to interrupt him: "I understand now perfectly
(which I guest at long before) what kind of angel and
protector you are; and, though your style in verse be
very much mended since you were wont to deliver
30 oracles, yet your doctrine is much worse than ever you
had formerly (that I heard of) the face to publish;
whether your long practice with mankind has increas'd
and improv'd your malice, or whether you think us in

this age to be grown so impudently wicked, that there needs no more art or disguises to draw us to your party."

"My dominion (said he hastily, and with a dreadful furious look) is so great in this world, and I am so 5 powerful a monarch of it, that I need not be ashamed that you should know me; and that you may see I know you too, I know you to be an obstinate and inveterate malignant; and for that reason I shall take you along with me to the next garrison of ours; from whence you 10 shall go to the Tower, and from thence to the court of justice, and from thence you know whither." I was almost in the very pounces of the great bird of prey:

WHEN, lo, ere the last words were fully spoke,
From a fair cloud, which rather ope'd than broke, 15
A flash of light, rather than lightning, came,
So swift and yet so gentle was the flame.
Upon it rode, and, in his full career,
Seem'd to my eyes no sooner there, than here,
The comeliest youth of all th'angelick race; 20
Lovely his shape, ineffable his face.
The frowns, with which he struck the trembling fiend,
All smiles of human beauty did transcend;
His beams of locks fell part dishevel'd down,
Part upwards curl'd, and form'd a nat'ral crown, 25
Such as the British monarchs us'd to wear;
If gold may be compar'd with angel's hair.
His coat and flowing mantle were so bright,
They seem'd both made of woven silver light:
Across his breast an azure ribon went, 30
At which a medal hung, that did present
In wondrous living figures to the sight,
The mystic champion's, and old dragon's fight;

And from his mantle's side there shone afar,
A fix't, and, I believe, a real star.
In his fair hand (what need was there of more?)
No arms, but th'English bloody cross, he bore,
5 Which when he towards th'affrighted tyrant bent,
And some few words pronounc'd (but what they meant,
Or were, could not, alas, by me be known,
Only, I well perceiv'd, Jesus was one)
He trembled, and he roar'd, and fled away;
10 Mad to quit thus his more than hop'd-for prey.
　　Such rage inflames the wolf's wild heart and eyes
(Robb'd, as he thinks, unjustly of his prize)
Whom unawares the shepheard spies, and draws
The bleating lamb from out his ravenous jaws:
15 The shepheard fain himself would he assail,
But fear above his hunger does prevail,
He knows his foe too strong, and must be gone:
He grins as he looks back, and howls as he goes on.

SEVERAL DISCOURSES BY WAY OF ESSAYS
IN VERSE AND PROSE.

I.

OF LIBERTY.

THE liberty of a people consists in being governed by laws which they have made themselves, under whatsoever form it be of government: the liberty of a private man, in being master of his own time and actions, as far as may 5 consist with the laws of God, and of his country. Of this latter only we are here to discourse, and to enquire what estate of life does best seat us in the possession of it. This liberty of our own actions is such a fundamental priviledge of humane nature, that God himself, not- 10 withstanding all his infinite power and right over us, permits us to enjoy it, and that too after a forfeiture made by the rebellion of Adam. He takes so much care for the entire preservation of it to us, that he suffers neither his providence nor eternal decree to break or 15 infringe it. Now for our time, the same God, to whom we are but tenants-at-will for the whole, requires but the seventh part to be paid to him as a small quit-rent

in acknowledgment of his title. It is man only that
has the impudence to demand our whole time, though
economy he neither gave it, nor can restore it, nor is able to pay
any considerable value for the least part of it. This
5 birth-right of mankind above all other creatures some
are forced by hunger to sell, like Esau, for bread and
broth: but the greatest part of men make such a
bargain for the delivery-up of themselves, as Thamer
did with Judah; instead of a kid, the necessary provisions
10 of human life, they are contented to do it for rings and
bracelets. The great dealers in this world may be divided
⟹ into the ambitious, the covetous, and the voluptuous;
and that all these men sell themselves to be slaves,
though to the vulgar it may seem a Stoical paradox, will
15 appear to the wise so plain and obvious, that they will
scarce think it deserves the labour of argumentation.

Let us first consider the ambitious; and those, both
in their progress to greatness, and after the attaining
of it. There is nothing truer than what Salust says,
20 "Dominationis in alios servitium suum mercedem dant:"
they are content to pay so great a price as their own
servitude, to purchase the domination over others. The
first thing they must resolve to sacrifice is their whole
time; they must never stop, nor ever turn aside whilst
25 they are in the race of glory, no not like Atalanta for
golden apples. Neither, indeed, can a man stop himself
if he would, when he's in this career:

Fertur equis auriga, neque audit currus habenas.

Pray, let us but consider a little, what mean servile
30 things men do for this imaginary food. We cannot
fetch a greater example of it, than from the chief men
of that nation which boasted most of liberty. To what
pitiful baseness did the noblest Romans submit them-

selves, for the obtaining of a prætorship, or the consular
dignity! They put on the habit of suppliants, and ran
about on foot, and in dirt, through all the tribes, to beg
voices; they flattered the poorest artisons; and carried
a nomenclator with them, to whisper in their ear every 5
man's name, lest they should mistake it in their salu-
tations; they shook the hand, and kiss'd the cheek,
of every popular tradesman; they stood all day at every
market in the publick places, to shew and ingratiate themselves to the rout; they imploy'd all their friends to 10
solicite for them; they kept open tables in every street;
they distributed wine, and bread, and money, even to
the vilest of the people. "En Romanos rerum dominos!"
Behold the masters of the world begging from door to
door. This particular humble way to greatness is now 15
out of fashion; but yet every ambitious person is still, in
some sort, a Roman candidate. He must feast and
bribe, and attend and flatter, and adore many beasts,
though not the beast with many heads. Catiline, who
was so proud that he could not content himself with a 20
less power than Sylla's, was yet so humble for the
attaining of it, as to make himself the most contemptible
of all servants. And, since I happen here to propose
Catiline for my instance (though there be thousands of
examples for the same thing,) give me leave to transcribe 25
the character which Cicero gives of this noble slave,
because it is a general description of all ambitious men,
and which Machiavel, perhaps, would say ought to be
the rule of their life and actions:

"This man (says he, as most of you may well re- 30
member) had many artificial touches and strokes, that
look'd like the beauty of great virtues; his intimate
conversation was with the worst of men, and yet he
seemed to be an admirer and lover of the best; he was

furnished with all the nets of lust and luxury, and yet
wanted not the arms of labour and industry: neither
do I believe that there was ever any monster in nature,
composed out of so many different and disagreeing parts.
5 Who more acceptable, sometimes, to the most honourable
persons? Who more a favourite to the most infamous?
Who, sometimes, appeared a braver champion; who,
at other times, a bolder enemy to his country? Who
more dissolute in his pleasures? Who more patient in
10 his toils? Who more rapacious in robbing? Who more
profuse in giving? Above all things, this was remarkable
and admirable in him, the arts he had to acquire the
good opinion and kindness of all sorts of men, to retain
it with great complaisance, to communicate all things to
15 them, watch and serve all the occasions of their fortune,
both with his money and his interest and his industry;
and, if need were, not by sticking at any wickedness
whatsoever that might be useful to them, to bend and
turn about his own nature and laveer with every wind;
20 to live severely with the melancholy, merrily with the
pleasant, gravely with the aged, wantonly with the young,
desperately with the bold, and debauchedly with the
luxurious: with this variety and multiplicity of his
nature—as he had made a collection of friendships with
25 all the most wicked and restless of all nations; so, by
the artificial simulation of some virtues, he made a shift
to ensnare some honest and eminent persons into his
familiarity. Neither could so vast a design as the
destruction of this empire have been undertaken by him,
30 if the immanity of so many vices had not been covered
and disguised by the appearances of some excellent
qualities."

I see, methinks, the character of an Anti-Paul, "who
became all things to all men," that he might destroy

all; who only wanted the assistance of fortune, to have been as great as his friend Cæsar was a little after him. And the ways of Cæsar to compass the same ends (I mean to the civil war, which was but another manner of setting his country on fire) were not unlike 5 these, though he used, afterward, his unjust dominion with more moderation, than I think the other would have done. Salust, therefore, who was well acquainted with them both, and with many such like gentlemen of his time, says, "that it is the nature of ambition, to make 10 men lyars and cheaters, to hide the truth in their breasts, and shew, like juglers, another thing in their mouths, to cut all friendships and enmities to the measure of their own interests, and to make a good countenance without the help of good will." And can 15 there be freedom with this perpetual constraint? what is it but a kind of rack, that forces men to say what they have no mind to?

I have wondred at the extravagant and barbarous stratagem of Zopyrus, and more at the praises which 20 I find of so deformed an action; who, though he was one of the seven grandees of Persia, and the son of Megabisus, who had freed, before, his country from an ignoble servitude, slit his own nose and lips, cut off his own ears, scourged and wounded his whole body, that 25 he might, under pretence of having been mangled so inhumanely by Darius, be received into Babylon (then besieged by the Persians,) and get into the command of it by the recommendation of so cruel a sufferance, and their hopes of his endeavouring to revenge it. It 30 is great pity, the Babylonians suspected not his falshood, that they might have cut off his hands too, and whipt him back again. But the design succeeded; he betrayed the city, and was made governor of it. What

brutish master ever punished his offending slave with
so little mercy, as ambition did this Zopyrus? and yet
how many are there, in all nations, who imitate him in
some degree for a less reward; who, though they endure
5 not so much corporal pain for a small preferment or
some honour (as they call it,) yet stick not to commit
actions, by which they are more shamefully and more
lastingly stigmatized! But you may say, though these
be the most ordinary and open ways to greatness, yet
10 there are narrow, thorny, and little-trodden paths too,
through which some men find a passage by virtuous
industry. I grant, sometimes they may; but then, that
industry must be such, as cannot consist with liberty,
though it may with honesty.

15 Thou'rt careful, frugal, painful; we commend a
servant so, but not a friend.

Well then, we must acknowledge the toil and
drudgery which we are forced to endure in this ascent;
but we are epicures and lords when once we are gotten
20 up into the high places. This is but a short appren-
tiship, after which we are made free of royal company. If we fall in love with any beauteous women,
we must be content that they would be our mistresses
whilst we woo them; as soon as we are wedded and
25 enjoy, 'tis we shall be the masters.

I am willing to stick to this similitude in the case
of greatness: we enter into the bonds of it, like those
of matrimony; we are bewitch'd with the outward
and printed beauty, and take it for better or worse,
30 before we know its true nature and interior inconveniences. A great fortune (says Seneca) is a great
servitude; but many are of that opinion which Brutus
imputes (I hope untruly) even to that patron of liberty,
his friend Cicero: "We fear (says he to Atticus) death,

and banishment, and poverty, a great deal too much.
Cicero, I am afraid, thinks these to be the worst of
evils; and if he have but some persons, from whom he
can obtain what he has a mind to, and others who will
flatter and worship him, seems to be well enough con- 5
tented with an honourable servitude, if any thing, indeed,
ought to be called honourable in so base and contume-
lious a condition." This was spoken as became the
bravest man who was ever born in the bravest commonwealth. But with us generally no condition passes 10
for servitude, that is accompanied with great riches,
and honors, and with the service of many inferiors.
This is but a deception of the sight through a false
medium; for if a groom serve a gentleman in his
chamber, that gentleman a lord, and that lord a prince; 15
the groom, the gentleman, and the lord, are as much
servants one as the other: the circumstantial difference
of the one getting only his bread and wages, the second
a plentiful, and the third a superfluous estate, is no
more intrinsical to this matter, than the difference be- 20
tween a plain, a rich, and gaudy livery. I do not say,
that he who sells his whole time and his own will for
one hundred thousand, is not a wiser merchant than he
who does it for one hundred pounds; but I will swear
they are both merchants, and that he is happier than 25
both, who can live contentedly without selling that
estate to which he was born. But this dependance
upon superiours is but one chain of the lovers of power:

Amatorem trecentæ
Pirithoum cohibent catenæ.   30

    Let's begin with him by break of day: for by that
time he's besieged by two or three hundred suitors;
and the hall and antichambers (all the outworks) possest by the enemy: as soon as his chamber opens,

they are ready to break into that, or to corrupt the guards, for entrance. This is so essential a part of greatness, that whosoever is without it, looks like a fallen favourite, like a person disgraced, and condemned
5 to do what he pleases all the morning. There are some who, rather than want this, are contented to have their rooms filled up every day with murmuring and cursing creditors, and to charge bravely through a body of them to get to their coach. Now, I would fain know
10 which is the worst duty, that of any one particular person who waits to speak with the great man, or the great man's, who waits every day to speak with all the company.

> Aliena negotia centum
15   Per caput, et circa saliunt latus—

a hundred businesses of other men (many unjust, and most impertinent) fly continually about his head and ears, and strike him in the face like dors. Let's contemplate him a little at another special scene of glory,
20 and that is, his table. Here he seems to be the lord of all nature: the earth affords him her best metals for his dishes, her best vegetables and animals for his food; the air and sea supply him with their choicest birds and fishes; and a great many men, who look like
25 masters, attend upon him; and yet, when all this is done, even all this is but *table d'host;* 'tis crowded with people for whom he cares not, with many parasites and some spies, with the most burdensome sort of guests, the endeavourers to be witty. .

30   But every body pays him great respect; every body commends his meat, that is, his money; every body admires the exquisite dressing and ordering of it, that is, his clark of the kitchen, or his cook; every body loves his hospitality, that is, his vanity. But I desire

to know why the honest inn-keeper, who provides a
public table for his profit, should be but of a mean
profession; and he, who does it for his honour, a
munificent prince? You'll say, because one sells,
and the other gives: nay, both sell, though for different 5
things; the one for plain money, the other for I know
not what jewels, whose value is in custom and in fancy.
If then his table be made a snare (as the Scripture
speaks) to his liberty, where can he hope for freedom?
There is always, and every where, some restraint upon 10
him. He's guarded with crowds, and shackled with
formalities. The half hat, the whole hat, the half smile,
the whole smile, the nod, the embrace, the positive
parting with a little bow, the comparative at the middle
of the room, the superlative at the door; and, if the 15
person be *pan huper sebastos*, there's a huper-superla-
tive ceremony then of conducting him to the bottom
of the stairs, or to the very gate: as if there were
such rules set to these Leviathans as are to the sea.
Hitherto shalt thou go, and no further. 20

Perditur hæc inter misero lux,

Thus wretchedly the precious day is lost.

How many impertinent letters and visits must he receive, and sometimes answer both too as impertinently!
He never sets his foot beyond his threshold, unless, like 25
a funeral, he have a train to follow him; as if, like the
dead corps, he would not stir, till the bearers were all
ready. "My life (says Horace, speaking to one of these
magnificos) is a great deal more easie and commodious
than thine; in that I can go into the market, and cheapen 30
what I please, without being wondered at; and take
my horse and ride as far as Tarentum, without being
mist." 'Tis an unpleasant constraint to be always under

the sight and observation, and censu▮▮▮▮▮
there may be vanity in it, so, methin▮▮
be vexation, too, of spirit: and I wo▮▮▮
can endure to have two or three hundred men stand
5 gazing upon them whilst they are at dinner, and take
notice of every bit they eat. Nothing seems - greater
and more lordly than the multitude of domestique servants; but even this too, if weighed seriously, is a piece
of servitude; unless you will be a servant to them (as
10 many men are,) the trouble and care of yours in the
government of them all is much more than that of every
one of them in their observance of you. I take the profession of a school-master to be one of the most useful,
and which ought to be of the most honourable in a
15 commonwealth; yet certainly all his fasces and. tyran-
nical authority over so many boys take away his own
liberty more than theirs.

I do but slightly touch upon all these particulars of
the slavery of greatness: I shake but a few of their
20 outward chains; their anger, hatred, jealousie, fear,
envy, grief, and all the *et cætera* of their passions, which
are the secret, but constant, tyrants and tortures of
their life, I omit here, because, though they be symp-
tomes most frequent and violent in this disease, yet they
25 are common too, in some degree, to the epidemical
disease of life itself.

But the ambitious man, though he be so many ways a
slave (*O toties servus!*) yet he bears it bravely and he-
roically: he struts and looks big upon the stage: he
30 thinks himself a real prince in his masking▮
deceives, too, all the foolish part of his spec▮
a slave *in Saturnalibus*. The covetous man▮▮▮
right servant, a draught-horse with bells or feathers;
ad metalla damnatus, a man condemned to work in mines,

▮▮▮▮and hardest condition of servitude ;
▮▮▮▮ misery, a worker there for he knows
▮▮▮▮*apeth up riches, and knows not who*
shall enjoy them; 'Tis only sure, that he himself neither
shall nor can enjoy them. He's an indigent needy 5
slave ; he will hardly allow himself cloaths and board-
wages :

> Unciatim vix de demenso suo,
> Suum defraudans genium, comparsit miser.

He defrauds not only other men, but his own genius ; 10
he cheats himself for money. But the servile and
miserable condition of this wretch is so apparent, that
I leave it, as evident to every man's sight, as well as
judgment.

It seems a more difficult work to prove that the 15
voluptuous man, too, is but a servant : what can be
more the life of a freeman, or, as we say ordinarily, of
a gentleman, than to follow nothing but his own pleasures ? Why, I'll tell you who is that true freeman, and
that true gentleman ; not he who blindly follows all 20
his pleasures (the very name of *followers* is servile) ; but
he who rationally guides them, and is not hindred by
outward impediments in the conduct and enjoyment of
them. If I want skill or force to restrain the beast that
I ride upon, though I bought it, and call it my own ; 25
yet, in the truth of the matter, I am at that time rather
his man, than he my horse. The voluptuous men
(whom we are fallen upon) may be divided, I think,
▮▮▮▮ lustful and luxurious, who are both servants of
▮▮▮▮her, whom we spoke of before, the am- 30
▮▮▮▮covetous, were κακὰ θηρία, *evil wild*
▮▮▮▮ γαστέρες ἀργαὶ, *slow bellies,* as our
translation renders it, but the word ἀργαὶ (which is a
fantastical word, with two directly opposite significations)

will bear as well the translation of *quick*, or *diligent bellies;* and both interpretations may be applied to these men.   Metrodorus said that he had learnt πλέον ἀληθῶς γαστρὶ χαρίζεσθαι, to give his belly just thanks for all
5 his pleasures.   This, by the calumniators of Epicurus his philosophy, was objected as one of the most scandalous of all their sayings; which, according to my charitable understanding, may admit a very virtuous sense, which is, that he thanked his own belly for that moderation,
10 in the customary appetites of it, which can only give a man liberty and happiness in this world.   Let this suffice at present to be spoken of those great triumviri of the world; the covetous man, who is a mean villain, like Lepidus; the ambitious, who is a brave one, like Octa-
15 vius; and the voluptuous, who is a loose and debauched one, like Mark Antony :

> Quisnam igitur liber? Sapiens, sibique imperiosus.

Not Oenomaus, who commits himself wholly to a cha- rioteer, that may break his neck : but the man,

20   Who governs his own course with steady hand,
        Who does himself with soveraign power command ;
        Whom neither death nor poverty does fright,
        Who stands not aukwardly in his own light
        Against the truth : who can, when pleasures knock
25   Loud at his door, keep from the bolt and lock.
        Who can, though honour at his gate should stay
        In all her masking cloaths, send her away,
        And cry, Be gone, I have no mind to play.

This, I confess, is a freeman : but it may be said, that
30 many persons are so shackled by their fortune, that they are hindred from enjoyment of that manumission which they have obtained from virtue.   I do both understand, and in part feel, the weight of this objection : all I can answer to it is, that we must get as much liberty as we
35 can, we must use our utmost endeavours, and, when all

that is done, be contented with the length of that line
which is allow'd us. If you ask me, what condition
of life I think the most allow'd; I should pitch upon
that sort of people, whom King James was wont to call
the happiest of our nation, the men placed in the country 5
by their fortune above an high-constable, and yet beneath the trouble of a justice of peace; in a moderate
plenty, without any just argument for the desire of increasing it by the care of many relations; and with so
much knowledge and love of piety and philosophy (that 10
is, of the study of God's laws, and of his creatures) as
may afford him matter enough never to be idle, though
without business; and never to be melancholy, though
without sin or vanity.

I shall conclude this tedious discourse with a prayer 15
of mine in a copy of Latine verses, of which I remember
no other part; and (*pour faire bonne bouche*) with some
other verses upon the same subject:

"Magne Deus, quod ad has vitæ brevis attinet horas,
Da mihi, da panem libertatemque, nec ultra 20
Sollicitas effundo preces: si quid datur ultra,
Accipiam gratus; sin non, contentus abibo."

For the few hours of life allotted me,
Give me (great God) but bread and libertie.
I'll beg no more: if more thou'rt pleas'd to give, 25
I'll thankfully that overplus receive:
If beyond this no more be freely sent,
I'll thank for this, and go away content.

MARTIAL, LIB. I. EP. 56.

"Vota tui breviter," &c.

WELL then, Sir, you shall know how far extend
The prayers and hopes of your poetic friend. 30

v He does not palaces nor mannors crave,
    Would be no lord, but less a lord would have;
    The ground he holds, if he his own can call,
    He quarrels not with heaven, because 'tis small:
5   Let gay and toilsome greatness others please,
    He loves of homely littleness · the ease.
    Can any man in guilded rooms attend,
    And his dear hours in humble visits spend;
    When in the fresh and beauteous fields he may
10 With various healthful pleasures fill the day?
    If there be man (ye gods!) I ought to hate,
    Dependance and attendance be his fate.
    Still let him busie be, and in a crowd,
    And very much a slave, and very proud:
15 Thus he perhaps pow'rful and rich may grow;
    No matter, O ye gods! that I'll allow:
    But let him peace and freedom never see;
    Let him not love this life, who loves not me.

MARTIAL, LIB. II. EP. 53.

"Vis fieri liber?" &c.

Would you be free? 'Tis your chief wish, you say:
20 Come on; I'll shew thee, friend, the certain way.
    If to no feasts abroad thou lov'st to go,
    Whilst bount'ous God does bread at home bestow;
    If thou the goodness of thy cloaths dost prize
    By thine own use, and not by others' eyes;
25 If (only safe from weathers) thou can'st dwell
    In a small house, but a convenient shell;
    If thou, without a sigh, or golden wish,
    Canst look upon thy beechen bowl, and dish;
    If in thy mind such power and greatness be,
30 The Persian king's a slave compar'd with thee.

MARTIAL, LIB. II. EP. 68.

"Quod te nomine," &c.

THAT I do you, with humble bowes no more,
And danger of my naked head, adore;
That I, who, Lord and master, cry'd erewhile,
Salute you, in a new and diff'rent stile,
By your own name, a scandal to you now,   5
Think not that I forget myself and you:
By loss of all things, by all others sought,
This freedom, and the freeman's hat is bought.
A lord and master no man wants, but he
Who o'er himself has no authority,   10
Who does for honours and for riches strive,
And follies, without which lords cannot live.
If thou from fortune dost no servant crave,
Believe it, thou no master need'st to have.

ODE.

UPON LIBERTY.

I.

FREEDOM with Virtue takes her seat;   15
Her proper place, her only scene,
⟨Is in the golden mean,⟩
She lives not with the poor, nor with the great.
The wings of those Necessity has clipt,
    And they're in Fortune's Bridewel whipt   20
    To the laborious task of bread;
These are by various tyrants captive led.
Now wild Ambition with imperious force
Rides, reins, and spurs them, like th' unruly horse.
    And servile Avarice yokes them now,   25

Like toilsom oxen, to the plow.
And sometimes Lust, like the misguided light,
Draws them through all the labyrinths of night.
If any few among the great there be
5   From these insulting passions free,
Yet we ev'n those, too, fetter'd see
By custom, business, crowds, and formal decencie.
And wheresoe'er they stay, and wheresoe'er they go,
Impertinencies round them flow :
10 These are the small uneasie things
Which about greatness still are found,
And rather it molest, than wound :
Like gnats, which too much heat of summer brings ;
But cares do swarm there, too, and those have stings :
15 As, when the honey does too open lie,
A thousand wasps about it flie :
Nor will the master ev'n to share admit ;
The master stands aloof, and dares not taste of it.

2.

'Tis morning : well ; I fain would yet sleep on ;
20   You cannot now ; you must be gone
To court, or to the noisie hall :
Besides, the rooms without are crowded all ;
The stream of business does begin,
And a spring-tide of clients is come in.
25 Ah, cruel guards, which this poor prisoner keep !
Will they not suffer him to sleep ?
Make an escape ; out at the postern flee,
And get some blessed hours of liberty :
With a few friends, and a few dishes dine,
30   And much of mirth and moderate wine.
To thy bent mind some relaxation give,
And steal one day out of thy life, to live.

Oh, happy man (he cries) to whom kind heaven
 Has such a freedom always given!
Why, mighty madman, what should hinder thee
 From being every day as free?

3.

In all the freeborn nations of the air,   5
Never did bird a spirit so mean and sordid bear,
As to exchange a native liberty
Of soaring boldly up into the sky,
His liberty to sing, to perch, or fly,
 When, and wherever he thought good, 10
And all his innocent pleasures of the wood,
For a more plentiful or constant food.
  Nor ever did ambitious rage
  Make him into a painted cage,
Or the false forest of a well-hung room, 15
  For honour and preferment, come.
Now, blessings on you all, ye heroick race,
Who keep their primitive powers and rights so well,
  Though men and angels fell.
Of all material lives the highest place 20
  To you is justly given;
  And ways and walks the nearest heaven.
Whilst wretched we, yet vain and proud, think fit
  To boast, that we look up to it.
Ev'n to the universal tyrant, Love, 25
  You homage pay but once a year:
None so degenerous and unbirdly prove,
  As his perpetual yoke to bear.
None, but a few unhappy household fowl,
  Whom human lordship does controul; 30
  Who from the birth corrupted were
By bondage, and by man's example here.

4.

He's no small prince, who every day
    Thus to himself can say;
Now will I sleep, now eat, now sit, now walk,
Now meditate alone, now with acquaintance talk.
5 This I will do, here I will stay,
    Or, if my fancy calleth me away,
My man and I will presently go ride;
(For we, before, have nothing to provide,
Nor, after, are to render an account)
10 To Dover, Berwick, or the Cornish mount.
       If thou but a short journey take,
      As if thy last thou wert to make,
Business must be despatch'd, ere thou canst part,
    Nor canst thou stir, unless there be
15   A hundred horse and men to wait on thee,
    And many a mule, and many a cart;
    What an unwieldy man thou art!
    The Rhodian Colossus so
    A journey, too, might go.

5.

20 Where honour, or where conscience, does not bind,
    No other law shall shackle me;
    Slave to myself I will not be,
Nor shall my future actions be confin'd
    By my own present mind.
25 Who by resolves and vows engag'd does stand
    For days, that yet belong to fate,
Does, like an unthrift, mortgage his estate,
    Before it falls into his hand:
    The bondman of the cloister so
30 All that he does receive, does always owe;

And still, as time comes in, it goes away
    Not to enjoy, but debts to pay.
Unhappy slave, and pupil to a bell,
Which his hour's work, as well as hours, does tell!
Unhappy, till the last, the kind releasing knell.   5

6.

If life should a well-order'd poem be
    (In which he only hits the white
Who joyns true profit with the best delight)
The more heroick strain let others take,
    Mine the Pindaric way I'll make;   10
The matter shall be grave, the numbers loose and free.
It shall not keep one settled pace of time,
In the same tune it shall not always chime,
Nor shall each day just to his neighbour rhime;
A thousand liberties it shall dispense,   15
And yet shall manage all without offence
Or to the sweetness of the sound, or greatness of the sense;
Nor shall it never from one subject start,
    Nor seek transitions to depart,
Nor its set way o'er stiles and bridges make,   20
    Nor thorough lanes a compass take,
As if it fear'd some trespass to commit,
    When the wide air's a road for it.
So the imperial eagle does not stay
    Till the whole carkass he devour,   25
    That's fallen into its power:
As if his generous hunger understood
That he can never want plenty of food,
    He only sucks the tastful blood;
And to fresh game flies cheerfully away;   30
To kites and meaner birds, he leaves the mangled prey.

II.

OF SOLITUDE.

" NUNQUAM minus solus, quam cum solus,"
is now become a very vulgar saying.   Every
man, and almost every boy, for these seven-
teen hundred years, has had it in his mouth.
5 But it was at first spoken by the excellent Scipio, who
was without question a most eloquent and witty person,
as well as the most wise, most worthy, most happy, and
the greatest of all mankind.   His meaning, no doubt,
was this, that he found more satisfaction to his mind,
10 and more improvement of it, by solitude than by company; and, to shew that he spoke not this loosly, or
out of vanity, after he had made Rome mistress of
almost the whole world, he retired himself from it by a
voluntary exile, and at a private house in the middle of
15 a wood near Linternum, passed the remainder of his
glorious life no less gloriously.   This house Seneca
went to see so long after with great veneration.; and,
among other things, describes his baths to have been
of so mean a structure, that now, says he, the basest
20 of the people would despise them, and cry out, "Poor
Scipio understood not how to live."   What an authority
is here for the credit of retreat ! and happy had it been
for Hannibal, if adversity could have taught him as

much wisdom as was learnt by Scipio from the highest
prosperities. This would be no wonder, if it were as
truly as it is colourably and wittily said by Monsieur
de Montaigne, "that ambition itself might teach us to
love solitude; there's nothing does so much hate to 5
have companions." 'Tis true, it loves to have its
elbows free, it detests to have company on either side;
but it delights above all things in a train behind, aye,
and ushers too before it. But the greatest part of men
are so far from the opinion of that noble Roman, that, 10
if they chance at any time to be without company, they're
like a becalmed ship; they never move but by the
wind of other men's breath, and have no oars of their
own to steer withal. It is very fantastical and contra-
dictory in humane nature, that men should love them- 15
selves above all the rest of the world, and yet never
endure to be with themselves. When they are in love with
a mistress, all other persons are importunate and burdensome to them. "Tecum vivere amem, tecum obeam
lubens," they would live and die with her alone. 20

> " Sic ego secretis possum bene vivere silvis,
>   Qua nulla humano sit via trita pede.
> Tu mihi curarum requies, tu nocte vel atrâ
>   Lumen, et in solis tu mihi turba locis."

> With thee for ever I in woods could rest, 25
> Where never human foot the ground has prest.
> Thou from all shades the darkness canst exclude,
> And from a desart banish solitude.

And yet our dear self is so wearisome to us, that we
can scarcely support its conversation for an hour to- 30
gether. This is such an odd temper of mind, as Catullus
expresses towards one of his mistresses, whom we may
suppose to have been of a very unsociable humour,

> "Odi, et amo : quare id faciam fortasse requiris.
>   Nescio; sed fieri sentio, et excrucior." 35

I hate, and yet I love thee too;
How can that be? I know not how;
Only that so it is I know,
And feel with torment that 'tis so.

5   It is a deplorable condition, this, and drives a man
sometimes to pitiful shifts in seeking how to avoid
himself.

The truth of the matter is, that neither he who is a
fop in the world, is a fit man to be alone; nor he who
10 has set his heart much upon the world, though he have
never so much understanding; so that solitude can be
well fitted and sit right, but upon a very few persons.
They must have enough knowledge of the world to see
the vanity of it, and enough virtue to despise all vanity;
15 if the mind be possessed with any lust or passions, a man
had better be in a fair, than in a wood alone.   They
may, like petty thieves, cheat us perhaps, and pick our
pockets, in the midst of company; but, like robbers,
they use to strip and bind, or murder us, when they
20 catch us alone.   This is but to retreat from men, and to
fall into the hands of devils.   'Tis like the punishment
of parricides among the Romans, to be sewed into a bag,
with an ape, a dog, and a serpent.

The first work, therefore, that a man must do, to
25 make himself capable of the good of solitude, is, the
very eradication of all lusts; for how is it possible for
a man to enjoy himself, while his affections are tyed to
things without himself? In the second place, he must
learn the art, and get the habit of thinking; for this, too,
30 no less than well speaking, depends upon much practice;
and cogitation is the thing which distinguishes the solitude of a God from a wild beast.   Now, because the
soul of man is not, by its own nature or observation,
furnisht with sufficient materials to work upon, it is

necessary for it to have continual recourse to learning
and books for fresh supplies, so that the solitary life will
grow indigent, and be ready to starve, without them;
but if once we be thoroughly engaged in the love of
letters, instead of being wearied with the length of any 5
day, we shall only complain of the shortness of our whole
life.

> "O vita, stulto longa, sapienti brevis !"
> O life, long to the fool, short to the wise!

The first minister of state has not so much business 10
in publick, as a wise man has in private : if the one have
little leasure to be alone, the other has less leasure to be
in company ; the one has but part of the affairs of one
nation, the other all the works of God and nature, under
his consideration. There is no saying shocks me so 15
much as that which I hear very often, that a man does
not know how to pass his time. 'Twould have been but
ill spoken by Methusalem in the nine hundred sixty-
ninth year of his life ; so far it is from us, who have not
time enough to attain to the utmost perfection of any 20
part of any science, to have cause to complain that we
are forced to be idle for want of work. But this, you'll
say, is work only for the learned ; others are not capable
either of the employments or divertisements that arrive
from letters. I know they are not ; and, therefore, can- 25
not much recommend solitude to a man totally illiterate.
But, if any man be so unlearned, as to want entertainment of the little intervals of accidental solitude, which
frequently occur in almost all conditions (except the
very meanest of the people, who have business enough 30
in the necessary provisions for life), it is truly a great
shame both to his parents and himself ; for a very small
portion of any ingenious art will stop up all those gaps
of our time : either musick, or painting, or designing,

or chymistry, or history, or gardening, or twenty other
things, will do it usefully and pleasantly; and, if he
happen to set his affections upon poetry (which I do not
advise him to immoderately), that will over-do it; no
5 wood will be thick enough to hide him from the impor-
tunities of company or business, which would abstract
him from his beloved.

> "―― O qui me gelidis in vallibus Hæmi
> Sistat, et ingenti ramorum protegat umbrâ?"

1.

10   HAIL, old patrician trees, so great and good!
     Hail, ye plebeian under-wood!
     Where the poetick birds rejoyce,
   And for their quiet nests and plenteous food
     Pay with their grateful voice.

2.

15   Hail, the poor Muses' richest mannor-seat!
     Ye country houses and retreat,
     Which all the happy gods so love,
   That for you oft they quit their bright and great
     Metropolis above.

3.

20   Here Nature does a house for me erect,
     Nature, the wisest architect,
     Who those fond artists does despise
   That can the fair and living trees neglect;
     Yet the dead timber prize.

4.

25   Here let me, careless and unthoughtful lying,
     Hear the soft winds, above me flying,
     With all their wanton boughs dispute,
   And the more tuneful birds to both replying,
     Nor be myself too mute.

5.

A silver stream shall roul his waters near,
    Gilt with sun-beams here and there,
    On whose enamel'd bank I'll walk,
And see how prettily they smile, and hear
    How prettily they talk. ·   5

6.

Ah wretched, and too solitary he,
    Who loves not his own companie!
    He'll feel the weight of't many a day,
Unless he call in sin or vanitie
    To help to bear't away.   10

7.

O Solitude, first state of human-kind!
    Which blest remain'd, till man did find
    Ev'n his own helper's companie.
As soon as two (alas!) together joyn'd,
    The serpent made up three.   15

8.

Though God himself, through countless ages, thee
    His sole companion chose to be,
    Thee, sacred Solitude, alone,
Before the branchy head of number's tree
    Sprang from the trunk of one.   20

9.

Thou (though men think thine an unactive part)
    Dost break and tame th' unruly heart,
    Which else would know no setled pace,
Making it move, well manag'd by thy art,
    With swiftness and with grace.   25

10.

Thou the faint beams of reason's scatter'd light
    Dost, like a burning glass, unite,
    Dost multiply the feeble heat,
And fortify the strength, till thou dost bright
5   And noble fires beget.

11.

Whilst this hard truth I teach, methinks I see
    The monster London laugh at me;
    I should at thee too, foolish city,
If it were fit to laugh at misery;
10   But thy estate I pity.

12.

Let but thy wicked men from out thee go,
    And all the fools that crowd thee so,
    Even thou, who dost thy millions boast,
A village less than Islington wilt grow,
15   A solitude almost.

III.

OF OBSCURITY.

"NAM neque divitibus contingunt gaudia solis;
"Nec vixit male, qui natus moriensque fefellit."

God made not pleasures only for the rich;
Nor have those men without their share too liv'd,
Who both in life and death the world deceiv'd.   5

THIS seems a strange sentence, thus litterally translated, and looks as if it were in vindication of the men of business (for who else can deceive the world?) whereas it is in commendation of those who live and die so obscurely, 10 that the world takes no notice of them. This Horace calls deceiving the world; and in another place uses the same phrase,

"——Secretum iter et fallentis semita vitæ."
The secret tracks of the deceiving life.   15

It is very elegant in Latine, but our English word will hardly bear up to that sense; and therefore Mr Broom translates it very well—

Or from a life, led, as it were, by stealth.

Yet we say, in our language, a thing deceives our sight, 20 when it passes before us unperceived: and we may say well enough, out of the same author,

Sometimes with sleep, sometimes with wine, we strive
The cares of life and troubles to deceive.

But that is not to deceive the world, but to deceive ourselves, as Quintilian says, "vitam fallere," to draw on
still, and amuse, and deceive our life, till it be advanced
insensibly to the fatal period, and fall into that pit which
5 nature hath prepared for it.   The meaning of all this is
no more than that most vulgar saying, "Bene qui latuit,
bene vixit," he has lived well, who has lain well hidden.
Which, if it be a truth, the world (I will swear) is
sufficiently deceived : for my part, I think it is, and that
10 the pleasantest condition of life is *in incognito.* What a
brave priviledge is it, to be free from all contentions,
from all envying or being envied, from receiving or
paying all kind of ceremonies ! It is, in my mind, a very
delightful pastime, for two good and agreable friends to
15 travel up and down together, in places where they are
by nobody known, nor know anybody.   It was the case
of Æneas and his Achates, when they walked invisibly
about the fields and streets of Carthage ; Venus herself

> A vail of thicken'd air around them cast,
20 >   That none might know, or see them, as they past.

The common story of Demosthenes' confession, that he
had taken great pleasure in hearing of a tanker-woman
say, as he past, "This is that Demosthenes," is wonderful
ridiculous from so solid an orator.   I myself have often
25 met with that temptation to vanity (if it were any); but
am so far from finding it any pleasure, that it only makes
me run faster from the place, till I get, as it were, out of
sight-shot.   Democritus relates, and in such a manner
as if he gloried in the good fortune and commodity of
30 it, that, when he came to Athens, nobody there did so
much as take notice of him ; and Epicurus lived there
very well, that is, lay hid many years in his gardens, so
famous since that time, with his friend Metrodorus :
after whose death, making in one of his letters a kind

commemoration of the happiness which they two had
enjoyed together, he adds at last, that he thought it no
disparagement to those great felicities of their life, that,
in the midst of the most talk'd-of and talking country in
the world, they had lived so long, not only without fame, 5
but almost without being heard of. And yet, within a
very few years afterward, there were no two names of
men more known, or more generally celebrated. If we
engage into a large acquaintance and various familiarities,
we set open our gates to the invaders of most of our 10
time : [we expose our life to a quotidian ague of frigid
impertinences, which would make a wise man tremble to
think of.] Now, as for being known much by sight, and
pointed at, I cannot comprehend the honour that lies
in that : whatsoever it be, every mountebank has it more 15
than the best doctor, and the hangman more than the
lord chief justice of a city. Every creature has it, both
of nature and art, if it be any ways extraordinary. It
was as often said, "This is that Bucephalus," or, "This
is that Incitatus," when they were led prancing through 20
the streets, as "This is that Alexander," or, "This is that
Domitian;" and truly, for the latter, I take Incitatus to
have been a much more honourable beast than his
master, and more deserving the consulship, than he the
empire.   25
    I love and commend a true good fame, because it is
the shadow of virtue; not that it doth any good to the
body which it accompanies, but 'tis an efficacious shadow,
and, like that of S. Peter, cures the diseases of others.
The best kind of glory, no doubt, is that which is re- 30
flected from honesty, such as was the glory of Cato and
Aristides; but it was harmful to them both, and is seldom
beneficial to any man, whilst he lives : what it is to
him after his death, I cannot say, because I love not

philosophy meerly notional and conjectural, and no man
who has made the experiment has been so kind as to
come back to inform us. Upon the whole matter, I
account a person who has a moderate mind and fortune,
5 and lives in the conversation of two or three agreeable
friends, with little commerce in the world besides, who
is esteemed well enough by his few neighbours that know
him, and is truly irreproachable by any body; and so,
after a healthful quiet life, before the great inconveniences
10 of old age, goes more silently out of it than he came in
(for I would not have him so much as cry in the exit):
this innocent deceiver of the world, as Horace calls him,
this "muta persona," I take to have been more happy in
his part, than the greatest actors that fill the stage with
15 show and noise, nay, even than Augustus himself, who
askt with his last breath, whether he had not played his
farce very well.

SENECA, EX THYESTE, ACT. II. CHOR.

"Stet, quicunque volet potens
Aulæ culmine lubrico," &c.

20 UPON the slippery tops of humane state,
The guilded pinnacles of fate,
Let others proudly stand, and, for a while
The giddy danger to beguile,
With joy, and with disdain, look down on all,
25 Till their heads turn, and down they fall.
Me, O ye gods, on earth, or else so near
That I no fall to earth may fear,
And, O ye gods, at a good distance seat
From the long ruins of the great.
30 Here wrapt in th' arms of quiet let me lye;
Quiet, companion of obscurity.

Here let my life with as much silence slide,
    As time, that measures it, does glide.
Nor let the breath of infamy or fame,
From town to town echo about my name.
Nor let my homely death embroidered be   5
    With scutcheon or with elogie.
    An old plebeian let me die,
Alas, all then are such as well as I.
    To him, alas, to him, I fear,
The face of death will terrible appear,   10
Who, in his life flattering his senseless pride,
By being known to all the world beside,
Does not himself, when he is dying, know,
Nor what he is, nor whither he's to go.

I, II, III : likely soldier chiv... ly

IV

OF AGRICULTURE.

THE first wish of Virgil (as you will find anon by his verses) was to be a good philosopher; the second, a good husbandman: and God (whom he seem'd to understand better than 5 most of the most learned heathens) dealt with him, just as he did with Solomon; because he prayed for wisdom in the first place, he added all things else, which were subordinately to be desir'd. He made him one of the best philosophers and the best husbandmen; and, to 10 adorn and communicate both those faculties, the best poet. He made him, besides all this, a rich man, and a man who desired to be no richer—

"O fortunatus nimium, et bona qui sua novit!"

To be a husbandman, is but a retreat from the city; to be a philosopher, from the world; or rather, a retreat from the world, as it is man's, into the world, as it is God's.

But, since nature denies to most men the capacity or appetite, and fortune allows but to a very few the 20 opportunites or possibility of applying themselves wholly to philosophy, the best mixture of humane affairs that we can make, are the employments of a country life. It is, as Columella calls it, "Res sine dubitatione proxima, et quasi consanguinea sapientiæ," the nearest neighbour, or rather next in kindred, to philosophy. Varro says, the principles of it are the same which Ennius made to be the principles of all nature, Earth, Water, Air, and 5 the Sun. It does certainly comprehend more parts of philosophy, than any one profession, art, or science, in the world besides: and therefore Cicero says, the pleasures of a husbandman, "mihi ad sapientis vitam proxime videntur accedere," come very nigh to those 10 of a philosopher. There is no other sort of life that affords so many branches of praise to a panegyrist: the utility of it, to a man's self; the usefulness, or rather necessity, of it to all the rest of mankind; the innocence, the pleasure, the antiquity, the dignity. 15

The utility (I mean plainly the lucre of it) is not so great, now in our nation, as arises from merchandise and the trading of the city, from whence many of the best sortes and chief honours of the kingdom are derived: we have no men now fetch't from the plow to be 20 made lords, as they were in Rome to be made consuls and dictators; the reason of which I conceive to be from an evil custom, now grown as strong among us as if it were a law, which is, that no men put their children to be bred up apprentices in agriculture, as in other 25 trades, but such who are so poor, that, when they come to be men, they have not where-withal to set up in it, and so can only farm some small parcel of ground, the rent of which devours all but the bare subsistence of the tenant: whilst they who are proprietors of the land 30 are either too proud, or, for want of that kind of education, too ignorant, to improve their estates, though the means of doing it be as easie and certain in this, as in any other track of commerce. If there were always two

L. C. 7

or three thousand youths, for seven or eight years,
bound to this profession, that they might learn the
whole art of it, and afterwards be enabled to be masters
in it, by a moderate stock, I cannot doubt but that we
5 should see as many aldermen's estates made in the
country, as now we do out of all kind of merchandizing
in the city. There are as many ways to be rich, and,
which is better, there is no possibility to be poor, without such negligence as can neither have excuse nor
10 pity; for a little ground will, without question, feed a
little family, and the superfluities of life (which are now
in some cases by custom made almost necessary) must
be supplyed out of the superabundance of art and
industry, or contemned by as great a degree of phi-
15 losophy.

As for the necessity of this art, it is evident enough,
since this can live without all others, and no one other
without this. This is like speech, without which the
society of men cannot be preserved; the others, 'st
20 figures and tropes of speech, which serve only to adorn
it. Many nations have lived, and some do still, without
any art but this: not so elegantly, I confess, but still
they live; and almost all the other arts, which are here
practised, are beholding to this for most of their materials.
25 The innocence of this life is the next thing for which
I commend it; and if husbandmen preserve not that,
they are much to blame, for no men are so free from
the temptations of iniquity. They live by what they can
get by industry from the earth; and others, by what
30 they can catch by craft from men. They live upon an
estate given them by their mother; and others, upon an
estate cheated from their brethren. They live, like
sheep and kine, by the allowances of nature; and others,
like wolves and foxes, by the acquisitions of rapine.

And, I hope, I may affirm (without any ~~re all, I~~
great) that sheep and kine are very usefu~~metaph~~.
wolves and foxes are pernicious creatures. ~~nor~~
without dispute, of all men, the most quiet and least
to be inflamed to the disturbance of the commonwealth:
their manner of life inclines them, and interest binds
them, to love peace: in our late mad and miserable
civil wars, all other trades, even to the meanest, set
forth whole troops, and raised up some great commanders, who became famous and mighty for the mis- 10
chiefs they had done: but I do not remember the name
of any one husbandman, who had so considerable a share
in the twenty years' ruine of his country, as to deserve
the curses of his countrymen.

And if great delights be joyn'd with so much inno- 15
cence, I think it is ill done of men, not to take them
here, where they are so tame, and ready at hand, rather
than hunt for them in courts and cities, where they are
so wild, and the chase so troublesome and dangerous.

We are here among the vast and noble scenes of 20
nature; we are there among the pitiful shifts of policy:
we walk here in the light and open ways of the divine
bounty; we grope there in the dark and confused
labyrinths of humane malice: our senses are here feasted
with the clear and genuine taste of their objects, which 25
are all sophisticated there, and for the most part overwhelmed with their contraries. Here, pleasure looks
(methinks) like a beautiful, constant, and modest wife;
it is there an impudent, fickle, and painted harlot.
Here, is harmless and cheap plenty; there, guilty and 30
expenceful luxury.

I shall only instance in one delight more, the most
natural and best-natured of all others, a perpetual
companion of the husbandman; and that is, the satisfac-

or three thou'round about him, and seeing nothing but
bound to thand improvements of his own art and
whole art; to be always gathering of some fruits of it,
in it, at the same time to behold others ripening, and
5 shthers budding : to see all his fields and gardens covered
with the beauteous creatures óf his own industry ; and
to see, like God, that all his works are good :——

——Hinc atque hinc glomerantur Orcades; ipsi
Agricolæ tacitum pertentant gaudia pectus.

10   On his heart-string a secret joy does strike.

The antiquity of his art is certainly not to be con-
tested by any other.   The three first men in the world,
were a gardener, a plowman, and a grazier; and if
any man object, that the second of these was a murtherer,
15 I desire he would consider, that as soon as he was so, he
quitted our profession, and turn'd builder.   It is for
this reason, I suppose, that Ecclesiasticus forbids us to
hate husbandry ; 'because (says he) the Most High has
created it.'   We were all born to this art, and taught by
20 nature to nourish our bodies by the same earth out of
which they were made, and to which they must return,
and pay at last for their sustenance.

Behold the original and primitive nobility of all those
great persons, who are too proud now, not only to till
25 the ground, but almost to tread upon it.   We may talk
what we please of lillies, and lions rampant, and spread-
eagles, in fields *d'or* or *d'argent;* but, if heraldry were
guided by reason, a plough in a field arable would be
the most noble and antient arms.

3o   All these considerations make me fall into the wonder
and complaint of Columella, how it should come to
pass that all arts or sciences (for the dispute, which is
an art, and which a science, does not belong to the curiosity of us husbandmen,) metaphysick, physick, morality,

mathematicks, logick, rhetorick &c. which are all, 1,
good and useful faculties, (except only metaph.
which I do not know whether it be anything or . ~
but even vaulting, fencing, dancing, attiring, cooke.,
carving, and such like vanities, should all have publick 5
schools and masters, and yet that we should never see
or hear of any man, who took upon him the profession of
teaching this so pleasant, so virtuous, so profitable, so
honourable, so necessary art.

A man would think, when he's in serious humour, 10
that it were but a vain, irrational, and ridiculous thing,
for a great company of men and women to run up and
down in a room together, in a hundred several postures
and figures, to no purpose, and with no design; and
therefore dancing was invented first, and only practised 15
antiently, in the ceremonies of the heathen religion,
which consisted all in mummery and madness; the latter
being the chief glory of the worship, and accounted
divine inspiration: this, I say, a severe man would
think; though I dare not determine so far against so 20
customary a part, now, of good-breeding. And yet, who
is there among our gentry, that does not entertain a
dancing-master for his children, as soon as they are able
to walk? But did ever any father provide a tutor for his
son, to instruct him betimes in the nature and improve- 25
ments of that land which he intended to leave him?
That is at least a superfluity, and this a defect, in our
manner of education; and therefore I could wish (but
cannot in these times much hope to see it) that one colledge in each university were erected, and appropriated 30
to this study, as well as there are to medicine and the
civil law: there would be no need of making a body of
scholars and fellows, with certain endowments, as in
other colledges; it would suffice, if, after the manner of

..n Oxford, there were only four professors consti-
or ' (for it would be too much work for only one
bo'er, or principal, as they call him there) to teach
w̌se four parts of it: First, Aration, and all things re-
5 lating to it. Secondly, Pasturage. Thirdly, Gardens,
Orchards, Vineyards, and Woods. Fourthly, all parts
of Rural Oeconomy, which would contain the government
of Bees, Swine, Poultry, Decoys, Ponds, &c. and all that
which Varro calls *villaticas pastiones*, together with the
10 sports of the field (which ought to be looked upon not
only as pleasures, but as parts of house-keeping), and
the domestical conservation and uses of all that is
brought in by industry abroad. The business of these
professors should not be, as is commonly practised in
15 other arts, only to read pompous and superficial lectures,
out of Virgil's Georgicks, Pliny, Varro, or Columella;
but to instruct their pupils in the whole method and
course of this study, which might be run through perhaps, with diligence, in a year or two: and the con-
20 tinual succession of scholars, upon a moderate taxation
for their diet, lodging, and learning, would be a sufficient constant revenue for maintenance of the house and
the professors, who should be men not chosen for the
ostentation of critical literature, but for solid and expe-
25 rimental knowledge of the things they teach; such men,
so industrious and publick-spirited, as I conceive Mr.
Hartlib to be, if the gentleman be yet alive: but it is
needless to speak further of my thoughts of this design,
unless the present disposition of the age allowed more
30 probability of bringing it into execution. What I have
further to say of the country life, shall be borrowed
from the poets, who were always the most faithful and
affectionate friends to it. Poetry was born among the
shepherds.

Nescio qua natale solum dulcedine Musas
  Ducit, et immemores non sinit esse sui.

The Muses still love their own native place;
'T has secret charms, which nothing can deface.

The truth is, no other place is proper for their work; 5
one might as well undertake to dance in a crowd, as to
make good verses in the midst of noise and tumult.

As well might corn, as verse, in cities grow;
In vain the thankless glebe we plow and sow;
Against th' unnatural soil in vain we strive; 10
'Tis not a ground, in which these plants will thrive.

It will bear nothing but the nettles or thorns of satyre,
which grow most naturally in the worst earth; and
therefore almost all poets, except those who were not
able to eat bread without the bounty of great men, that 15
is, without what they could get by flattering of them,
have not only withdrawn themselves from the vices and
vanities of the grand world,

———— pariter vitiisque jocisque
  Altius humanis exeruere caput, 20

into the innocent happiness of a retired life; but have
commended and adorned nothing so much by their ever-
living poems. Hesiod was the first or second poet in
the world that remains yet extant (if Homer, as some
think, preceded him, but I rather believe they were 25
contemporaries); and he is the first writer too of the
art of husbandry : " he has contributed (says Columella)
not a little to our profession;" I suppose, he means not
a little honour, for the matter of his instructions is not
very important: his great antiquity is visible through 30
the gravity and simplicity of his stile. The most acute
of all his sayings concerns our purpose very much, and
is couched in the reverend obscurity of an oracle. Πλέον
ἥμισυ παντός, The half is more than the whole. The

occasion of the speech is this; his brother Perses had, by corrupting some great men (βασιλῆας δωροφάγους, great bribe-eaters he calls them), gotten from him the half of his estate. It is no matter (says he); they have
5 not done me so much prejudice, as they imagine.

> Νήπιοι, οὐδ᾽ ἴσασιν ὅσῳ πλέον ἥμισυ παντός,
> Οὐδ᾽ ὅσον ἐν μαλάχῃ τε καὶ ἀσφοδέλῳ μέγ᾽ ὄνειαρ,
> Κρύψαντες γὰρ ἔχουσι θεοὶ βίον ἀνθρώποισι.

> Unhappy they, to whom God ha'n't reveal'd,
10   By a strong light which must their sense controul,
> That half a great estate's more than the whole.
> Unhappy, from whom still conceal'd does lye,
> Of roots and herbs, the wholesom luxury.

This I conceive to be honest Hesiod's meaning. From
15 Homer, we must not expect much concerning our affairs. He was blind, and could neither work in the country, nor enjoy the pleasures of it; his helpless poverty was likeliest to be sustained in the richest places; he was to delight the Grecians with fine tales of the wars and ad-
20 ventures of their ancestors; his subject removed him from all commerce with us, and yet, methinks, he made a shift to shew his good-will a little. For, though he could do us no honour in the person of his hero Ulysses (much less of Achilles), because his whole time was con-
25 sumed in wars and voyages; yet he makes his father Laertes a gardener all that while, and seeking his con- solation for the absence of his son in the pleasure of planting, and even dunging his own grounds. Ye see, he did not contemn us peasants; nay, so far was he
30 from that insolence, that he always stiles Eumæus, who kept the hogs, with wonderful respect, δῖον ὑφορβόν, the divine swine herd; he could ha' done no more for Menelaus or Agamemnon. And Theocritus (a very antient poet, but he was one of our own tribe, for he

wrote nothing but pastorals) gave the same epithete to.
an husbandman,

—ἠμείβετο δῖος ἀγρώστης.

The divine husbandman replyed to Hercules, who was
but δῖος himself. These were civil Greeks, and who 5
understood the dignity of our calling! Among the
Romans we have, in the first place, our truly divine
Virgil, who, though, by the favour of Mæcenas and
Augustus, he might have been one of the chief men of
Rome, yet chose rather to employ much of his time in 10
the exercise, and much of his immortal wit in the praise
and instructions, of a rustique life; who, though he had
written, before, whole books of pastorals and georgics,
could not abstain, in his great and imperial poem, from
describing Evander, one of his best princes, as living 15
just after the homely manner of an ordinary countryman. He seats him in a throne of maple, and lays him
but upon a bear's skin; the kine and oxen are lowing
in his court-yard; the birds under the eves of his
window call him up in the morning; and when he goes 20
abroad, only two dogs go along with him for his guard:
at last, when he brings Æneas into his royal cottage, he
makes him say this memorable complement, greater than
ever yet was spoken at the Escurial, the Louvre, or our
Whitehal: 25

— Hæc (inquit) limina victor
Alcides subiit, hæc illum regia cepit:
Aude, hospes, contemnere opes: et te quoque dignum
Finge Deo, rebúsque veni non asper egenis.

This humble roof, this rustick court, (said he) 30
Receiv'd Alcides, crown'd with victorie:
Scorn not, great guest, the steps where he has trod;
But contemn wealth, and imitate a God.

The next man, whom we are much obliged to, both

for his doctrine and example, is the next best poet in
the world to Virgil, his dear friend Horace; who, when
Augustus had desired Mæcenas to perswade him to come
and live domestically and at the same table with him,
5 and to be secretary of state of the whole world under
him, or rather jointly with him, for he says, "ut nos in
epistolis scribendis adjuvet," could not be tempted to
forsake his Sabin, or Tiburtin mannor, for so rich and
so glorious a trouble. There was never, I think, such
10 an example as this in the world, that he should have so
much moderation and courage as to refuse an offer of
such greatness, and the emperor so much generosity and
good-nature as not to be at all offended with his refusal,
but to retain still the same kindness, and express it often
15 to him in most friendly and familiar letters, part of which
are still extant. If I should produce all the passages of
this excellent author upon the several subjects which I
treat of in this book, I must be obliged to translate half
his works; of which I may say more truly than, in my
20 opinion, he did of Homer,

> Qui, quid sit pulchrum, quid turpe, quid utile, quid non,
> Planius et melius Chrysippo et Crantore dicit.

I shall content myself upon this particular theme
with three only, one out of his Odes, the other out of
25 his Satires, the third out of his Epistles; and shall for-
bear to collect the suffrages of all other poets, which
may be found scattered up and down through all their
writings, and especially in Martial's. But I must not
omit to make some excuse for the bold undertaking of
30 my own unskilful pencil upon the beauties of a face
that has been drawn before by so many great masters;
especially, that I should dare to do it in Latine verses
(though of another kind), and have the confidence to

translate them. I can only say that I love the matter, and that ought to cover many faults; and that I run not to contend with those befote me, but follow to applaud them.

A TRANSLATION OUT OF VIRGIL.

GEORG. LIB. II. 458.

O fortunatos nimium &c.

OH happy (if his happiness he knows)   5
The country swain, on whom kind heaven bestows
At home all riches, that wise nature needs;
Whom the just earth with easie plenty feeds.
'Tis true, no morning tide of clients comes,
And fills the painted channels of his rooms,   10
Adoring the rich figures, as they pass,
In tap'stry wrought, or cut in living brass;
Nor is his wooll superfluously dy'd
With the dear poison of Assyrian pride:
Nor do Arabian perfumes vainly spoil   15
The native use and sweetness of his oil.
Instead of these, his calm and harmless life,
Free from th' allarms of fear, and storms of strife,
Does with substantial blessedness abound,
And the soft wings of peace cover him round: 20
Through artless grots the murm'ring waters glide;
Thick trees both against heat and cold provide,
From whence the birds salute him; and his ground
With lowing herds, and bleating sheep, does sound;
And all the rivers, and the forests nigh,   25
Both food, and game, and exercise, supply.
Here, a well-hard'ned active youth we see,
Taught the great art of chearful povertie.

Here, in this place alone, there still do shine
Some streaks of love, both humane and divine;
From hence Astræa took her flight, and here
Still her last foot-steps upon earth appear.
5 'Tis true, the first desire, which does controul
All the inferior wheels that move my soul,
Is, that the Muse me her high priest would make,
Into her holiest scenes of myst'ry take,
And open there to my mind's purged eye
10 Those wonders, which to sense the gods deny.
How in the moon such change of shapes is found;
The moon, the changing world's eternal bound.
What shakes the solid earth, what strong disease
Dares trouble the firm centre's antient ease;
15 What makes the sea retreat, and what advance:
"Varieties too regular for chance."
What drives the chariot on of winter's light,
And stops the lazy wagon of the night.
But, if my dull and frozen blood deny
20 To send forth th' sp'rits, that raise a soul so high!
In the next place, let woods and rivers be
My quiet, though inglorious, destinie.
In life's cool vale let my low scene be laid:
Cover me, gods, with Tempe's thickest shade.
25 Happy the man, I grant, thrice happy he,
Who can through gross effects their causes see:
Whose courage from the deeps of knowledge springs,
Nor vainly fears inevitable things;
But does his walk of virtue calmly go
30 Through all th' alarms of death and hell below.
Happy! but, next such conqu'rors, happy they,
Whose humble life lies not in fortune's way.
They, unconcern'd, from their safe distant seat
Behold the rods and scepters of the great.

The quarrels of the mighty without fear,
And the descent of foreign troops they hear.
Nor can ev'n Rome their steady course misguide,
With all the lustre of her per'shing pride.
Them never yet did strife or av'rice draw   5
Into the noisie markets of the law,
The camps of gowned war; nor do they live
By rules or forms, that many madmen give.
Duty for nature's bounty they repay,
And her sole laws religiously obey.   10
   Some with bold labour plough the faithless main,
Some rougher storms in princes' courts sustain.
Some swell up their slight sails with pop'lar fame,
Charm'd with the foolish whistlings of a name.
Some their vain wealth to earth again commit;   15
With endless cares some brooding o'er it sit.
Country and friends are by some wretches sold,
To lie on Tyrian beds, and drink in gold;
No price too high for profit can be shown;
Not brother's blood, nor hazards of their own.   20
Around the world in search of it they roam;
It makes ev'n their antipodes their home;
Meanwhile, the prudent husbandman is found,
In mutual duties, striving with his ground,
And half the year the care of that does take,   25
That half the year grateful returns does make.
Each fertile month does some new gifts present,
And with new work his industry content.
This, the young lamb, that the soft fleece doth yield;
This, loads with hay, and that, with corn, the field;   30
All sorts of fruit crown the rich autumn's pride;
And on a swelling hill's warm stony side,
The pow'rful princely purple of the vine,
Twice dy'd with the redoubled sun, does shine.

In th' evening to a fair ensuing day,
With joy he sees his flocks and kids to play;
And loaded kyne about his cottage stand,
Inviting with known sound the milker's hand;
5 And, when from wholsome labour he doth come,
With wishes to be there, and wish'd for home,
He meets at door the softest humane blisses,
His chaste wife's welcome, and dear children's kisses.
When any rural holidays invite
10 His genius forth to innocent delight,
On earth's fair bed, beneath some sacred shade,
Amidst his equal friends carelessly laid,
He sings thee, Bacchus, patron of the vine.
The beechen bowl foams with a flood of wine,
15 Not to the loss of reason, or of strength:
To active games and manly sport, at length,
Their mirth ascends, and with fill'd veins they see,
Who can the best at better tryals be.
From such the old Hetrurian virtue rose;
20 Such was the life the prudent Sabins chose;
Such, Remus and the god, his brother, led;
From such firm footing Rome grew the world's head.
Such was the life that, ev'n till now, does raise
The honour of poor Saturn's golden days.
25 Before men, born of earth and buried there,
Let in the sea their mortal fate to share:
Before new ways of perishing were sought,
Before unskilful death on anvils wrought:
Before those beasts, which humane life sustain,
30 By men, unless to the gods' use, were slain.

HOR. EPOD. ODE II.

Beatus ille qui procul &c.

HAPPY the man, whom bount'ous gods allow
With his own hands paternal grounds to plough!
Like the first golden mortals happy, he,
From business and the cares of money free!
No human storms break off, at land, his sleep;   5
No loud alarms of nature on the deep:
From all the cheats of law he lives secure,
Nor does th'affront of palaces endure;
Sometimes, the beaut'ous marriageable vine
He to the lusty bridegroom elm does joyn;   10
Sometimes, he lops the barren trees around,
And grafts new life into the fruitful wound;
Sometimes, he shears his flock, and, sometimes, he
Stores up the golden treasures of the bee.
He sees his lowing herds walk o'er the plain,   15
Whilst neighb'ring hills low back to them agin
And when the season, rich as well as gay,
All her autumnal bounty does display,
How is he pleas'd th' increasing use to see,
Of his well-trusted labours, bend the tree!   20
Of which large shares, on the glad sacred days,
He gives to friends, and to the gods repays.
With how much joy does he, beneath some shade
By aged trees' rev'rend embraces made,
His careless head on the fresh green recline,   25
His head uncharg'd with fear or with design.
By him a river constantly complains,
The birds above rejoyce with various strains,
And in the solemn scene their orgies keep,
Like dreams, mixt with the gravity of sleep;   30

Sleep, which does always there for entrance wait,
And nought within against it shuts the gate.
   Nor does the roughest season of the sky,
Or sullen Jove, all sports to him deny.
5 He runs the mazes of the nimble hare,
His well-mouth'd dogs' glad concert rends the air;
Or with game bolder, and rewarded more,
He drives into a toil the foaming bore;
Here flies the hawk t'assault, and there the net,
10 To intercept the trave'ling fowl, is set;
And all his malice, all his craft, is shown
In innocent wars, on beasts and birds alone;
This is the life from all misfortunes free,
From thee, the great one, tyrant love, from thee;
15 And, if a chaste and clean, though homely, wife
Be added to the blessings of this life,
Such as the antient sun-burnt Sabins were,
Such as Apulia, frugal still, does bear,
Who makes her children and the house her care,
20 And joyfully the work of life does share,
Nor thinks herself too noble or too fine
To pin the sheepfold or to milk the kine,
Who waits at door against her husband come
From rural duties, late, and wearied home,
25 Where she receives him with a kind embrace,
A chearful fire, and a more chearful face;
And fills the bowl up to her homely lord,
And with domestick plenty loads the board,
Not all the lustful shell-fish of the sea,
30 Drest by the wanton hand of luxury,
Nor ortolans nor godwits, nor the rest
Of costly names that glorifie a feast,
Are at the princely tables better cheer,
Than lamb and Kid, lettice and olives, here.

THE COUNTRY MOUSE.

A Paraphrase upon Horace, Book II. Sat. VI.

At the large foot of a fair hollow tree,
Close to plow'd ground, seated commodiously,
His antient and hereditary house,
There dwelt a good substantial country mouse;
Frugal, and grave, and careful of the main,   5
Yet one who once did nobly entertain
A city mouse, well coated, sleek, and gay,
A mouse of high degree, which lost his way,
Wantonly walking forth to take the air,
And arriv'd early, and belighted there,   10
For a day's lodging: the good hearty host,
(The antient plenty of his hall to boast)
Did all the store produce, that might excite,
With various tastes, the courtier's appetite.
Fitches and beans, peason, oats, and wheat,   15
And a large chesnut, the delicious meat
Which Jove himself, were he a mouse, would eat.
And, for a *haut goust*, there was mixt with these
The swerd of bacon, and the coat of cheese:
The precious reliques, which, at harvest, he   20
Had gathered from the reapers' luxurie.
Freely (said he) fall on, and never spare,
The bounteous gods will for to-morrow care.
And thus at ease, on beds of straw, they lay,
And to their genius sacrific'd the day: 25
Yet the nice guest's epicurean mind,
(Though breeding made him civil seem, and kind)
Despis'd this country feast; and still his thought
Upon the cakes and pies of London wrought.

Your bounty and civility, (said he)
Which I'm surpris'd in these rude parts to see,
Shews that the gods have given you a mind
Too noble for the fate, which here you find.
5　Why should a soul, so virt'ous, and so great,
Lose itself thus in an obscure retreat?
Let savage beasts lodge in a country den;
You should see towns, and manners know, and men;
And taste the gen'rous luxury of the court,
10　Where all the mice of quality resort;
Where thousand beaut'ous shes about you move,
᛫And, by high fare, are plyant made to love.
We all, ere long, must render up our breath;
No cave or hole can shelter us from death.
15　　Since life is so uncertain, and so short,
Let's spend it all in feasting and in sport.
Come, worthy sir, come with me, and partake
All the great things, that mortals happy make.
　　Alas! what virtue hath sufficient arms,
20　T' oppose bright honour, and soft pleasure's charms?
What wisdom can their magick force repel?
It draws this rev'rend hermit from his cell.
It was the time, when witty poets tell,
"That Phœbus into Thetis' bosome fell:
25　She blush'd at first, and then put out the light,
And drew the modest curtains of the night."
Plainly the troth to tell, the sun was set.
When to the town our wearied trav'llers get,
To a lord's house, as lordly as can be,
30　Made for the use of pride and luxurie,
They come; the gentle courtier at the door
Stops, and will hardly enter in before.
But 'tis, sir, your command, and being so,
I'm sworn t' obedience; and so in they go.

Behind a hanging in a spacious room,
(The richest work of Mortlacke's noble loom)
They wait a while their wearied limbs to rest,
Till silence should invite them to their feast.
"About the hour that Cynthia's silver light   5
Had touch'd the pale meridies of the night,"
At last, the various supper being done,
It happen'd that the company was gone
Into a room remote, servants and all,
To please their noble fancies with a ball.   10
Our host leads forth his stranger, and does find
All fitted to the bounties of his mind.
Still on the table half-fill'd dishes stood,
And with delicious bits the floor was strow'd.
The court'ous mouse presents him with the best,   15
And both with fat varieties are blest.
Th' industrious peasant every where does range,
And thanks the gods for his life's happy change.
Lo! in the midst of a well-fraighted pie,
They both at last glutted and wanton lie.   20
When see the sad reverse of prosp'rous fate,
And what fierce storms on mortal glories wait!
With hid'ous noise, down the rude servants come,
Six dogs before run barking into th' room;
The wretched gluttons fly with wild affright,   25
And hate the fulness which retards their flight.
Our trembling peasant wishes now in vain,
That rocks and mountains cover'd him again.
Oh how the change of his poor life he curst!
This, of all lives (said he) is sure the worst.   30
Give me again, ye gods, my cave and wood;
With peace, let tares and acorns be my food.

A PARAPHRASE UPON THE 10TH EPISTLE OF THE FIRST BOOK OF HORACE.

HORACE TO FUSCUS ARISTIUS.

HEALTH, from the lover of the country, me,
Health to the lover of the city, thee;
A difference in our souls, this only proves;
In all things else, we agree like married doves.
5 But the warm nest and crowded dove-house thou
Dost like; I loosely fly from bough to bough,
And rivers drink, and all the shining day,
Upon fair trees or mossy rocks, I play;
In fine, I live and reign, when I retire
10 From all that you equal with heav'n admire.
Like one at last from the priest's service fled,
Loathing the honied cakes, I long for bread.
Would I a house for happiness erect,
Nature alone should be the architect,
15 She'd build it more convenient, than great,
And, doubtles, in the country chuse her seat.
Is there a place, doth better helps supply,
Against the wounds of winter's cruelty?
Is there an air, that gentlier does asswage
20 The mad celestial dog's, or lyon's rage?
Is it not there that sleep (and only there)
Nor noise without, nor cares within, does fear?
Does art through pipes a purer water bring,
Than that, which nature strains into a spring?
25 Can all your tap'stries, or your pictures, show
More beauties, than in herbs and flow'rs do grow?
Fountains and trees our wearied pride do please,
Ev'n in the midst of gilded palaces.

And in your towns, that prospect gives delight,
Which opens round the country to our sight.
Men to the good, from which they rashly fly,
Return at last; and their wild luxury
Does but in vain with those true joys contend,   5
Which nature did to mankind recommend.
The man, who changes gold for burnisht brass,
Or small right gems for larger ones of glass,
Is not, at length, more certain to be made
Ridiculous, and wretched by the trade,   10
Than he, who sells a solid good to buy
The painted goods of pride and vanity.
If thou be wise, no glorious fortune choose,
Which 'tis but pain to keep, yet grief to lose.
For, when we place ev'n trifles in the heart,   15
With trifles too, unwillingly we part.
An humble roof, plain bed, and homely board,
More clear, untainted pleasures do afford,
Than all the tumult of vain greatness brings
To kings, or to the favorites of kings.   20
The horned deer, by nature arm'd so well,
Did with the horse in common pasture dwell;
And, when they fought, the field it always wan,
Till the ambitious horse begg'd help of man,
And took the bridle, and thenceforth did reign   25
Bravely alone, as lord of all the plain;
But never after could the rider get
From off his back, or from his mouth the bit.
So they, who poverty too much do fear,
T' avoid that weight, a greater burden bear;   30
That they might pow'r above their equals have,
To cruel masters they themselves enslave.
For gold, their liberty exchang'd we see,
That fairest flower, which crowns humanitie.

And all this mischief does upon them light,
Only because they know not how, aright,
That great, but secret, happiness to prize,
That 's laid up in a little, for the wise:
5   That is the best and easiest estate,
Which to a man sits close, but not too strait;
'Tis like a shoe; it pinches, and it burns,
Too narrow; and too large, it overturns.
My dearest friend, stop thy desires at last,
10 And chearfully enjoy the wealth thou hast.
And, if me still seeking for more you see,
Chide, and reproach, despise and laugh at me.
Money was made, not to command our will,
But all our lawful pleasures to fulfill.
15 Shame and woe to us, if we our wealth obey;
The horse doth with the horseman run away.

THE COUNTRY LIFE.

LIB. IV. PLANTARUM.

BLEST be the man (and blest he is) whom e'er
(Plac'd far out of the roads of hope or fear)
A little field, and little garden, feeds:
20 The field gives all that frugal nature needs;
The wealthy garden liberally bestows
All she can ask, when she luxurious grows.
The specious inconveniences, that wait
Upon a life of business, and of state,
25 He sees (nor does the sight disturb his rest)
By fools desir'd, by wicked men possest.
Thus, thus (and this deserv'd great Virgil's praise)
The old Corycian yeoman past his days;

Thus his wise life Abdolonymus spent:
Th' ambassadors, which the great emperour sent
To offer him a crown, with wonder found
The rev'rend gard'ner howing of his ground;
Unwillingly and slow and discontent, 5
From his lov'd cottage, to a throne he went.
And oft he stopt in his triumphant way,
And oft look'd back, and oft was heard to say,
Not without sighs, Alas, I there forsake
A happier kingdom than I go to take! 10
Thus Aglaus (a man unknown to men,
But the gods knew, and therefore lov'd him then,)
Thus liv'd obscurely then without a name,
Aglaus, now consign'd t' eternal fame.
For Gyges, the rich king, wicked and great, 15
Presum'd, at wise Apollo's Delphick seat
Presum'd, to ask, Oh thou, the whole world's eye,
See'st thou a man, that happier is than I?
The god, who scorn'd to flatter men, reply'd,
Aglaus happier is. But Gyges cry'd, 20
In a proud rage, who can that Aglaus be?
W' have heard, as yet, of no such king as he.
And true it was, through the whole earth around
No king of such a name was to be found.
Is some old hero of that name alive, 25
Who his high race does from the gods derive?
Is it some mighty gen'ral, that has done
Wonders in fight, and god-like honours won?
Is it some man of endless wealth, said he?
None, none of these. Who can this Aglaus be? 30
After long search, and vain inquiries past,
In an obscure Arcadian vale at last,
(Th' Arcadian life has always shady been)
Near Sopho's town (which he but once had seen)

This Aglaus, who monarchs' envy drew,
Whose happiness the gods stood witness to,
This mighty Aglaus was labouring found,
With his own hands, in his own little ground.
5   So, gracious God, (if it may lawful be,
Among those foolish gods to mention thee)
So let me act, on such a private stage,
The last dull scenes of my declining age;
After long toils and voyages in vain,
10   This quiet port, let my tost vessel gain;
Of heavenly rest, this earnest to me lend,
Let my life sleep, and learn to love her end.

V.

THE GARDEN.

TO J. EVELYN, *Esquire.*

I NEVER had any other desire so strong, and so like to covetousness, as that one which I have had always, that I might be master at last of a small house and large garden, with very moderate conveniences joyned to them, and there 5 dedicate the remainder of my life only to the culture of them, and study of nature;

And there (with no design beyond my wall) whole and entire
    to lye,
In no unactive ease, and no unglorious poverty. 10

Or, as Virgil has said, shorter and better for me, that I might there
      "Studiis florere ignobilis otii;"
(though I could wish that he had rather said, "Nobilis oti," when he spoke of his own.) But several accidents 15 of my ill fortune have disappointed me hitherto, and do still, of that felicity; for though I have made the first and hardest step to it, by abandoning all ambitions and hopes in this world, and by retiring from the noise of all business and almost company, yet I stick still in the inn of a hired 20

house and garden, among weeds and rubbish: and without that pleasantest work of human industry, the improvement of something which we call (not very properly, but yet we call) our own.   I am gone out from Sodom, but I am not yet arrived at my little Zoar.   *O let me escape thither (is it not a little one?) and my soul shall live.*   I do not look back yet; but I have been forced to stop, and make too many halts.   You may wonder, Sir, (for this seems a little too extravagant and Pindarical for prose) what I mean by all this preface; it is to let you know, that though I have mist, like a chymist, my great end, yet I account my affections and endeavours well rewarded by something that I have met with by the by; which is, that they have procured to me some part in your kindness and esteem; and thereby the honour of having my name so advantagiously recommended to posterity, by the epistle you are pleased to prefix to the most useful book that has been written in that kind, and which is to last as long as months and years.

Among many other arts and excellencies, which you enjoy, I am glad to find this favourite of mine the most predominant; that you choose this for your wife, though you have hundreds of other arts for your concubines; though you know them, and beget sons upon them all (to which, you are rich enough to allow great legacies), yet, the issue of this seems to be designed by you to the main of the estate; you have taken most pleasure in it, and bestowed most charges upon its education: and I doubt not to see that book, which you are pleased to promise to the world, and of which you have given us a large earnest in your calendar, as accomplish'd, as any thing can be expected from an extraordinary wit, and no ordinary expences, and a long experience.   I know nobody that possesses more private happiness than you do in your

garden; and, yet no man, who makes his happiness more publick by a free communication of the art and know-ledge of it to others. All that I myself am able yet to do, is only to recommend to mankind the search of that felicity, which you instruct them how to find and to 5 enjoy.

1.

HAPPY art thou, whom God does bless
With the full choice of thine own happiness;
    And happier yet, because thou'rt blest
    With prudence, how to choose the best;   10
In books and gardens, thou hast plac'd aright
    (Things well which thou dost understand;
And both dost make with thy laborious hand)
    Thy noble, innocent delight:
And in thy virtuous wife, where thou again dost meet 15
    Both pleasures more refin'd and sweet;
    The fairest garden in her looks,
    And in her mind the wisest books.
Oh, who would change these soft, yet solid joys,
    For empty shows, and sensless noise;   20
    And all which rank ambition breeds,
Which seem such beauteous flowers, and are such poi-
    sonous weeds?

2.

When God did man to his own likeness make,
As much as clay, though of the purest kind,   25
    By the great potter's art refin'd,
    Could the divine impression take,
    He thought it fit to place· him, where
    A kind of heav'n too did appear,
As far as earth could such a likeness bear: 30
    That man no happiness might want,

Which earth to her first master could afford,
    He did a garden for him plant
By the quick hand of his omnipotent word.
As the chief help and joy of human life,
5 He gave him the first gift; first, even before a wife.

3.

For God, the universal architect,
    'T had been as easy to erect
A Louvre or Escurial, or a tower,
That might with heaven communication hold,
10 As Babel vainly thought to do of old—
    He wanted not the skill or power;
    In the world's fabrick those were shown,
And, the materials were all his own.
But well he knew, what place would best agree
15 With innocence, and with felicity:
And we elsewhere still seek for them in vain
If any part of either yet remain,
If any part of either we expect,
This may our judgment in the search direct;
20 God the first garden made, and the first city Cain.

4.

O blessed shades! O gentle cool retreat
    From all th' immoderate heat,
In which the frantick world doth burn and sweat!
This does the lion-star, ambition's rage;
25 This avarice, the dog-star's thirst asswage;
Every where else their fatal power we see,
They make and rule man's wretched destinie:
    They neither set, nor disappear,
    But tyrannize o'er all the year;
30 Whilst we ne'er feel their flame or influence here.

'The birds, that dance from bough to bough,
And sing above in every tree,
Are not from fears and cares more free,.
Than we, who lie, or walk below,
And should by right be singers too. 5
What prince's choir of musick can excel
That which within this shade does dwell?
To which we nothing pay or give;
They, like all other poets, live
Without reward, or thanks for their obliging pains: 10
'Tis well, if they become not prey:
The whistling winds add their less artful strains,
And a grave base the murmuring fountains play;
Nature does all this harmony bestow,—
But to our plants, art's musick too, 15
The pipe, theorbo, and guitar we owe;
The lute itself, which once was green and mute,
When Orpheus struck th' inspired lute,
The trees danc'd round, and understood
By sympathy the voice of wood. 20

5.

These are the spells, that to kind sleep invite,
And nothing does within resistance make,
Which yet we moderately take;
Who would not choose to be awake,
While he's incompas'd round with such delight, 25
To th' ear, the nose, the touch, the taste, and sight?
When Venus would her dear Ascanius keep
A pris'ner in the downy bands of sleep,
She od'rous herbs and flowers beneath him spread,
As the most soft and sweetest bed; 30
Not her own lap would more have charm'd his head.

Who, that has reason, and his smell,
Would not among roses and jasmin dwell,
 Rather than all his spirits choak
With exhalations of dirt and smoak?
5 And all th' uncleanness, which does drown
In pestilential clouds a populous town?
The earth itself breathes better perfumes here,
Than all the female men, or women, there,
Not without cause, about them bear.

6.

10 When Epicurus to the world had taught,
 That pleasure was the chiefest good,
(And was, perhaps, i' th' right, if rightly understood)
 His life he to his doctrine brought,
And in a garden's shade that soveraign pleasure sought.
15 Whoever a true epicure would be,
May there find cheap and virtuous luxurie.
Vitellius his table, which did hold
As many creatures as the ark of old;
That fiscal table, to which every day
20 All countries did a constant tribute pay,
Could nothing more delicious afford
 Than nature's liberality,
Helpt with a little art and industry,
Allows the meanest gard'ner's board.
25 The wanton taste no fish or fowl can choose,
For which the grape or melon she would lose;
Though all th' inhabitants of sea and air
Be listed in the glutton's bill of fare;
 Yet still the fruits of earth we see
30 Plac'd the third story high in all her luxurie.

7.

But with no sense the garden does comply,
None courts, or flatters, as it does the eye.
When the great Hebrew king did almost strain
The wond'rous treasures of his wealth and brain,
His royal southern guest to entertain;   5
    Though she on silver floors did tread,
With bright Assyrian carpets on them spread,
    To hide the metal's poverty;
Though she look'd up to roofs of gold,
And nought around her could behold,   10
      But silk and rich embroidery,
      And Babylonian tapestry,
    And wealthy Hiram's princely dy;
Though Ophir's starry stones met every where her eye;
Though she herself and her gay host were drest   15
With all the shining glories of the East;
When lavish art her costly work had done,
    The honour and the prize of bravery
Was by the garden from the palace won;
And every rose and lilly there did stand   20
    Better attir'd by nature's hand:
The case thus judg'd against the king we see,
By one, that would not be so rich, though wiser far than he.

8.

Nor does this happy place only dispense
    Such various pleasures to the sense;   25
      Here health itself does live,
That salt of life, which does to all a relish give,
It's standing pleasure, and intrinsick wealth,
The body's virtue, and the soul's good fortune, health.

The tree of life, when it in Eden stood,
Did its immortal head to heaven rear;
It lasted a tall cedar, till the flood;
Now a small thorny shrub it does appear;
5   Nor will it thrive too every where:
It always here is freshest seen;
'Tis only here an evergreen.
If, through the strong and beauteous fence
Of temperance and innocence,
10 And wholsome labours, and a quiet mind,
Any diseases passage find,
They must not think here to assail
A land unarmed, or without a guard;
They must fight for it, and dispute it hard,
15   Before they can prevail:
Scarce any plant is growing here,
Which against death some weapon does not bear.
Let cities boast, that they provide
For life the ornaments of pride;
20   But 'tis the country and the field,
That furnish it with staff and shield.

9.

Where does the wisdom and the power divine
In a more bright and sweet reflection shine?
Where do we finer strokes and colours see
25 Of the Creator's real poetrie,
Than when we with attention look
Upon the third day's volume of the book?
If we could open and intend our eye,
We all, like Moses, should espy
30 Ev'n in a bush the radiant Deity.
But we despise these his inferior ways
(Though no less full of miracle and praise):

Upon the flowers of heaven we gaze;
The stars of earth no wonder in us raise,
   Though these perhaps do more than they
     The life of mankind sway,
Although no part of mighty nature be   5
More stor'd with beauty, power, and mysterie;
Yet, to encourage humane industrie,
God has so order'd, that no other part
Such space and such dominion leaves for art.

           10.

We nowhere art do so triumphant see,   10
   As when it grafts or buds the tree:
In other things we count it to excel,
If it a docile scholar can appear
To Nature, and but imitate her well;
It over-rules, and is her master here.   15
It imitates her Maker's power divine,
And changes her sometimes, and sometimes does refine:
It does, like grace, the fallen tree restore
To its blest state of Paradice before:
Who would not joy to see his conquering hand   20
O'er all the vegetable world command?
And the wild giants of the wood receive
   What law he's pleas'd to give?
He bids th' ill-natur'd crab produce
The gentle apple's winy juice,   25
   The golden fruit, that worthy is
   Of Galatea's purple kiss:
He does the savage hawthorn teach
To bear the medlar and the pear;
He bids the rustic plum to rear   30
A noble trunk, and be a peach.

L. C.   9

Even Daphne's coyness he does mock,
And weds the cherry to her stock,
Though she refus'd Apollo's suit;
Even she, that chaste and virgin tree,
5   Now wonders at herself, to see
That she's a mother made, and blushes in her fruit.

II.

Methinks, I see great Dioclesian walk
In the Salonian garden's noble shade,
Which by his own imperial hands was made:
10 I see him smile (methinks) as he does talk
With the ambassadors, who come in vain,
    T' entice him to a throne again.
If I, my friends (said he), should to you show
All the delights, which in these gardens grow,
15 'Tis likelier.much, that you should with me stay,
Than 'tis, that you should carry me away:
.And trust me not, my friends, if, every day,
    I walk not here with more delight
Than ever, after the most happy fight,
20 In triumph to the capitol I rod,
    To thank the gods, and to be thought myself almost
        a god.

VI.

OF GREATNESS.

INCE we cannot attain to greatness (says the Sieur de Montagne,) let us have our revenge by railing at it:" this he spoke but in jest. I believe he desired it no more than I do, and had less reason; for he enjoyed so plentiful and honourable a fortune in a most excellent country, as allowed him all the real conveniencies of it, separated and purged from the incommodities. If I were but in his condition, I should think it hard measure, without being convinced of any crime, to be sequestred from it, and made one of the principal officers of state. But the reader may think that what I now say is of small authority, because I never was, nor ever shall be, put to the trial: I can therefore only make my protestation,

If ever I more riches did desire
Than cleanliness and quiet do require:
If e'er ambition did my fancy cheat,
With any wish, so mean as to be great,
Continue, heaven, still from me to remove
The humble blessing of that life I love.

I know very many men will despise, and some pity me,

for this humour, as a poor-spirited fellow; but I am
content, and, like Horace, thank God for being so.

> Di bene fecerunt, inopis me quodque pusilli
> Finxerunt animi.

I confess, I love littleness almost in all things. A
little convenient estate, a little chearful house, a little
company, and a very little feast; and, if I were ever to
fall in love again (which is a great passion, and therefore,
I hope, I have done with it) it would be, I think, with
prettiness, rather than with majestick beauty. I would
neither wish that my mistress, nor my fortune, should
be a *bona roba*, nor, as Homer uses to describe his beauties, like a daughter of great Jupiter, for the stateliness
and largeness of her person; but, as Lucretius says,

> Parvula, pumilió, Χαρίτων μία, tota merum sal.

Where there is one man of this, I believe there are a
thousand of Senecio's mind, whose ridiculous affectation
of grandeur, Seneca the elder describes to this effect:
Senecio was a man of a turbid and confused wit, who
could not endure to speak any but mighty words and
sentences, till this humour grew at last into so notorious
a habit, or rather a disease, as became the sport of the
whole town: he would have no servants, but huge,
massy fellows; no plate or household stuff, but thrice
as big as the fashion: you may believe me, for I speak
it without railery, his extravigancy came at last into
such a madness, that he would not put on a pair of
shoes, each of which was not big enough for both his
feet: he would eat nothing but what was great, nor
touch any fruit but horse-plums and pound-pears: he
kept a concubine, that was a very gyantess, and made
her walk too always in chiopins, till, at last, he got the
surname of Senecio Grandio, which, Messala said, was

not his *cognomen*, but his *cognomentum :* when he de-
claimed for the three hundred Lacedæmonians, who
alone opposed Xerxes's army of above three hundred
thousand, he stretch'd out his arms, and stood on tip-
toes, that he might appear the taller, and cryed out, in a 5
very loud voice: "I rejoyce, I rejoyce"—We wondred,
I remember, what new great fortune had befaln his
eminence. "Xerxes (says he) is all mine own. He,
who took away the sight of the sea, with canvas veils
of so many ships"—and then he goes on so, as I 10
know not what to make of the rest, whether it be the
fault of the edition, or the orator's own burly way of
nonsence.

This is the character that Seneca gives of this hyper-
bolical fop, whom we stand amazed at, and yet there 15
are very few men who are not in some things, and to
some degrees, *Grandios.* Is any thing more common,
than to see our ladies of quality wear such high shoes
as they cannot walk in, without one to lead them ; and
a gown as long again as their body, so that they cannot 20
stir to the next room, without a page or two to hold it
up ? I may safely say, that all the ostentation of our
grandees is, just like a train, of no use in the world, but
horribly cumbersom and incommodius. What is all
this, but a spice of *Grandio ?* how tedious would this be, 25
if we were always bound to it ! I do believe there is no
king, who would not rather be deposed, than endure,
every day of his reign, all the ceremonies of his coronation.

The mightiest princes are glad to fly often from these 30
majestick pleasures (which is, methinks, no small disparagement to them) as it were for refuge, to the most
contemptible divertisements, and meanest recreations of
the vulgar, nay, even of children. One of the most

powerful and fortunate princes of the world, of late, could find out no delight so satisfactory, as the keeping of little singing birds, and hearing of them, and whistling to them. What did the emperors of the whole world?
5 If ever any men had the free and full enjoyment of all humane greatness (nay that would not suffice, for they would be gods too), they certainly possest it : and yet one of them, who stiled himself lord and god of the earth, could not tell how to pass his whole day pleasant-
10 ly, without spending constantly two or three hours in catching of flies, and killing them with a bodkin, as if his godship had been Beelzebub. One of his predecessors, Nero (who never put any bounds, nor met with any stop to his appetite), could divert himself with no pastime
15 more agreeable, than to run about the streets all night in a disguise, and abuse the women, and affront the men whom he met, and sometimes to beat them, and some-times to be beaten by them : this was one of his imperial nocturnal pleasures. His chiefest in the day was, to sing,
20 and play upon a fiddle, in the habit of a minstrel, upon the publick stage : he was prouder of the garlands that were given to his divine voice (as they called it then) in those kind of prizes, than all his forefathers were, of their triumphs over nations : he did not at his death
25 complain that so mighty an emperor, and the last of all the Cæsarian race of deities, should be brought to so shameful and miserable an end; but only cried out, "Alas, what pity 'tis that so excellent a musician should perish in this manner!" His uncle Claudius spent half
30 his time at playing at dice; that was the main fruit of his soveraignty. I omit the madnesses of Caligula's delight, and the execrable sordidness of those of Tiberius. Would one think that Augustus himself, the highest and most fortunate of mankind, a person endowed too with many

excellent parts of nature, should be so hard put to it sometimes for want of recreations, as to be found playing at nuts and bounding-stones, with little Syrian and Moorish boys, whose company he took delight in, for their prating and their wantonness? 5

> Was it for this, that Rome's best blood he spilt
>   With so much falsehood, so much guilt?
> Was it for this, that his ambition strove
> To equal Cæsar, first; and after, Jove?
> Greatness is barren, sure, of solid joys; 10
> Her merchandize (I fear) is all in toys:
> She could not else, sure, so uncivil be,
> To treat his universal majesty,
>   His new-created Deity,
>   With nuts and bounding-stones and boys. 15

But we must excuse her for this meager entertainment; she has not really wherewithal to make such feasts as we imagine. Her guests must be contented sometimes with but slender cates, and with the same cold meats served over and over again, even till they 20 become nauseous. When you have pared away all the vanity, what solid and natural contentment does there remain, which may not be had with five hundred pounds a year? Not so many servants or horses; but a few good ones, which will do all the business as well: not so 25 many choice dishes at every meal; but at several meals all of them, which makes them both the more healthy, and the more pleasant: not so rich garments, nor so frequent changes; but as warm and as comely, and so frequent change too, as is every jot as good for the 30 master, though not for the tailor or *valet de chambre:* not such a stately palace, nor gilt rooms, or the costliest sorts of tapestry; but a convenient brick house, with decent wanscot, and pretty forest-work hangings. Lastly, (for I omit all other particulars, nd will end with that which I 35

love most in both conditions) not whole woods cut in
walks, nor vast parks, nor fountain or cascade gardens;
but herb, and flower, and fruit gardens, which are more
useful, and the water every whit as clear and wholsom as
5 if it darted from the breasts of a marble nymph, or the
urn of a river-god.

If, for all this, you like better the substance of that
former estate of life, do but consider the inseparable
accidents of both: servitude, disquiet, danger, and
10 most commonly guilt, inherent in the one; in the other,
liberty, tranquility, security, and innocence. And when
you have thought upon this, you will confess that to be
a truth which appeared to you before but a ridiculous
paradox, that a low fortune is better guarded and
15 attended than a high one. If, indeed, we look only
upon the flourishing head of the tree, it appears a most
beautiful object,

> "—sed quantum vertice ad auras
> "Ætherias, tantum radice in Tartara tendit."

20
> As far as up towards heaven the branches grow,
> So far the roots sink down to hell below.

Another horrible disgrace to greatness is, that it is
for the most part in pitiful want and distress. What a
wonderful thing is this! Unless it degenerate into a-
25 varice, and so cease to be greatness, it falls perpetually
into such necessities, as drive it into all the meanest
and most sordid ways of borrowing, cousenage, and
robbery:

> Mancipiis locuples, eget æris Cappadocum rex.

30 This is the case of almost all great men, as well as of
the poor king of Cappadocia: they abound with slaves,
but are indigent of money. The ancient Roman emperors, who had the riches of the whole world for their

revenue, had wherewithall to live (one would have thought) pretty well at ease, and to have been exempt from the pressures of extream poverty. But, yet with most of them it was much otherwise; they fell perpetually into such miserable penury, that they were 5 forced to devour or squeeze most of their friends and servants, to cheat with infamous projects, to ransack and pillage all their provinces. This fashion of imperial grandeur is imitated by all inferior and subordinate sorts of it, as if it were a point of honour. They must be 10 cheated of a third part of their estates; two other thirds they must expend in vanity; so that they remain debtors for all the necessary provisions of life, and have no way to satisfie those debts, but out of the succours and supplies of rapine. As riches encrease (says Solomon), 15 so do the mouths that devour them. The master mouth has no more than before. The owner, methinks, is like Ocnus in the fable, who is perpetually winding a rope of hay, and an ass at the end perpetually eating it.

Out of these inconveniences arises naturally one more, 20 which is, that no greatness can be satisfied or contented with itself: still, if it could mount up a little higher, it would be happy; if it could gain but that point, it would obtain all its desires; but yet at last, when it is got up to the very top of the Pic of Tenariff, it is in very great 25 danger of breaking its neck downwards, but in no possibility of ascending upwards into the seat of tranquillity above the moon. The first ambitious men in the world, the old giants, are said to have made an heroical attempt of scaling heaven in despight of the gods; and they 30 cast Ossa upon Olympus, and Pelion upon Ossa: two or three mountains more, they thought, would have done their business; but the thunder spoil'd all their work, when they were come up to the third story:

And what a noble plot was crost !
And what a brave design was lost !

A famous person of their off-spring, the late gyant of
our nation, when, from the condition of a very incon-
5 siderable captain, he had made himself lieutenant general
of an army of little Titans, which was his first mountain,
and afterwards general, which was the second, and after
that, absolute tyrant of three kingdoms, which was the
third, and almost touch'd the heaven which he affected,
10 is believed to have died with grief and discontent, because he could not attain to the honest name of a king,
and the old formality of a crown, though he had before
exceeded the power by a wicked usurpation. If he could
have compass'd that, he would perhaps have wanted
15 something else that is necessary to felicity, and pined
away for the want of the title of an emperor or a god.
The reason of this is, that greatness has not reality in
nature, but is a creature of the fancy, a notion that
consists only in relation and comparison : it is indeed an
20 idol ; but St Paul teaches us, that an idol is nothing in
the world. There is, in truth, no rising or meridian of
the sun, but only in respect to several places : there is no
right nor left, no upper-hand, in nature ; every thing is
little, and every thing is great, according as it is diversly
25 compared. There may be perhaps some village in
Scotland or Ireland, where I might be a great man ;
and 'in that case I should be like Cæsar (you would
wonder how Cæsar and I should be like one another in
any thing) ; and choose rather to be the first man of the
30 village, than second at Rome. Our country is called
Great Britany, in regard only of a lesser of the same
name ; it would be but a ridiculous epithete for it, when
we consider it together with the kingdom of China.
That, too, is but a pitiful rood of ground, in comparison

of the whole earth besides: and this whole globe of
earth, which we account so immense a body, is but one
point or atome in relation to those numberless worlds
that are scattered up and down in the infinite space of
the sky which we behold. 5

The other many inconveniences of grandeur I have
spoken of disperstly in several chapters; and shall end
this with an ode of Horace, not exactly copied, but
rudely imitated.

HORACE, LIB. III. ODE I.

"Odi profanum vulgus et arceo."

1.

HENCE, ye prophane; I hate ye all 10
    Both the great vulgar, and the small.
To virgin minds, which yet their native whitness hold,
Not yet discolour'd with the love of gold,
    (That jaundice of the soul,
Which makes it look so gilded and so foul,) 15
To you, ye very few, these truths I tell;
The muse inspires my song; hark, and observe it well.

2.

We look on men, and wonder at such odds
    'Twixt things that were the same by birth,
We look on kings as giants of the earth, 20
These giants are but pigmeys to the gods.
    The humblest bush and proudest oak
Are but of equal proof against the thunder-stroke.
Beauty, and strength, and wit, and wealth, and power,
    Have their short flourishing hour; 25

And love to see themselves, and smile,
And joy in their pre-eminence a while;
    Even so in the·same land,
Poor weeds, rich corn, gay flowers, together stand;
5 Alas, death mows down all with an impartial hand.

3

And all you men, whom greatness does so please,
    Ye feast, I fear, like Damocles:
    If ye your eyes could upwards move,
(But ye, I fear, think nothing is above)
10 Ye would perceive by what a little thread
    The sword still hangs over your head.
No tide of wine would drown your cares;
No mirth or musick over-noise your fears,
The fear of death would you so watchful keep,
15 As not t'admit the image of it, sleep.

4.

Sleep is a god too proud to wait in palaces,
And yet so humble too, as not to scorn
    The meanest country cottages;
    "His poppey grows among the corn."
20 The halycon sleep will never build his nest
    In any stormy breast.
    'Tis not enough that he does find
    Clouds and darkness in their mind;
     , Darkness but half·his work will do;
25 'Tis not enough; he must find quiet too.

5.

The man, who, in all wishes he does make,
    Does only nature's counsel take,
That wise and happy man will never fear
    The evil aspects of the year;
30 Nor tremble, though two comets should appear.

He does not look in almanacks, to see
    Whether he fortunate shall be ;
Let Mars and Saturn in the heavens conjoyn,
And what they please against the world design,
    So Jupiter within him shine.   5

6.

If of your pleasures and desires no end be found,
God to your cares and fears will set no bound.
    What would content you? who can tell?
Ye fear so much to lose what ye have got,
    As if you lik'd it well :   10
Ye strive for more, as if you lik'd it not.
    Go, level hills, and fill up seas,
Spare nought that may your wanton fancy please ;
    But, trust me, when you have done all this,
Much will be missing still, and much will be amiss. 15

VII.

OF AVARICE.

THERE are two sorts of avarice: the one is but of a bastard kind, and that is, the rapacious appetite of gain; not for its own sake, but for the pleasure of refunding it immediately through all the channels of pride and luxury./ The other is the true kind, and properly so called; which is a restless and unsatiable desire of riches, not for any farther end or use, but only to hoard, and preserve, and perpetually encrease them. The covetous man, of the first kind, is like a greedy ostrich, which devours any metal; but 'tis with an intent to feed upon it, and in effect it makes a shift to digest and excern it. The second is like the foolish chough, which loves to steal money only to hide it. The first does much harm to mankind; and a little good too, to some few: the second does good to none; no, not to himself. The first can make no excuse to God, or angels, or rational men, for his actions: the second can give no reason or colour, not to the devil himself, for what he does; he is a slave to Mammon, without wages. The first makes a shift to be beloved; ay, and envyed, too, by some people: the second is the universal object of hatred and contempt. There is no

vice has been so pelted with good sentences, and especially
by the poets, who have pursued it with stories and fables,
and allegories, and allusions; and moved, as we say,
every stone to fling at it: among all which, I do not
remember a more fine and gentleman-like correction than 5
that which was given it by one line of Ovid.

"Desunt luxuriæ multa, avaritiæ omnia."

Much is wanting to luxury, all to avarice.

To which saying, I have a mind to add one member,
and tender it thus; 10

Poverty wants some, luxury many, avarice all things.

Somebody says of a virtuous and wise man, "that
having nothing, he has all:" this is just his antipode,
who, having all things, yet has nothing.

And, oh, what man's condition can be worse 15
Than his, whom plenty starves, and blessings curse;
The beggars but a common fate deplore,
The rich poor man's emphatically poor.

I wonder how it comes to pass, that there has never
been any law made against him: against him, do I say? 20
I mean, for him: as there are public provisions made for
all other mad-men: it is very reasonable that the king
should appoint some persons (and I think the courtiers
would not be against this proposition) to manage his
estate during his life (for his heirs commonly need not 25
that care); and out of it to make it their business to see,
that he should not want alimony befitting his condition,
which he could never get out of his own cruel fingers.
We relieve idle vagrants, and counterfeit beggars; but
have no care at all of these really poor men, who are 30
(methinks) to be respectfully treated, in regard of their
quality. I might be endless against them, but I am
almost choakt with the super-abundance of the matter;

too much plenty impoverishes me, as it does them. I will conclude this odious subject with part of Horace's first satire, which take in his own familiar stile:

I ADMIRE, Mæcenas, how it comes to pass,
5 That no man ever yet contented was,
Nor is, nor perhaps will be, with that state
In which his own choice plants him, or his fate.
Happy the merchant! the old souldier cries.
The merchant, beaten with tempestuous skies,
10 Happy the souldier! one half-hour to thee
Gives speedy death, or glorious victory.
The lawyer, knockt up early from his rest
By restless clyents, calls the peasant blest;
The peasant, when his labours ill succeed,
15 Envies the mouth, which only talk does feed.
'Tis not (I think you'll say) that I want store
Of instances, if here I add no more;
They are enough to reach at least a mile
Beyond long orator Fabius his stile.
20 But hold, you whom no fortune e'er endears,
Gentlemen, malecontents, and mutineers,
Who bounteous Jove so often cruel call,
Behold, Jove's now resolv'd to please you all.
Thou, souldier, be a merchant; merchant, thou
25 A souldier be; and, lawyer, to the plow.
Change all your stations strait: why do they stay?
The devil a man will change, now, when he may.
Were I in gen'ral Jove's abused case,
By Jove I'de cudgel this rebellious race:
30 But he's too good; be all then, as you were:
However, make the best of what you are,
And in that state be chearful and rejoyce,
Which either was your fate, or was your choice:

No, they must labour yet, and sweat and toil,
And very miserable be a while.
But 'tis with a design only to gain
What may their age with plenteous ease maintain.
The prudent pismire does this lesson teach, 5
And industry to lazy mankind preach.
The little drudge does trot about and sweat,
Nor does he strait devour all he can get;
But in his temperate mouth carries it home
A stock for winter, which he knows must come. 10
And, when the rowling world to creatures here
Turns up the deform'd wrong side of the year,
And shuts him in, with storms, and cold, and wet,
He chearfully does his past labours eat:
O, does he so? your wise example, th' ant, 15
Does not, at all times, rest and plenty want.
But, weighing justly a mortal ant's condition,
Divides his life 'twixt labour and fruition.
Thee, neither heat, nor storms, nor wet, nor cold,
From thy unnatural diligence can withhold: 20
To th' Indies thou would'st run, rather than see
Another, though a friend, richer than thee.
Fond man! what good or beauty can be found
In heaps of treasure, buried under ground?
Which rather than diminisht e'er to see, 25
Thou would'st thyself, too, buried with them be:
And what's the diff'rence? is't not quite as bad
Never to use, as never to have had?
In thy vast barns millions of quarters store;
Thy belly, for all that, will hold no more 30
Than mine does. Every baker makes much bread:
What then? He's with no more, than others, fed.
Do you within the bounds of nature live,
And to augment your own you need not strive;

One hundred acres will no less for you
Your life's whole business, than ten thousand, do.
But pleasant 'tis to take from a great store.
What, man? though you're resolv'd to take no more
5 Than I can from a small one? If your will
Be but a pitcher or a pot to fill,
To some great river for it must you go,
When a clear spring just at your feet does flow?
Give me the spring, which does to humane use
10 Safe, easie, and untroubled stores produce;
He who scorns these, and needs will drink at Nile,
Must run the danger of the crocodile,
And of the rapid stream itself, which may,
At unawares, bear him perhaps away.
15 In a full flood Tantalus stands, his skin
Washt o'er in vain, for ever dry within;
He catches at the stream with greedy lips,
From his toucht mouth the wanton torrent slips:
You laugh now, and expand your careful brow;
20 'Tis finely said, but what's all this to you?
Change but the name, this fable is thy story,
Thou in a flood of useless wealth dost glory,
Which thou canst only touch, but never taste;
Th' abundance still, and still the want, does last.
25 The treasures of the gods thou would'st not spare:
But, when they're made thine own, they sacred are,
And must be kept with reverence; as if thou
No other use of precious gold didst know,
But that of curious pictures, to delight
30 With the fair stamp thy virtuoso sight.
The only true and genuine use is this,
To buy the things, which nature cannot miss
Without discomfort; oyl, and vital bread,
And wine, by which the life of life is fed,

And all those few things else by which we live,
All that remains, is given for thee to give;
If cares and troubles, envy, grief, and fear,
The bitter fruits be, which fair riches bear;
If a new poverty grow out of store;   5
The old plain way, ye gods! let me be poor.

PARAPHRASE ON HORACE, B. III. OD. XVI.

Beginning thus *Inclusam Danaen turris ahenea.*

I.

A TOWER of brass, one would have said,
And locks, and bolts, and iron bars,
And guards, as strict as in the heat of wars,
Might have at least preserv'd one innocent maid.   10
The jealous father thought, he well might spare
      All further jealous care;
And, as he walkt, t' himself alone he smil'd,
    To think how Venus' arts he had beguil'd;
    And, when he slept, his rest was deep,   15
But Venus laught to see and hear him sleep.
      She taught the amorous Jove
      A magical receipt in love,
Which arm'd him stronger, and which help'd him more,
Than all his thunder did, and his almighty-ship before. 20

2.

She taught him love's elixir, by which art
His godhead into gold he did convert:
    No guards did then his passage stay,
    He pass'd with ease; gold was the word;

Subtle as lightning, bright and quick and fierce,
    Gold through doors and walls did pierce.
    The prudent Macedonian king,
To blow up towns, a golden mine did spring.
5   He broke through gates with this petar,
'Tis the great art of peace, the engine 'tis of war;
    And fleets and armies follow it afar:
The ensign 'tis at land, and 'tis the seamen's star.

3.

Let all the world slave to this tyrant be,
10 Creature to this disguised deitie,
    Yet it shall never conquer me.
A guard of virtues will not let it pass,
And wisdom is a tower of stronger brass.
The Muse's lawrel, round my temples spred,
15 Does from this lightning's force secure my head.
    Nor will I lift it up so high,
As in the violent meteor's way to lye.
Wealth for its power do we honour and adore?
The things we hate, ill fate, and death, have more.

4.

20 From towns and courts, camps of the rich and great,
The vast Xerxean army, I retreat,
    And to the small Laconick forces fly,
    Which hold the streights of poverty.
Sellers and granaries in vain we fill,
25   With all the summer's store,
    If the mind thirst and hunger still:
        The poor rich man's emphatically poor.
        Slave to things we too much prize,
We masters grow of all that we despise.

5.

A field of corn, a fountain, and a wood,
 Is all the wealth by nature understood.
The monarch, on whom fertile Nile bestows
 All which that grateful earth can bear,
 Deceives himself, if he suppose   5
That more than this falls to his share.
Whatever an estate does beyond this afford,
 Is not a rent paid to the lord;
But is a tax illegal and unjust,
Exacted from it by the tyrant lust.   10
 Much will always wanting be
 To him who much desires. Thrice happy he
To whom the wise indulgency of heaven,
 With sparing hand, but just enough has given.

VIII.

THE DANGERS OF AN HONEST MAN IN MUCH COMPANY.

IF twenty thousand naked Americans were not able to resist the assaults of but twenty well-armed Spaniards, I see little possibility for one honest man to defend himself against

5 twenty thousand knaves, who are all furnisht *cap a pe*, with the defensive arms of worldly prudence, and the offensive too of craft and malice. He will find no less odds than this against him, if he have much to do in human affairs. The only advice therefore that I can

10 give him is, to be sure not to venture his person any longer in the open campagne, to retreat and entrench himself, to stop up all avenues, and draw up all bridges against so numerous an enemy.

The truth of it is, that a man in much business must

15 either make himself a knave, or else the world will make him a fool : and, if the injury went no farther than the being laught at, a wise man would content himself with the revenge of retaliation ; but the case is much worse, for these civil cannibals too, as well as the wild ones, not

20 only dance about such a taken stranger, but at last devour him. A sober man cannot get too soon out of drunken company, though they be never so kind and

merry among themselves; 'tis not unpleasant only, but
dangerous to him.

Do ye wonder that a virtuous man should love to be
alone? It is hard for him to be otherwise; he is so,
when he is among ten thousand: neither is the solitude 5
so uncomfortable to be alone without any other creature,
as it is to be alone in the midst of wild beasts. Man is
to man all kind of beasts; a fawning dog, a roaring lion,
a thieving fox, a robbing wolf, a dissembling crocodile, a
treacherous decoy, and a rapacious vultur. The civilest, 10
methinks, of all nations, are those, whom we account the
most barbarous; there is some moderation and good-
nature in the Toupinambaltians, who eat no men but
their enemies, whilst we learned and polite and Christian Europeans, like so many pikes and sharks, prey upon 15
everything that we can swallow. It is the greatest boast
of eloquence and philosophy, that they first congregated
men disperst, united them into societies, and built up
the houses and the walls of cities. I wish they could un-
ravel all they had woven; that we might have our woods 20
and our innocence again, instead of our castles and our
policies. They have assembled many thousands of scattered people into one body: 'tis true, they have done so;
they have brought them together into cities to cozen, and
into armies to murder one another: they found them 25
hunters and fishers of wild creatures; they have made
them hunters and fishers of their brethren; they boast
to have reduced them to a state of peace, when the truth
is, they have only taught them an art of war; they have
framed, I must confess, wholesome laws for the restraint 30
of vice, but they rais'd first that devil, which now they
conjure and cannot bind; though there were before no
punishments for wickedness, yet there was less committed because there were no rewards for it.

But the men, who praise philosophy from this topick are much deceived; let oratory answer for itself, the tinkling perhaps of that may unite a swarm: it never was the work of philosophy to assemble multitudes, but 5 to regulate only, and govern them, when they were assembled; to make the best of an evil, and bring them, as much as is possible, to unity again. Avarice and ambition only were the first builders of towns, and founders of empire; they said, *Go to, let us build us a city and a tower* 10 *whose top may reach unto heaven, and let us make us a name, lest we be scattered abroad upon the face of the earth.* What was the beginning of Rome, the metropolis of all the world? what was it, but a concourse of thieves, and a sanctuary of criminals? It was justly named by the 15 augury of no less than twelve vulturs, and the founder cemented his walls with the blood of his brother. Not unlike to this was the beginning even of the first town too in the world, and such is the original sin of most cities: their actual encrease daily with their age and 20 growth: the more people, the more wicked all of them; every one brings in his part to enflame the contagion, which at last becomes so universal and so strong, that no precepts can be sufficient preservatives, nor any thing secure our safety, but flight from among the infected.

25 We ought, in the choice of a situation, to regard, above all things, the healthfulness of the place, and the healthfulness of it for the mind, rather than for the body. But suppose (which is hardly to be supposed) we had antidote enough against this poison; 30 nay, suppose further, we were always and at all pieces armed and provided, both against the assaults of hostility, and the mines of treachery, 'twill yet be but an uncomfortable life to be ever in alarms; though we were compass'd round with fire, to defend ourselves

from wild beasts, the lodgings would be unpleasant, because we must always be obliged to watch that fire, and to fear no less the defects of our guard, than the diligences of our enemy. The sum of this is, that a virtuous man is in danger to be trod upon and destroyed in the crowd of his contraries, nay, which is worse, to be changed and corrupted by them; and that 'tis impossible to escape both these inconveniencies without so much caution, as will take away the whole quiet, that is, the happiness, of his life.

Ye see, then, what he may lose; but, I pray, what can he get there?

Quid Romæ faciam? Mentiri nescio.

What should a man of truth and honesty do at Rome? He can neither understand nor speak the language of the place; a naked man may swim in the sea, but 'tis not the way to catch fish there; they are likelier to devour him, than he them, if he bring no nets, and use no deceits. I think, therefore, it was wise and friendly advice, which Martial gave to Fabian, when he met him newly arrived at Rome:

> Honest and poor, faithful in word and thought;
> What has thee, Fabian, to the city brought?
> Thou neither the buffoon nor bawd canst play,
> Nor with false whispers th' innocent betray;
> Nor corrupt wives, nor from rich beldams get
> A living by thy industry and sweat;
> Nor with vain promises and projects cheat,
> Nor bribe or flatter any of the great.
> But you're a man of learning, prudent, just;
> A man of courage, firm, and fit for trust.
> Why you may stay, and live unenvied here;
> But (faith) go back, and keep you where you were.

Nay, if nothing of all this were in the case, yet the very sight of uncleanness is loathsome to the cleanly; the sight of folly and impiety, vexatious to the wise and pious.

Lucretius, by his favour, though a good poet, was but an ill-natur'd man, when he said, it was delightful 5 to see other men in a great storm. And no less ill-natur'd should I think Democritus, who laughs at all the world, but that he retired himself so much out of it, that we may perceive he took no great pleasure in that kind of mirth. I have been drawn twice or thrice by 10 company to go to Bedlam, and have seen others very much delighted with the fantastical extravagancy of so many various madnesses, which upon me wrought so contrary an effect, that I always returned, not only melancholy, but even sick with the sight. My compas-15 sion there was perhaps too tender, for I meet a thousand madmen abroad, without any perturbation; though, to weigh the matter justly, the total loss of reason is less deplorable than the total depravation of it. An exact judge of human blessings, of riches, honours, beauty, 20 even of wit itself, should pity the abuse of them more than the want.

Briefly, though a wise man could pass never so securely through the great roads of human life, yet he will meet perpetually with so many objects and occasions of com-25 passion, grief, shame, anger, hatred, indignation, and all passions but envy (for he will find nothing to deserve that), that he had better strike into some private path; nay, go so far, if he could, out of the common way, "ut nec facta audiat Pelopidarum;" that he might not so 30 much as hear of the actions of the sons of Adam. But, whither shall we fly then? into the deserts like the antient hermites?

—Qua terra patet, fera regnat Erinnys,
In facinus jurasse putes.

One would think that all mankind had bound themselves by an oath to do all the wickedness they can; that
they had all (as the Scripture speaks) sold themselves to
sin : the difference only is, that some are a little more
crafty (and but a little, God knows), in making of the 5
bargain.   I thought, when I went first to dwell in the
country, that, without doubt, I should have met there
with the simplicity of the old poetical golden age; I
thought to have found no inhabitants there, but such as
the shepherds of Sir Philip Sydney in Arcadia, or of 10
Monsieur d'Urfe upon the banks of Lignon ; and began
to consider with myself, which way I might recommend
no less to posterity the happiness and innocence of the
men of Chertsea : but, to confess the truth, I perceived
quickly, by infallible demonstrations, that I was still in 15
Old England, and not in Arcadia, or La Forrest; that,
if I could not content myself with any thing less than
exact fidelity in humane conversation, I had almost as
good go back and seek for it in the Court, or the Exchange, or Westminster-hall.   I ask again then, whither 20
shall we fly, or what shall we do?   The world may so
come in a man's way, that he cannot choose but salute
it.   If, by any lawful vocation, or just necessity, men
happen to be married to it, I can only give them St. Paul's
advice : Brethren, the time is short; it remains, that 25
they, that have wives, be as though they had none.—
But I would that all men were even as I myself.

In all cases, they must be sure, that they do *mundum
ducere*, and not *mundo nubere*.   They must retain the
superiority and headship over it; happy are they, who 30
can get out of the sight of this deceitful beauty, that
they may not be led so much as into temptation ; who
have not only quitted the metropolis, but can abstain
from ever seeing the next market town of their country.

CLAUDIAN'S OLD MAN OF VERONA.

"Felix, qui patriis ævum," &c.

HAPPY the man, who his whole time doth bound
Within th' inclosure of his little ground.
Happy the man, whom the same humble place
(Th' hereditary cottage of his race)
5 From his first rising infancy has known,
And by degrees sees gently bending down,
With natural propension, to that earth
Which both preserv'd his life, and gave him birth.
Him no false distant lights, by fortune set,
10 Could ever into foolish wand'rings get.
He never dangers either saw, or fear'd:
The dreadful storms at sea he never heard.
He never heard the shril alarms of war,
Or the worse noises of the lawyers' bar.
15 No change of consuls marks to him the year,
The change of seasons is his calendar.
The cold and heat, winter and summer shows;
Autumn by fruits, and spring by flow'rs he knows,
He measures time by land-marks, and has found
20 For the whole day the dial of his ground.
A neighbouring wood, born with himself, he sees,
And loves his old contemporary trees.
He's only heard of near Verona's name,
And knows it, like the Indies, but by fame.
25 Does with a like concernment notice take
Of the Red sea, and of Benacus' lake.
Thus health and strength he to a third age enjoys,
And sees a long posterity of boys.
About the spacious world let others roam,
30 The voyage, life, is longest made at home.

IX.

THE SHORTNESS OF LIFE, AND
UNCERTAINTY OF RICHES.

F you should see a man, that were to cross from Dover to Calais, run about very busie and solicitous, and trouble himself many weeks before in making provisions for his voyage, would you commend him for a cautious and 5 discreet person, or laugh at him for a timerous and impertinent coxcomb? A man, who is excessive in his pains and diligence, and who consumes the greatest part of his time in furnishing the remainder with all conveniencies and even superfluities, is to angels and wise men 10 no less ridiculous; he does as little consider the shortness of his passage, that he might proportion his cares accordingly. It is, alas, so narrow a straight betwixt the womb and the grave, that it might be called the *Pas de Vie*, as well as that the *Pas de Calais*. 15

We are all ἐφήμεροι, (as Pindar calls us,) creatures of a day, and therefore our Saviour bounds our desires to that little space; as if it were very probable that every day should be our last, we are taught to demand even bread for no longer a time. The sun ought not to set 20 upon our covetousness, no more than upon our anger; but, as to God Almighty a thousand years are as one

day, so, in direct opposition, one day to the covetous man is as a thousand years; "tam brevi fortis jaculatur ævo multa," so far he shoots beyond his butt: one would think, he were of the opinion of the Millenaries, and
5 hoped for so long a reign upon earth. The patriarchs before the flood, who enjoy'd almost such a life, made, we are sure, less stores for the maintaining of it; they, who lived nine hundred years, scarcely provided for a few days; we, who live but a few days, provide at least
10 for nine hundred years. What a strange alteration is this of human life and manners! and yet we see an imitation of it in every man's particular experience; for we begin not the cares of life, till it be half spent, and still encrease them, as that decreases.

15 What is there among the actions of beasts so illogical and repugnant to reason? When they do any thing which seems to proceed from that which we call reason, we disdain to allow them that perfection, and attribute it only to a natural instinct: and are not we fools, too,
20 by the same kind of instinct? If we could but learn to number our days (as we are taught to pray that we might), we should adjust much better our other accounts; but, whilst we never consider an end of them, it is no wonder if our cares for them be without end,
25 too. Horace advises very wisely, and in excellent good words,

—Spatio brevi
Spem longam reseces—

from a short life cut off all hopes that grow too long.
30 They must be pruned away, like suckers, that choak the mother-plant, and hinder it from bearing fruit. And in another place, to the same sence,

Vitæ summa brevis spem nos vetat inchoare longam;

which Seneca does not mend when he says, "O! quanta

dementia est spes longas inchoantium !" but he gives an
example there of an acquaintance of his, named Senecio,
who, from a very mean beginning, by great industry in
turning about of money through all ways of gain, had
attained to extraordinary riches, but died on a sudden 5
after having supped merrily, "In ipso actu bene ceden-
tium rerum, in ipso procurrentis fortunæ impetu," in
the full course of his good fortune, when she had a high
tide, and a stiff gale, and all her sails on; upon which
occasion he cries, out of Virgil,   10

    "Insere nunc, Meliboe, pyros; pone ordine vites !"

                ——Go, Meliboeus, now,
    Go graff thy orchards, and thy vineyards plant;
    Behold the fruit!

For this Senecio I have no compassion, because he 15
was taken, as we say, *in ipso facto*, still labouring in the
work of avarice; but the poor rich man in St. Luke
(whose case was not like this) I could pity, methinks, if
the Scripture would permit me; for he seems to have
been satisfied at last, he confesses he had enough for 20
many years, he bids his soul take its ease; and yet, for all
that, God says to him, Thou fool, this night thy soul
shall be required of thee; and the things thou hast laid
up, who shall they belong to? Where shall we find the
causes of this bitter reproach and terrible judgment? We 25
may find, I think, two; and God, perhaps, saw more.
First, that he did not intend true rest to his soul, but
only to change the employments of it from avarice to
luxury; his design is, to eat and to drink, and to be
merry. Secondly, that he went on too long before he 30
thought of resting; the fulness of his old barns had not
sufficed him, he would stay till he was forced to build
new ones; and God meted out to him in the same

measure; since he would have more riches than his life could contain, God destroy'd his life, and gave the fruits of it to another.

Thus God takes away sometimes the man from his 5 riches, and no less frequently riches from the man : what hope can there be of such a marriage, where both parties are so fickle and uncertain? by what bonds can such a couple be kept long together?

1.

WHY dost thou heap up wealth, which thou must quit,
10   Or, what is worse, be left by it?
Why dost thou load thyself, when thou'rt to flie,
      Oh man, ordain'd to die?

2.

Why dost thou build up stately rooms on high,
      Thou who art under ground to lie?
15 Thou sow'st and plantest, but no fruit must sce,
      For death, alas! is sowing thee.

3.

Suppose, thou fortune could'st to tameness bring
      And clip or pinion her wing;
Suppose, thou could'st on fate so far prevail,
20   As not to cut off thy entail;

4.

Yet death at all that subtilty will laugh,
      Death will that foolish gard'ner mock,
Who does a slight and annual plant engraff,
      Upon a lasting stock.

5.

Thou. dost thyself wise and industrious deem;
    A mighty husband thou would'st seem;
Fond man! like a bought slave, thou all the while
    Dost but for others sweat and toil.

6.

Officious fool! that needs must meddling be   5
    In bus'ness, that concerns not thee!
For when to future years thou extend'st thy cares,
    Thou deal'st in other men's affairs.

7.

Even aged men, as if they truly were
    Children again, for age prepare;   10
Provisions for long travail they design,
    In the last point of their short line.

8.

Wisely the ant against poor winter hoards
    The stock, which summer's wealth affords;
In grasshoppers, that must at autumn die,   15
    How vain were such an industry!

9.

Of power and honour the deceitful light
    Might half excuse our cheated sight,
If it of life the whole small time would stay,
    And be our sun-shine all the day;   20

10.

Like lightning, that, begot but in a cloud,
    (Though shining bright, and speaking loud)
Whilst it begins, concludes its violent race,
    And where it gilds, it wounds the place.

L. C.   11

11.

Oh, scene of fortune, which dost fair appear,
  Only to men that stand not near!
Proud poverty, that tinsel brav'ry wears!
  And, like a rainbow, painted tears!

12.

5 Be prudent, and the shore in prospect keep,
  In a weak boat trust not the deep.
Plac'd beneath envy, above envying rise;
  Pity great men, great things despise.

13.

The wise example of the heavenly lark,
10 Thy fellow-poet, Cowley, mark;
Above the clouds, let thy proud musick sound
  Thy humble nest build on the ground.

X.

THE DANGER OF PROCRASTINATION.

A LETTER TO MR S. L.

I AM glad that you approve and applaud my design, of withdrawing myself from all tumult and business of the world; and consecrating the little rest of my time to those studies, to which nature had so motherly inclined me, and from 5 which fortune, like a step-mother, has so long detained me. But nevertheless (you say), which, *but*, is "ærugo mera," a rust which spoils the good metal it grows upon. But (you say) you would advise me not to precipitate that resolution, but to stay a while longer with patience 10 and complaisance, till I had gotten such an estate as might afford me (according to the saying of that person, whom you and I love very much, and would believe as soon as another man) "cum dignitate otium." This were excellent advice to Joshua, who could bid the sun 15 stay too. But there is no fooling with life, when it is once turn'd beyond forty. The seeking for a fortune then is but a desperate after-game: 'tis a hundred to one, if a man fling two sixes, and recover all; especially, if his hand be no luckier than mine. 20

There is some help for all the defects of fortune; for if a man cannot attain to the length of his wishes, he may have his remedy by cutting of them shorter. Epicurus writes a letter to Idomeneus who was then a very powerful, wealthy, and (it seems), a bountiful person to recommend to him, who had made so many rich, one Pythocles, a friend of his, whom he desired might be made a rich man too; "but I intreat you that you would not do it just the same way as you have done to many less deserving persons, but in the most gentlemanly manner of obliging him, which is, not to add any thing to his estate, but to take something from his desires."

The sum of this is, that, for the uncertain hopes of some conveniences, we ought not to defer the execution of a work that is necessary; especially, when the use of those things, which we would stay for, may otherwise be supplyed; but the loss of time, never recovered: nay, farther yet, though we were sure to obtain all that we had a mind to, though we were sure of getting never so much by continuing the game, yet, when the light of life is so near going out, and ought to be so precious, "le jeu ne vaut pas la chandelle," the play is not worth the expence of the candle: after having been long tost in a tempest, if our masts be standing, and we have still sail and tackling enough to carry us to our port, it is no matter for the want of streamers and top-gallants;

———utere velis,
· Totos pande sinus—

A gentleman in our late civil wars, when his quarters were beaten up by the enemy, was taken prisoner, and lost his life afterwards, only by staying to put on a band, and adjust his perriwig; he would escape like a person of quality, or not at all, and dyed the noble martyr of

ceremony and gentility.   I think, your counsel of "Festina lente" is as ill to a man who is flying from the world,
as it would have been to that unfortunate well-bred
gentleman, who was so cautious as not to fly undecently
from his enemies; and therefore I prefer Horace's advice 5
before yours,

——sapere aude,

Incipe—

Begin; the getting out of doors is the greatest part of
the journey.   Varro teaches us that Latin proverb, 10
"portam itineri longissimam esse:" but to return to
Horace,

> "— Sapere aude :
> Incipe; vivendi recte qui prorogat horam,
> Rusticus exspectat, dum labitur amnis, at ille   15
> Labitur, et labetur in omne volubilis ævum."

Begin, be bold, and venture to be wise;
He who defers this work from day to day,
Does on a river's bank expecting stay,
Till the whole stream, which stopt him, should be gone,   20
That runs, and as it runs, for ever will run on.

Cæsar (the man of expedition above all others) was
so far from this folly, that whensoever, in a journey, he
was to cross any river, he never went one foot out of his
way for a bridge, or a ford, or a ferry; but flung himself 25
into it immediately, and swam over: and this is the
course we ought to imitate, if we meet with any stops in
our way to happiness.   Stay till the waters are low; stay
till some boats come by to transport you; stay till a
bridge be built for you: you had even as good stay, till 30
the river be quite past.   Persius (who, you use to say,
you do not know whether he be a good poet or no,
because you cannot understand him, and whom, therefore,
I say, I know to be not a good poet) has an odd expres-

sion of these procrastinators, which, methinks, is full of fancy:

> "Jam cras hesternum consumpsimus; ecce aliud cras
>   Egerit hos annos."

5 Our yesterday's to-morrow now is gone,
And still a new to-morrow does come on;
We by to-morrows draw up all our store,
Till the exhausted well can yield no more.

And now, I think, I am even with you, for your
10 "Otium cum dignitate," and "Festina lente," and three
or four other more of your new Latine sentences: if I
should draw upon you all my forces out of Seneca and
Plutarch upon this subject, I should overwhelm you;
but I leave those, as *Triarii*, for your next charge. I
15 shall only give you now a light skirmish out of an epi-
grammatist, your special good friend; and so, *vale*.

MARTIALIS, LIB. V. EPIGR. LVIII.

"Cras te victurum," &c.

To-morrow you will live, you always cry!
In what far country does this morrow lye,
That 'tis so mighty long ere it arrive?
20 Beyond the Indies does this morrow live?
'Tis so far fetch't this morrow, that I fear
'Twill be both very old and very dear.
To-morrow I will live, the fool does say:
To-day itself's too late; the wise lived yesterday.

MARTIAL, LIB. II. EPIGR. XC.

"Quintiliane, vagæ moderator," &c.

25 Wonder not, Sir, (you who instruct the town
In the true wisdom of the sacred gown)

That I make haste to live, and cannot hold
Patiently out, till I grow rich and old.
Life for delays and doubts no time does give,
None ever yet made haste enough to live.
Let him defer it, whose preposterous care   5
Omits himself, and reaches to his heir.
Who does his father's bounded stores despise,
And whom his own too never can suffice:
My humble thoughts no glittering roofs require,
Or rooms, that shine with aught but constant fire.   10
I well content the avarice of my sight
With the fair gildings of reflected light: .
Pleasures abroad, the sport of nature yields
Her living fountains, and her smiling fields;
And then at home, what pleasure is't to see   15
A little cleanly chearful familie!
Which if a chaste wife crown, no less in her
Than fortune, I the golden mean prefer.
Too noble, nor too wise, she should not be,
No, nor too rich, too fair, too fond of me.   20
Thus let my life slide silently away,
With sleep all night, and quiet all the day.

XI.

OF MYSELF.

T is a hard and nice subject for a man to write of himself; it grates his own heart to say any thing of disparagement, and the reader's ears to hear any thing of praise from him. There 5 is no danger from me of offending him in this kind; neither my mind, nor my body, nor my fortune, allow me any materials for that vanity. It is sufficient for my own contentment, that they have preserved me from being scandalous, or remarkable on the defective side. 10 But, besides that, I shall here speak of myself, only in relation to the subject of these precedent discourses, and shall be likelier thereby to fall into the contempt, than rise up to the estimation, of most people.

As far as my memory can return back into my past 15 life, before I knew, or was capable of guessing, what the world, or the glories or business of it, were, the natural affections of my soul gave me a secret bent of aversion from them, as some plants are said to turn away from others, by an antipathy imperceptible to themselves, and 20 inscrutable to man's understanding. Even when I was a very young boy at school, instead of running about on holydays and playing with my fellows, I was wont to steal from them, and walk into the fields, either alone

with a book, or with some one companion, if I could
find any of the same temper.   I was then, too, so much
an enemy to all constraint, that my masters could never
prevail on me, by any perswasions or encouragements,
to learn without book the common rules of grammar; in 5
which they dispenced with me alone, because they found
I made a shift to do the usual exercise out of my own -
reading and observation.   That I was then of the same
mind as I am now (which, I confess, I wonder at, myself)
may appear by the latter end of an ode, which I made 10
when I was but thirteen years old, and which was then
printed with many other verses.   The beginning of it is
boyish; but of this part, which I here set down (if a
very little were corrected), I should hardly now be much
ashamed.   15

9.

THIS only grant me, that my means may lye
Too low for envy, for contempt too high.
    Some honour I would have,
Not from great deeds, but good alone;
The unknown are better, than ill known: 20
    Rumour can ope the grave.
Acquaintance I would have, but when 't depends
Not on the number, but the choice of friends.

10.

Books should, not business, entertain the light,
And sleep, as undisturb'd as death, the night.   25
    My house a cottage more
Than palace; and should fitting be
For all my use, no luxurie.
    My garden painted o'er

With nature's hand, nor art's; and pleasures yield,
Horace might envy in his Sabine field.

II.

Thus would I double my life's fading space;
For he, that runs it well, twice runs his race.
5   And in this true delight,
These unbought sports, that happy state,
I would not fear, nor wish, my fate;
      But boldly say each night,
To-morrow let my sun his beams display,
10 Or, in clouds hide them; I have liv'd, to-day.

You may see by it, I was even then acquainted with
the poets (for the conclusion is taken out of Horace);
and perhaps it was the immature and immoderate love
of them, which stampt first, or rather engraved, the
15 characters in me : they were like letters cut into the bark
of a young tree, which with the tree still grow propor-
tionably.   But, how this love came to be produced in me
so early, is a hard question : I believe, I can tell the
particular little chance that filled my head first with such
20 chimes of verse, as have never since left ringing there :
for I remember, when I began to read, and take some
pleasure in it, there was wont to lye in my mother's
parlour (I know not by what accident, for she herself
never in her life read any book but of devotion) but there
25 was wont to lye Spenser's works: this I happened to fall
upon, and was infinitely delighted with the stories of the
knights, and gyants, and monsters, and brave houses,
which I found every where there (though my understanding had little to do with all this); and, by degrees, with
30 the tinkling of the rhyme and dance of the numbers ; so

that, I think, I had read him all over before I was twelve
years old.

With these affections of mind, and my heart wholly
set upon letters, I went to the university; but was soon
torn from thence by that violent public storm, which 5
would suffer nothing to stand where it did, but rooted
up every plant, even from the princely cedars to me
the hyssop. Yet, I had as good fortune as could have
befallen me in such a tempest; for I was cast by it into
the family of one of the best persons, and into the court 10
of one of the best princesses, of the world. Now, though
I was here engaged in ways most contrary to the original
design of my life, that is, into much company, and no
small business, and into a daily sight of greatness, both
militant and triumphant (for that was the state then of 15
the English and French courts); yet all this was so far
from altering my opinion, that it only added the confir-
mation of reason to that which was before but natural
inclination. I saw plainly all the paint of that kind of
life, the nearer I came to it; and that beauty, which I 20
did not fall in love with, when, for aught I knew, it
was real, was not like to bewitch or intice me, when I
saw that it was adulterate. I met with several great
persons, whom I liked very well; but could not perceive
that any part of their greatness was to be liked or de- 25
sired, no more than I would be glad or content to be in
a storm, though I saw many ships which rid safely and
bravely in it : a storm would not agree with my stomach,
if it did with my courage. Though I was in a crowd of
as good company as could be found any where, though I 30
was in business of great and honourable trust, though I
eat at the best table, and enjoyed the best conveniences
for present subsistence that ought to be desired by a
man of my condition in banishment and publick distresses;

yet I could not abstain from renewing my old school-boy's
wish, in a copy of verses to the same effect :

1.

WELL then ; I now do plainly see
This busie world and I shall ne'er agree.
5   The very Honey of all earthly joy
    Does of all meats the soonest cloy,
    And they (methinks) deserve my pity,
Who for it can endure the stings,
The crowd, and buzz, and murmurings
10   Of this great hive, the city.

2.

Ah, yet, ere I descend to th' grave,
May I a small house and large garden have !
And a few friends, and many books, both true,
    Both wise, and both delightful too !
15   And since love ne'er will from me flee,
A Mistress moderately fair,
And good as guardian-angels are,
    Only beloved, and loving me !

3.

O Fountains, when in you shall I
20   Myself, eas'd of unpeaceful thoughts espy ?
Oh fields ! Oh woods ! when, when shall I be made,
    The happy tenant of your shade ?
    Here's the spring-head of pleasure's flood ;
Where all the riches lye, that she
25   Has coyn'd and stampt for good.

4.

Pride and Ambition here
Only in far fetcht metaphors appear ;
Here nought but winds can hurtful murmurs scatter,
    And nought but Echo flatter,

The gods when they descended hither
From heaven, did always chuse their way;
And therefore we may boldly say,
    That 'tis the way to thither.

5.

How happy here should I   5
And one dear she live, and embracing dye!
She who is all the world, and can exclude
    In desarts solitude
    I should have then this only fear,
Lest men, when they my pleasures see,   10
Should hither throng to live like me,
    And so make a city here.

And I never then proposed to myself any other advantage from his majesty's happy restauration, but the getting into some moderately convenient retreat in the country; which I thought, in that case, I might easily have compassed, as well as some others, who with no greater probabilities or pretences, have arrived to extraordinary fortunes: but I had before written a shrewd prophesie against myself; and I think Apollo inspired me in the truth, though not in the elegance, of it:

Thou neither great at court, nor in the war,
Nor at th' exchange shalt be, nor at the wrangling bar.
Content thyself with the small barren praise,
    That neglected verse does raise.   25
  She spake; and all my years to come
    Took their unlucky doom.
Their several ways of life let others chuse,
    Their several pleasures let them use;
But I was born for Love, and for a Muse.   30

4.

With Fate what boots it to contend?
Such I began, such am, and so must end.

The Star, that did my being frame,
Was but a lambent flame,
And some small light it did dispence,
But neither heat nor influence.
5 No matter, Cowley; let proud Fortune see,
That thou canst her despise no less than she does thee.
Let all her gifts the portion be
Of folly, lust, and flatterie,
Fraud, extortion, calumnie,
10   Murder, infidelitie,
Rebellion and hypocrisie.
Do thou not grieve nor blush to be,
As all th' inspired tuneful men,
And all thy great forefathers were, from Homer down
15   to Ben.

However, by the failing of the forces which I had
expected, I did not acquit the design which I had resolved
on; I cast myself into it a *corps perdu*, without making
capitulations, or taking counsel of fortune. But God
20 laughs at a man, who says to his soul, *Take thy ease:*
I met presently not only with many little incumbrances
and impediments, but with so much sickness (a new
misfortune to me) as would have spoiled the happiness
of an emperor as well as mine: yet I do neither repent,
25 nor alter my course. "Non ego perfidum dixi sacra·
mentum;" nothing shall separate me from a mistress,
which I have loved so long, and have now at last
married; though she neither has brought me a rich
portion, nor lived yet so quietly with me as I hoped
30 from her:

————"Nec vos, dulcissima mundi
Nomina, vos Musæ, libertas, otia, libri,
Hortique sylvæque, anima remanente, relinquam."

Nor by me e'er shall you,
You, of all names the sweetest, and the best,
You, Muses, books, and liberty, and rest;
You, gardens, fields, and woods, forsaken be,
As long as life itself forsakes not me.   5

But this is a very pretty ejaculation; because I have
concluded all the other chapters with a copy of verses,
I will maintain the humour to the last.

MARTIAL, LIB. X. EPIGR. XLVII.

"Vitam quæ faciunt beatiorem," etc.

SINCE, dearest friend, 'tis your desire to see
A true receipt of happiness from me;   10
These are the chief ingredients, if not all:
Take an estate neither too great nor small,
Which *quantum sufficit* the doctors call.
Let this estate from parents' care descend;
The getting it too much of life does spend.   15
Take such a ground, whose gratitude may be
A fair encouragement for industry.
Let constant fires the winter's fury tame;
And let thy kitchen's be a vestal flame.
Thee to the town let never suit at law,   20
And rarely, very rarely, business draw.
Thy active mind in equal temper keep,
In undisturbed peace, yet not in sleep.
Let exercise a vigorous health maintain,
Without which all the composition's vain.   25
In the same weight prudence and innocence take,
Ana of each does the just mixture make.
But a few friendships wear, and let them be
By nature and by fortune fit for thee.

Instead of art and luxury in food,
Let mirth and freedom make thy table good.
If any cares into thy day-time creep,
At night, without wine's opium, let them sleep.
5   Let rest, which nature does to darkness wed,
And not lust, recommend to thee thy bed.
Be satisfied, and pleas'd with what thou art,
Act chearfully and well th' allotted part;
Enjoy the present hour, be thankful for the past,
10   And neither fear, nor wish, th' approaches of the last.

MARTIAL, LIB. X. EPIGR. XÇVI.

" Sæpe loquar nimium gentes," &c.

ME, who have liv'd so long amóng the great,
You wonder to hear talk of a retreat:
And a retreat so distant, as may show
No thoughts of a return, when once I go.
15   Give me a country, how remote so e'er,
Where happiness a moderate rate does bear,
Where poverty itself in plenty flows,
And all the solid use of riches knows.
The ground about the house maintains it there,
20   The house maintains the ground about it here.
Here even hunger's dear; and a full board
Devours the vital substance of the lord.
The land itself does there the feast bestow,
The land itself must here to market go.
25   Three or four suits one winter here does wast,
One suit does there three or four winters last.
Here every frugal man must oft be cold,
And little luke-warm fires are to you sold.
There fire's an element, as cheap and free,
30   Almost as any of the other three.

Stay you then here, and live among the great,
Attend their sports, and at their tables eat.
When all the bounties here of men you score,
The place's bounty there shall give me more.

EPITAPHIUM VIVI AUCTORIS.

"HIC, o viator, sub lare parvulo   5
  Couleius hic est conditus, hic jacet;
    Defunctus humani laboris
      Sorte, supervacuaque vita.

Non indecora pauperie nitens,
Et non inerti nobilis otio,   10
    Vanoque dilectis popello
      Divitiis animosus hostis.

Possis ut illum dicere mortuum;
En terra jam nunc quantula sufficit!
    Exempta sit curis, viator,   15
      Terra sit illa levis, precare.

Hic sparge flores, sparge breves rosas,
Nam vita gaudet mortua floribus,
    Herbisque odoratis corona
      Vatis adhuc cinerem calentem."   20

PREFACE TO "CUTTER OF COLEMAN STREET."

A COMEDY, call'd the Guardian, and made by me when I was very young, was acted formerly at Cambridge; and several times after, privately during the troubles, as I am told, with
5 good approbation, as it has been lately too at Dublin. There being many things in it which I dislik'd, and finding myself for some days idle, and alone in the country, I fell upon the changing of it almost wholly, as now it is, and it was play'd since at his Royal Highness's
10 theatre, under this new name. It met at the first representation with no favourable reception, and I think there was something of faction against it, by the early appearance of some men's disapprobation before they had seen enough of it to build their dislike upon their judgment.
15 Afterwards it got some ground, and found friends, as well as adversaries. In which condition I should willingly let it die, if the main imputation under which it suffer'd had been shot only against my wit or art in these matters, and not directed against the tenderest parts of
20 human reputation, good nature, good manners, and piety itself.

The first clamour, which some malicious persons rais'd, and made a great noise with, was, that it was a piece intended for abuse and satyre against the King's party. Good God! against the King's party? After having served it twenty years during all the time of their misfortunes and afflictions, I must be a very rash and imprudent person, if I chose out that of their restitution to begin a quarrel with them. I must be too much a madman to be trusted with such an edg'd tool as comedy. But first, why should either the whole party (as it was once distinguish'd by that name, which I hope is abolish'd now by universal loyalty), or any man of virtue or honour in it, believe themselves injur'd, or at all concern'd, by the representation of the faults and follies of a few, who, in the general division of the nation, had crowded in among them? In all mix'd numbers (which is the case of parties), nay, in the most entire and continu'd bodies, there are often some degenerated and corrupted parts, which may be cast away from that, and even cut off from this unity, without any infection of scandal to the remaining body. The church of Rome, with all her arrogance, and her wide pretences of certainty in all truths, and exemption from all errors, does not clap on this enchanted armour of infallibility upon all her particular subjects, nor is offended at the reproof of her greatest doctors. We are not, I hope, become such Puritans ourselves, as to assume the name of the congregation of the spotless. It is hard for any party to be so ill as that no good, impossible to be so good as that no ill, should be found among them. And it has been the perpetual privilege of satyre and comedy, to pluck their vices and follies, tho' not their persons, out of the sanctuary of any title. A cowardly ranting soldier, an ignorant charlatanical doctor, a foolish cheating lawyer, a

silly pedantical scholar, have always been, and still are, the principal subjects of all comedies, without any scandal given to those honourable professions, or even taken by their severest professors. And, if any good physician or
5 divine should be offended with me here, for inveighing against a quack, or for finding Deacon Soaker too often in the butteries, my respect and reverence to their callings would make me troubled at their displeasure, but I could not abstain from taking them for very cholerick and
10 quarrelsome persons. What does this therefore amount to, if it were true which is objected? But it is far from being so; for the representation of two sharks about the town (fellows merry and ingenious enough, and therefore admitted into better companies than they deserve, yet·
15 withal two very scoundrels, which is no unfrequent character at London), the representation, I say, of these as pretended officers of the royal army, was made for no other purpose but to show the world, that the vices and extravagances imputed vulgarly to the cavaliers, were
20 really committed by aliens who only usurp'd that name, and endeavour'd to cover the reproach of their indigency, or infamy of their actions, with so honourable a title. So that the business was not here to correct or cut off any natural branches, though never so corrupted or luxuriant, but to
25 separate and cast away that vermin, which, by sticking so close to them, had done great and considerable prejudice both to the beauty and fertility of the tree; and this is as plainly said, and as often inculcated, as if one should write round about a sign, *This is a dog, This is a*
30 *dog*, out of over-much caution lest some might happen to mistake it for a lion.

Therefore, when this calumny could not hold (for the case is clear, and will take no colour,) some others sought out a subtler hint, to traduce me upon the same score,

and were angry, thàt the person whom I made a true
gentleman, and one both of considerable quality and
sufferings in the royal party, should not have a fair and
noble character throughout, but should submit, in his
great extremities, to wrong his niece for his own relief. 5
This is a refin'd exception, such as I little foresaw, nor
should, with the dulness of my usual charity, have found
out against another man in twenty years. The truth is,
I did not intend the character of a hero, one of exemplary
virtue, and, as Homer often terms such men, unblameable, 10
but an ordinary jovial gentleman, commonly called a
good-fellow, one not so conscientious as to starve rather
than do the least injury, and yet endow'd with so much
sense of honour, as to refuse, when that necessity was
removed, the gain of five thousand pounds, which he might 15
have taken from his niece by the rigour of a forfeiture :
and let the frankness of this latter generosity so expiate
for the former frailty, as may make us not ashamed of his
company ; for, if his true metal is but equal to his allay,
it will not indeed render him one of the finest sorts of 20
men, but it will make him current, for aught I know, in
any party that ever yet was in the world. If you be to
chuse parts for a comedy out of any noble or elevated
rank of persons, the most proper for that work are the
worst of that kind. Comedy is humble of her nature, 25
and has always been bred low, so that she knows not
how to behave herself with the great and accomplish'd.
She does not pretend to the brisk and bold qualities of
wine, but to the stomachal acidity of vinegar ; and therefore is best plac'd among that sort of people which the 30
Romans call The lees of Romulus. If I had design'd
here the celebration of the virtues of our friends, I would
have made the scene nobler where I intended to erect
their statues. They should have stood in odes and

tragedies, and epick poems (neither have I totally omitted those great testimonies of my esteem of them)—"Sed
nunc non erat his locus," &c.

  And so much for this little spiny objection, which a
5 man cannot see without a magnifying-glass. The next
is enough to knock a man down, and accuses me of no.
less than prophaneness. Prophane, to deride the hypocrisie of those men whose skulls are not yet bare upon
the gates since the publick and just punishment of it?
10 But there is some imitation of Scripture-phrases : God
forbid! there is no representation of the true face of
Scripture, but only of that vizard which these hypocrites
(that is, by interpretation, actors with a vizard) draw
upon it. Is it prophane to speak of Harrison's return to
15 life again, when some of his friends really profest their
belief of it, and he himself had been said to promise it?
A man may be so imprudently scrupulous as to find
prophaneness in any thing, either said or written, by
applying it under some similitude or other to some
20 expressions in scripture. This nicety is both vain and
endless. But I call God to witness, that, rather than one
tittle should remain among all my writings, which, according to my severest judgment, should be found
guilty of the crime objected, I would myself burn and
25 extinguish them all together. Nothing is so detestably
leud and wretchless as the derision of things sacred;
and would be in me more unpardonable than any man
else, who have endeavour'd to root out the ordinary
weeds of poetry, and to plant it almost wholly with
30 divinity. I am so far from allowing any loose or
irreverent expressions in matters of that religion which I
believe, that I am very tender in this point, even for the
grossest errors of conscientious persons; they are the
properest object (methinks) both of our pity and charity

too : they are the innocent and white sectaries, in comparison of another kind, who engraft pride upon ignorance,
tyranny upon liberty, and upon all their heresies, treason
and rebellion.   These are principles so destructive to the
peace and society of mankind, that they deserve to be 5
pursu'd by our serious hatred ; and the putting a mask
of sanctity upon such devils, is so ridiculous, that it ought
to be exposed to contempt and laughter.   They are indeed
prophane, who counterfeit the softness of the voice of
holiness, to disguise the roughness of the hands of 10
impiety ; and not they, who, with reverence to the thing
which others dissemble, deride nothing but their dissimulation.   If some piece of an admirable artist should be ill
copy'd, even to ridiculousness, by an ignorant hand ; and
another painter should undertake to draw that copy, and 15
make it yet more ridiculous, to shew apparently the
difference of the two works, and deformity of the latter ;
will not every man see plainly, that the abuse is intended
to the foolish imitation, and not to the excellent original ?
I might say much more, to confute and confound this 20
very false and malicious accusation ; but this is enough, I
hope, to clear the matter, and is, I am afraid, too much
for a preface to a work of so little consideration.
    As for all other objections, which have been or may
be made against the invention or elocution, or any thing 25
else which comes under the critical jurisdiction, let it
stand or fall as it can answer for itself, for I do not lay
the great stress of my reputation upon a structure of this
nature, much less upon the slight reparations only of an
old and unfashionable building.   There is no writer but 30
may fail sometimes in point of wit ; and it is no less
frequent for the auditors to fail in point of judgment.   I
perceive plainly, by daily experience, that Fortune is
mistress of the theatre, as Tully says it is of all popular

assemblies. No man can tell sometimes from whence the invisible winds rise that move them. There are a multitude of people, who are truly and only spectators at a play, without any use of their understanding; and
5 these carry it sometimes by the strength of their numbers. There are others, who use their understandings too much; who think it a sign of weakness and stupidity, to let any thing pass by them unattack'd, and that the honour of their judgments (as some brutals imagine of
10 their courage) consists in quarrelling with every thing. We are therefore wonderful wise men, and have a fine business of it, we, who spend our time in poetry. I do sometimes laugh, and am often angry with myself, when I think on it; and if I had a son inclined by nature to
15 the same folly, I believe I should bind him from it by the strictest conjurations of a paternal blessing. For what can be more ridiculous, than to labour to give men delight, whilst they labour, on their part, more earnestly to take offence? To expose one's self voluntarily and
20 frankly to all the dangers of that narrow passage to unprofitable fame, which is defended by rude multitudes of the ignorant, and by armed troops of the malicious? If we do ill, many discover it, and all despise us; if we do well, but few men find it out, and fewer entertain it
25 kindly. If we commit errors, there is no pardon; if we could do wonders, there would be but little thanks, and that, too, extorted from unwilling givers.

But some perhaps may say, Was it not always thus? do you expect a particular privilege, that was never yet
30 enjoyed by any poet? Were the ancient Grecian or noble Roman authors, was Virgil himself, exempt from this possibility:

Qui multis, melior quàm tu, fuit, improbe, rebus;

who was, in many things, thy better far, thou impudent

pretender? As was said by Lucretius to a person, who took it ill that he was to die, though he had seen so many do it before him, who better deserv'd immortality; and this is to repine at the natural condition of a living poet, as he did at that of a living mortal. I do not 5 only acknowledge the pre-eminence of Virgil (whose footsteps I adore), but submit to many of his Roman brethren; and I confess, that even they, in their own times, were not so secure from the assaults of detraction (though Horace brags at last, 10

Jam dente minus mordeor invido;)

but then the barkings of a few were drown'd in the applause of all the rest of the world, and the poison of their bitings extinguish'd by the antidote of great rewards and great encouragements, which is a way of 15 curing now out of use; and I really profess, that I neither expect, nor think I deserve it. Indolency would serve my turn instead of pleasure: but the case is not so well; for, though I comfort myself with some assurance of the favour and affection of very many candid and good- 20 natur'd (and yet too, judicious and even critical) persons; yet this I do affirm, that from all which I have written I never receiv'd the least benefit, or the least advantage, but, on the contrary, have felt sometimes the effects of malice and misfortune. 25

A PROPOSITION FOR THE ADVANCEMENT
OF EXPERIMENTAL PHILOSOPHY.

NOTES.

PAGE 1.

The title-page to the first Edition of this 'Proposition' sets forth that it was published in London : 'Printed by J. M. for Henry Herringman, and are to be sold at his shop at the sign of the Blew Anchor in the Lower Walk of the New Exchange, 1661.' The publisher who signs himself P.P. says that he puts forth the book during the author's absence in France, and in his address he presents it to the 'Honourable Society for the Advancement of Experimental Philosophy.'

5. *mediate creatures.* Defined in the next line as 'the creatures of God's creature man.' We have to bear in mind that the sense of the Latin *creatura* is 'anything created.' In English 'creature' has now become in a great measure restricted to *living creatures.* God's *mediate* creatures are all things fashioned or wrought out by the *medium* or means of man.

7. *humane.* This is Cowley's constant orthography. We now distinguish two senses from the same Latin root *humanus.* 'Human' is that which concerns or belongs to man, as 'human life' 'human race' &c. 'humane' is confined to those tender and kindly feelings which ought to characterise the family of man.

The orthography of this edition is that of the earliest published copies and it was thought at first that some principles of spelling might have been traced throughout, but there will be found a great degree of inconsistency. This however, as it in no case interferes with the comprehension of Cowley's sense, it has been decided to preserve, especially as some of the peculiarities are among the spelling reforms at present widely advocated, e.g. *mixt* for *mixed*, in line 14, *mist* for missed p. 122, l. 11, and many others.

15. *then.* The distinction between 'then' as an adverb of time and 'than' as the adverbial form to follow the comparative degree was not strictly observed in Cowley's day, though 'then' after the comparative as here is not of frequent occurrence in his works. We find it however on page 2, line 24. Cf. also Sir Thomas Brown, *Vulgar Errors* iii. 25 : 'There was no sarcophagie before the

flood, and without the eating of flesh, our fathers from vegetable aliments preserved themselves unto longer lives, *then* their posterity by any other.'

30. *Aristotle.* The famous Greek philosopher, founder of the Peripatetic school. He was born at Stagira in Thrace about 384 B.C. and died in 322 B.C.

Macrobius. Macrobius was a Latin writer who lived at the close of the 4th century A. D. His chief works were a commentary on Cicero's Dream of Scipio, in two books, and seven books of *Saturnalia.* In the former (*Somn. Scip.* lib. 1. Pontani ed. 1697) p. 28, he speaks of Hippocrates (the famous physician of Cos) as one 'qui tam fallere quam falli nescit.'

12. *hundred years ago.* We should now say 'hundreds of years ago.'

14. *have been discovered.* How much more would Cowley have used language like this had he lived in our day! But in the many applications of steam, electricity, photography, &c. we are reaping fruits such as he saw, though but to a small extent, would result from the pursuit of science in the systematic manner which he advocated. Many 'terræ incognitæ' have been discovered, and there is the certainty that many are still 'behind to exercise our diligence.'

23. *purchases.* The original sense of 'purchase' was 'to procure,' 'to acquire,' by diligent effort, hence the noun here = acquisitions. The French *pourchasser* from which it comes to us has nothing of the meaning of 'buying for a price,' which is the usual sense of the word at present. So Wycliffe translates in 1 Pet. ii. 9, the Latin *populus acquisitionis,* 'a people of *purchasying,*' cf. Dryden, *Palamon and Arcite* bk. 1, line 382, where speaking of the liberty granted to Arcite on the promise of Pirithous,

'And who but Arcite mourns his bitter fate,
Finds his dear *purchase* and repents too late.'

30. *sensible objects.* The need for observation by the senses in addition to and in distinction from the contemplation by reason only, without experiment, is the great argument for Cowley's scheme. Cf. what he says in his ode on Harvey, the discoverer of the circulation:

'Thus Harvey sought for truth in truth's own book,
The creatures which by God himself was writ,
And wisely thought 'twas fit
Not to read comments only upon it,
But on the original itself to look.'

4. *commentating.* We now say 'commenting' but still preserve the longer form in the noun 'commentators.'

9. *above a thousand years.* He intends to embrace the period anterior to Bacon, going back from 1600 A.D. to 600 A.D.

11. *guns.* Gunpowder seems to have been known in the 13th century and Roger Bacon, who died in 1292 appears to have been acquainted with it. It was used in war at the battle of Crecy (1346) and it appears to have been employed at the siege of Algeziras by the Spaniards in 1343.

printing. Introduced into England by Caxton in 1471 but discovered in Germany and practised at Mainz by Gutenberg as early as 1457.

15. *abounded with excellent inventions.* Cowley died in 1667. He is alluding here specially to the discoveries which had been made between Bacon's time and his own. Among these were such discoveries as he mentions p. 8, line 11.

24. *his sacred Majesty.* As the first edition was printed in 1661, the Monarch alluded to here is Charles II. The publisher of the 'Proposition' says that Cowley had allowed him to make it public since his going into France. Cowley went to France immediately after Cromwell's death.

PAGE 5.

1. *the...colledge be situated.* The reason for this choice of position is seen pp. 10—11, where an arrangement for lectures once or twice a week is proposed to be given 'in the hours in the afternoon most convenient for auditors from London.' Cowley designed his College to be under the constant influence of the public eye and public opinion. The proximity to the river is also specified because in his day the journey could be best and soonest made by water.

9. *scholars, servants to the professors.* The relation between student and tutor in former times much resembled that between servant and master. So too apprentices when bound to a trade, undertook while learning it, many household duties and services in no way appertaining to the craft which they were to be taught. Cf. on p. 92, l. 22.

10. *a baily.* We have now returned more nearly to the derivation of the word (which is from the low Latin *ballivus*), in spelling it *bailiff.* The sense is seen in the French 'bailler'='to deliver,' 'put into the charge of any one.' So, Holland's Plutarch, fol. 812, sleep is called 'a false baily' because she takes half of life for herself.

a manciple. From the Latin 'manceps' used specially of the officer who *takes in hand* the provisioning of a college or inn. Cf. Chaucer's Prologue, 569:

> 'A gentil *manciple* was there of a temple
> Of which achatours myghten take ensample
> For to ben wise in bying of vitaille.'

13. *a chirurgeon.* From the Greek χειρουργός, but through the French the hard consonant was softened and the word became *cirurgion*, and from that was contracted into *surgeon*.

14. *lungs, or chymical servants.* In the Glossary to Ben Jonson we find '*Lungs*, a name given to an alchemist's servant...from his blowing the bellows of the furnace.'

See *The Alchemist* II. i. 28, where Sir Epicure Mammon speaking of Face, the alchemist's servant, says

> 'That is his fire-drake,
> His *Lungs*, his Zephyrus, he that puffs his coals.'

And later on in the same scene, line 141,

> '*Lungs*, I will manumit thee from the furnace,
> I will restore thee thy complexion, Puffe,
> Lost in the embers, and repair this brain
> Hurt with the fumes o' the metals.'

Bacon, in the same fanciful way, in his 'New Atlantis' had made 'the father of Solomon's house' say 'We have three that take care to direct new experiments. These we call *lamps*.'

17. *beast*. This word is often used in the singular form with a collective sense = cattle. Thus Judges xx. 48: 'They smote...as well the men of every city, as the *beast* and all that came to hand.'

26. *diet*, i.e. food, as distinguished from the cost of lodging and other service.

27. *entertainment*, the rest of their expenses. These two words represent what the Germans call 'kost und logis.'

PAGE 6.

14. *operatories*, i.e. rooms for the various operations which are to be carried on; work or operating-rooms. We have the form in 'laboratories.'

26. *from leases*. It was the custom to let trust-property on long leases, for the renewal of which a fine, sometimes of considerable amount was payable. It is to this occasional source of additional income that the allusion is made.

PAGE 7.

18. *if he pretend*, i.e. lay a claim, or make an application, for the place. The word often conveys a notion of the groundlessness of the claim. Hence unsuccessful claimants of thrones have been often styled *pretenders*.

30. *the Chartreux*, i.e. the Carthusian monks. This order was founded in 1084 by St Bruno, who built an oratory and a cell on a mountain near Grenoble which subsequently was extended into the magnificent Benedictine convent known as *La Grande Chartreuse*. See also p. 49, l. 30.

31. *lined*. The sense is that all round this inner court or cloister shall run a gravel walk to form the outermost inclosure, then all along the inner side of the walk shall be the row of trees.

PAGE 8.

11. *the circulation of the blood*. Discovered by William Harvey between 1619 and 1628. That the blood circulated through the lungs was known to Michael Servetus, a Spanish physician in 1553.

the milky veins, otherwise called the lacteals, were first noticed in 1622, by Gaspar Asellius, professor of anatomy at Pavia. Further advance was made in the researches on this subject, in 1634 by Wesling, professor of anatomy at Venice, and the discovery was completed by Pecquet, a French physician and anatomist in 1647. These discoveries were very recent in 1661, when Cowley's 'Proposition' was published.

12. *elogies.* (See also p. 12, l. 19.) An *elogy* properly signifies 'a title or description' without any necessary connexion with praise or compliment, but it is sometimes used as if equivalent to *eulogy,* i.e. a complimentary description. Cf. p. 95, l. 6.

13. *portraictures.* The latter part of the word is derived from the Latin *traho,* whose participle is *tractus,* and in the earlier English writers there is a tendency to preserve the 'c' of the original in this derivative. Thus North, Plutarch, II. 49 has 'Artemisia, whose *pourtraicture* I do herewith present you.'

28. *lardry.* The store-room for meat &c. So Holinshed, *Henry III.* (anno 1235). 'The citizens of Winchester had oversight of the kitchen and *larderie.*'

PAGE 9.

24. *Solomon's house in my Lord Bacon.* Solomon's house, or as it is otherwise named, 'The college of the six days' works,' is an order or society described in Bacon's 'New Atlantis.' The Utopian nature of the scheme, 'experiments that can never be experimented,' to which Cowley alludes, is seen in such matters as the provision of houses for imitating and demonstrating meteors, snow, hail and rain; the growing of plants without seeds, and making one tree or plant turn into another, &c. all which things are set forth by 'the father of Solomon's house,' who among other matters says 'We imitate also flights of birds; we have some degrees of flying in the air; we have ships and boats for going under water.'

PAGE 10.

4. *professors itinerate.* We now use *itinerant* in the sense of travelling.

11. *simples,* i.e. herbs used for medicines. Cf. Browne, *Britannia's Pastorals* bk. 2, song 4:

'On every hillside and each vale he looks,
If 'mongst their store of *simples* may be found
An herb to draw and heal his smarting wound.'

28. *the facture.* Superseded now by *manufacture.* The word is not common, but is found in Bacon's Essay 'on Learning.' 'There is no doubt but the *facture* or framing of the inward parts is as full of difference as the outward?'

29. *natural magick.* 'A magician (according to the Persian word) is no other than *divinorum cultor et interpres,* a studious

observer and expounder of divine things; and the art itself (I mean
the art of natural magick) no other than *naturalis philosophiæ
absoluta consummatio,* the absolute perfection of natural philosophy.'
Ralegh, *History of the World,* I. xi. 3.

31. *Lord Bacon's Organon.* Bacon's work is entitled 'Novum
Organum sive indicia vera de interpretatione naturæ.' The catalogue of natural histories to which Cowley here alludes is a list of
130 subjects into which natural science may be subdivided, and the
history of which might form subjects of investigation. The first 40
of these divisions relate to natural phenomena, the elements, and the
vegetable and animal world, the rest to man and the circumstances
in which he lives and the operations in which he is engaged.

PAGE 11.

14. *take place,* i.e. 'take precedence,' 'be at the head of.'
arbitri duarum mensarum, i.e. presidents of the two tables, at
which it is appointed below (line 25) that the professors shall dine
twice a week.
18. *double voice,* i.e. he shall have two votes, or as is now commonly arranged, he shall have a casting vote in the case of equality.
21. *if it be an extraordinary,* i.e. an extraordinary order.
The ordinary orders might be given by word of mouth, but this must
be in writing.

PAGE 12.

15. *that may bring in profit.* Cowley's scheme was in time to
be self-supporting from the profits of inventions. We see too from
p. 10, l. 15, that from time to time as the revenues improved the
itinerant professors were to be better paid.
20. *denison.* We now write *denizen.* The word is said to be
Welsh.
28. *furnish,* i.e. provide the money. Cf. Shaks. *Timon,* III. 1.
20: 'My lord, having great and instant occasion to use fifty talents,
hath sent to your lordship to *furnish* him.'

PAGE 13.

2. *evinced.* Demonstrated and proved to be errors, and so conquered (Lat. *vinco*) and driven away, cf. Burton, *Anatomy,* p. 368:
'Arion made fishes follow him, which as common experience *evinceth,*
are much affected with music.'
8. *triennial.* Here used to signify 'during the course of three
years.' The usual sense of the word now is 'at the end of every
three years.'
34. *mulct,* a fine. The word is from the Italian *multare,* to
fine. The verb is still in use but the noun is more rare.

'A *mulct* thy poverty could never pay,
Had not eternal wisdom found the way.'

Dryden, *Rel. Laici,* 104.

10. *every month.* Probably once a month was the usual rule for the administration of the Holy Communion in Cowley's day. Such incidental notices of the habits of the time are valuable, cf. p. 17, l. 7.

18. *into six.* Thus we see the 6 forms of a public school to have been the rule then.

2. *so near concernment,* i.e. of such great importance and value. Cf. Jer. Taylor, *Rule of Conscience,* bk. I. ch. i. 'In things of great *concernment* we pray God to conduct and direct our choice.'

19. *Varro.* Marcus Terentius Varro, a Latin author, contemporary with Cicero. His work here alluded to is entitled *De re rustica.* He was born B.C. 116 and died B.C. 28.

Cato. M. Porcius Cato wrote a work also entitled *De re rustica.* He lived before Varro, dying B.C. 149.

Columella. He was born at Cadiz, and flourished in the early part of the first century of the Christian era. He was one of the most voluminous Latin writers on rural matters.

20. *Pliny.* C. Plinius Secundus, the famous author of the *Historia Naturalis.* He was born A.D. 22 and died A.D. 79.

Celsus. A. Corn. Celsus lived in the reigns of Augustus and Tiberius. The work of his which remains is a treatise 'de medicina.' He is often alluded to by Columella.

Seneca. Best known as the tutor of the Emperor Nero. But among his other works he produced 'Quaestionum naturalium libri septem,' which is the reason why he is included here in Cowley's list. He was put to death by order of Nero A.D. 65.

22. *Grotius.* Hugo Grotius, a Dutch Statesman and Jurist, born in Delft A.D. 1583, died 1645. Among his works, which are numerous, the larger part however dealing with religious subjects, the only one which Cowley can have intended his philosophical students to read must have been the *De jure belli et pacis.*

Nemetianus. M. Aurelius Nemetianus was a native of Africa, who lived in Italy about A.D. 243. He wrote on fishing, hunting and kindred subjects. Only portions of his works have been preserved to us.

Manilius. The date of this writer is altogether uncertain. A work by him *de Astrologia* is all that remains, and its date has given rise to much discussion.

25. *indulging to.* Where we now should say 'indulgent to.'

29. *parcels.* The word was used in Cowley's day for a small portion of anything. Cf. Shakespeare, *Merry Wives,* I. 1. 237: 'Divers philosophers hold that the lips is *parcel* of the mouth.'

31. *unuseful.* A rather uncommon form.

PAGE 16.

7. *Plautus his.* This mode of representing the possessive case in English was common in the 16th and 17th century writings. The idea was that the 's' of the possessive was a contraction for the personal pronoun. This notion is however at once dispelled when we remember that 'Mary's' could not be a contraction for 'Mary his.' We have instance of this form in the Prayer-book where the prayer 'For all sorts and conditions of men' concludes with the words 'for Jesus Christ his sake.' Cf. also 'Epicurus his philosophy,' p. 76, l. 5, also 'Vitellius his table,' p. 126, l. 17.

10. *Nicander.* A Greek poet and physician who was born at Claros and flourished B.C. 135. He wrote a poem called 'Theriaca' on venomous animals, and the treatment of their wounds.

Oppianus. A Greek writer at the close of the 2nd century of the Christian era. He has left two poems, one on fishing, the other on hunting, and a prose work on hawking.

Scaliger. Joseph Julius Scaliger, born 1540, died in Leyden (where he was Professor in the University) in 1609. He was a learned scholar, and devoted himself largely to criticism and correction of classical texts.

11. *doubt*, i.e. 'hesitate.' Cf. Spenser, *F. Q.* IV. i. 48:

'Fond knight, said she, the thing that with this eye
I saw, why should I *doubt* to tell the same?'

13. *Theophrastus.* A Greek philosopher, born in Lesbos. He was a contemporary of Plato. The books of his to which Cowley here refers are two works on botany, and some fragments on fire, the winds and matters of meteorology.

Dioscorides. The name of several Greek physicians, one of whom was at the court of Cleopatra, B.C. 41—30. Under his name we have a treatise which deals with the plants growing in Greece, which was most likely the work in Cowley's thoughts.

16. *Hermogenes.* A Greek rhetorician A.D. 161—180. His book on the 'Art of Rhetoric' teaches how to speak in courts of justice. It has been frequently edited and commented on.

Longinus. Dionysius Cassius Longinus, a Greek philosopher who lived in the 3rd century of the Christian era. He has left among many other works a treatise on Rhetoric, and had such wide general knowledge that he was styled 'a living library.'

21. *errors.* An attempt had been made to disabuse the minds of men of such errors as are here alluded to by Sir Thomas Brown in his famous treatise on 'Vulgar Errors,' known also by the more learned-sounding title 'Pseudodoxia Epidemica.' As specimens of the errors with which he deals we may mention : 'That crystal is nothing else but ice strongly congealed:' 'That a diamond is made soft or broke by the blood of a goat:' 'That a pot full of ashes will contain as much water as it would without them:' 'That an elephant has no joints:' 'That a wolf first seeing a man begets a dumbness in him:' 'That a salamander lives in the fire:' 'That

the flesh of peacocks corrupteth not:' 'That men weigh heavier dead than alive, and before meat than after.'

26. *they should likewise use,* i.e. 'practise.' Cf. Shakes. *Troilus,* II. I. 52: 'If thou *use* to beat me, I will...tell what thou art.'

28. *travel.* For which we now write 'travail'=trouble, labour. The two forms are from the same root, French *travailler,* cf. Beaumont and Fletcher, *Pilgrim,* Act I.

'The saints ye kneel to hear and ease your *travels.*'

PAGE 17.

1. *scholars,* i.e. of the sixteen young scholars, servants to the professors (p. 5, l. 8). Cowley uses *scholars* both for them and for the other pupils who are to have teaching in the College.

3. *learn to dance.* Cowley is not the first poet who has commended dancing. Perhaps the best known laudation of it is the 'Orchestra' of Sir John Davies, which is in the form of a dialogue between Penelope and one of her wooers.

7. *days of devotion,* i.e. fast and festival days appointed of the Church. See above on p. 14, l. 10.

16. *expences.* Apparently in the sense of 'means,' 'ability,' 'what they were able to expend.'

29. *hospital-like.* The word 'hospital,' at first applied to a place for the reception and entertainment of strangers, later on became restricted to houses for the poor or sick. So 'hospital-like'=meagre, poverty-stricken, pinched.

PAGE 18.

1. *abused,* led astray, misled. Cf. Shak. *Cymb.* I. 4. 124: 'You are a great deal *abused* in too bold a persuasion.'

15. *explode.* The original idea is 'to hiss a bad actor off the stage,' and hence, 'to drive away anything that is bad and false.' Cf. Milton, *P. L.* XI. 669:
'Him old and young
Exploded.'
See also below p. 48, l. 31.

16. *false moneys.* Cowley thus names any wrong opinions which have come to pass current for truth. We keep to the same metaphor in the expression 'pass current.'

24. *by the by,* i.e. superadded, in addition to all other good effects.

28. *indifferently,* 'impartially.' 'Judge of my life or death *indifferently*', Spenser, *F. Q.* I. i. 51.

PAGE 19.

1. *encounter with.* In more modern English the preposition is omitted. But the full phrase is common in Shakespeare, cf. *All's Well,* I. 3. 214: 'Let not your hate *encounter with* my love.'

9. *reliques.* Cowley has a liking for this orthography, which connects it with the Latin 'reliquiæ' from which it comes. Cf. also p. 113, l. 20.

A DISCOURSE BY WAY OF VISION CONCERNING THE GOVERNMENT OF OLIVER CROMWELL.

PAGE 20.

1. *It was the funeral day.* Cromwell was buried in Westminster Abbey on Monday, 22nd Nov. 1658. He had died on his lucky day, 3rd Sept., the anniversary of the victories of Dunbar and Worcester. Evelyn notices the funeral in his diary: 'Saw the superb funerall of the Protector. He was carried from Somerset House in a velvet bed of state drawn by six horses, houssed with the same: the pall held by his new Lords: Oliver lying in effigie in royal robes, and crowned with a crown, sceptre and globe like a king. The pendants and guidons were carried by the officers of the army; the imperial banners, atchievements &c. by the heraulds in their coates; a rich caparisoned horse, embroidered all over with gold; a knight of honour armed cap a pie, and after all, his guards, souldiers, and innumerable mourners. In this equipage they proceeded to Westminster; but it was the joyfullest funeral I ever saw, for there were none that cried but dogs, which the souldiers hooted away with a barbarous noise, drinking and taking tobacco in the streets as they went.'

3. *little affection.* In his 'verses upon His Majesty's Restauration' Cowley speaks thus of Cromwell:

'Where's now that *ignis fatuus* that ere while
Misled our wandering isle?
Where's the impostor Cromwell gone?'

9. *singular virtuosos.* 'Virtuoso' is generally used of those persons who have skill in some special art. Here it would seem to mean those who had come to see the pageant out of curiosity. For the word cf. Glanvill, Essay 3, 'Another excellent *virtuoso*, Mr John Evelyn, hath very considerably advanced the history of fruit and forest-trees.'

10. *the mount in Cornwall,* i.e. St Michael's Mount, the southern extremity of the land, and a little beyond it; just as the *Orcades,* the Orkneys, in the next line are a little past the northern limit of our islands. All were assembled, as it were from Dan to Beersheba.

16. *their brother.* Such being the style in which royal personages were spoken of by each other. Cf. 1 Kings xx. 32, 33. See also below p. 27, l. 3, 'a *brother* to the gods of the earth.'

17. *the herse.* The ornamented carriage to bear the coffin at a

funeral. Of the magnificence of the hearse on this occasion Evelyn's description bears witness. The word is now commonly spelt 'hearse.'

the idol. At royal funerals there was often borne in the procession a figure or effigy of the dead on a bier, and some of these are still preserved in the Abbey at Westminster, though not often shewn to the public. This image (Gk. εἴδωλον) is what Cowley refers to, which on this occasion wore a crown, though he whom it represented had not done so.

PAGE 21.

3. *methoughts.* A strange form, the 's' being due to the same letter at the end of 'methinks', but entirely without warrant in language. Cowley uses it in *The Mistress*, p. 11 :

' But then, *methoughts*, there something shined within.'

16. *vision.* In *visions* a higher degree of revelation was supposed to be imparted than in *dreams*, mentioned in the,next line. Cf. *Select Discourses of John Smith*, p. 184: 'The Jews are wont to make a vision superior to a dream, as representing things more to the life.'

18. *father of poets*, i.e. Homer. The allusion is to *Iliad*, I. 63: καὶ γάρ τ' ὄναρ ἐκ Διός ἐστιν. 'For indeed a vision comes from Zeus.'

22. *like St Paul.* The allusion, which perhaps a very reverent taste would have dispensed with, is to 2 Cor. xii. 2, 3. That Cowley meant to be very reverent in all his employment of Scriptural language we see from p. 132, l. 30.

23. *famous hill in the island of Mona*, i.e. Snowfield in the Isle of Man, which island is called Mona by Cæsar (*Bell. Gall.* v. 13).

28. *these twenty years.* Meaning the time of Cromwell's power, and the troublous years by which it was preceded, going back to the days of the 'Solemn League and Covenant.' Cf. p. 25, l. 4. The civil war dates from 1641.

30. *a sighing.* The *a* thus used before the gerundive is a corruption of the preposition *on.* Cf. Shakes. *Romeo*, III. 1. 194:

'My blood for your rude brawls doth lie *a* bleeding.'

PAGE 22.

3. *forsook.* For '*forsaken.*' Cf. Shakes. *Othello*, IV. 2. 125: 'Hath she *forsook* so many noble matches.'

24. *turned only into noise.* The 'face and substance' to which Cowley alludes in these lines was the regular appointed order of prayer; whereas, during the Commonwealth, the Prayer-book was superseded by the 'Directory for Publique Worship,' which left much to the discretion of the minister. This our author compares to a real personality being turned into mere noise.

PAGE 23.

6. *will hardly be*, i.e. that will hardly be.

10. *Bedlam.* A corrupted form of *Bethlehem*, the name of the hospital in London devoted to the treatment of the insane. See p. 154, l. 10.

14. *barbarous Britons.* Alluding to the custom of the early inhabitants of this island to paint their bodies with woad. There is another allusion to the practice on p. 24, l. 24.

22. *French inconstancie.* The fickleness of the Gallic race has long been proverbial. Cæsar, *B. G.* II. I, speaks of their *mobilitas et levitas animi.*

PAGE 24.

4. *threat.* For 'threaten.' Used only in verse and as a present tense. Cf. Shakespeare, *Macbeth,* II. I. 60:

> 'Whiles I *threat,* he lives.'

13. *the royal martyr's prayer.* There is a prayer at the close of each section of the '*Eikon Basilike,*' a work long supposed to be the composition of King Charles I., and by some still thought to be so. There are also, appended to the book, four private prayers used by his Majesty in the time of his sufferings.

16. *his bloud below.* This would cry for vengeance, and for this the soul of the king is supposed not to pray, but only for blessings on the land.

21. *in the evening,* i.e. when shadows would be longest.

27. *the battel of Naseby.* This, which was the most fatal battle to the cause of the Royalists, might be expected to be prominently depicted on the body of such a being as this 'strange and terrible apparition' turns out to be. Naseby was fought on 15 June, 1645, and from that time the death of Charles seems to have begun to form a part of the plans of Cromwell.

29. *guest,* i.e. guessed. Cowley uses largely, but with much inconsistency, these forms of the preterite in 't' for 'ed.' Here the form appears the stranger by reason of the omission of one 's' from the root.

PAGE 25.

2. i.e. 'Peace is sought by war.'

4. *Acts, Ordinances.* Enactments of the nature here described under various titles were multiplied during the period of the Commonwealth.

7. *quelled,* i.e. 'quailed,' 'terrified.' The original sense of the word is 'to kill.' So by Shakespeare (*2 Hen. IV.* II. I. 58) murderers are called 'manquellers.' For the sense in the text, cf. Dryden, *Annus Mirabilis,* lxxvi. 1,

> 'If number English courages could *quell.*'

11. *north-west principality.* That being the quarter in which Great Britain lies in respect of the other countries of Europe.

26. *Richard III.,* brother to Edward IV., and therefore uncle to Edward V. and his brother the Duke of York, whom he caused to be murdered in the Tower.

27. *he presently slew the commonwealth.* This has reference to

the way in which Cromwell, finding the Long Parliament not so obedient to him as he expected, dissolved it in conjunction with his council of officers (April 20, 1653). Cf. p. 26, l. 25, 'to trample upon them too &c.'

30. *did but murder a murderer.* For the Parliament had already put to death the King.

33. *Turk.* This word was used as the impersonation of the worst of enemies. Even such a one however, if his purpose had been understood and constant, would have been better than Cromwell with his perpetual changes.

PAGE 26.

5. *use,* i.e. are wont. See below, p. 50, l. 29, and p. 86, l. 19, and cf. Shakes. 2 *Henry IV.* v. 2. 114,

'The unstained sword which you have *used* to bear.'

7. *jealousie,* i.e. suspicion that he was not the angel he professed to be.

9. *forreign correspondences.* Cromwell's influence abroad was very great. He was in the closest correspondence with France, Christina queen of Sweden esteemed him highly, he exercised great influence over the Dutch, and his friendship was sought after by the Spaniards. Bp. Warburton compares him to Julius Cæsar. See below on p. 27, l. 14.

PAGE 27.

6. *a new and unheard-of monster.* This was the Parliament which assembled on July 4th, 1653. It was nominated by Cromwell, as Lord General, and his council of war, and was intended to consist exclusively of men distinguished by holiness of life and piety of conversation. The Ministers of the Congregational Churches sent in lists of men 'faithful, fearing God, and hating covetousness,' and from these lists Cromwell made choice of about 150 members. As there was no pretence of any election Cowley calls this gathering 'a new and unheard-of monster.'

7. *stifle that in the very infancy.* The innovations proposed by the Barebones' parliament, as the new and unheard-of monster was called, were so startling, including the abolition of the court of Chancery, the repeal of all the old laws, and the formation of a new and simple code, &c. that Cromwell soon found he had mistaken his instruments, and the military council resolved that these troublesome legislators should be sent back to their parishes. Thus the government came entirely into the hands of the Lord General and his officers. This was on 12th Dec. 1653, and four days afterwards Cromwell was installed as 'Lord Protector.' The large powers given to the Protector by the 'Instrument of Government' are alluded to in the next line.

12. *each corner of the three nations.* That England was completely subservient to him is manifest from what has been just said in the previous notes. In Ireland he had taken Drogheda, Wexford had been betrayed to him, as also Cork, and his command had been

so successful that when he was sent for by the parliament, he could leave Ireton as his deputy. Scotland was entirely broken after the battle of Dunbar, and there Monk was left as Cromwell's representative.

14. *feared and courted by all forreign princes.* On this cf. Clarendon, XV. 152, who says among other things: "His greatness at home was but a shadow of the glory he had abroad. It was hard to discover which feared him most, France, Spain or the Low Countries, where his friendship was current at the value he put upon it. And as they did all sacrifice their honour and their interest to his pleasure, so there is nothing he could have demanded, that either of them would have denied him."

19. *two millions a year.* This alludes to the 'Humble petition and advice' by which there was assigned to the Protector a million a year as a perpetual revenue for the pay of the army and the fleet and £300,000 for the support of the civil government. Other funds had previously been assigned to him by the 'Instrument of Government.'

25. *to bequeath all this with one word to his posterity.* Cf. Clarendon XV. 146: "He did not think he should die till even the time that his spirits failed him, and then he declared that he did appoint his son to succeed him, his eldest son Richard."

PAGE 28.

1. *what kind of angel.* Cf. p. 30, l. 2, 'to give even the devil (as they say) his right.'

11. *by an angel.* The allusion is probably to Gal. i. 8. So the words 'Christ forbids' must be taken as signifying 'Christ in the person of His apostle St Paul.'

12. *rather to try than to tempt,* i.e. to test rather than to lead astray.

25. *taxes of scarce two hundred thousand pounds a year.* The whole revenue of Charles I. was £800,000, of these little more than a quarter appear to have been of the nature of taxation.

27. *the loss of three or four ears.* Alluding to the mutilation suffered under Charles I. by Prynne, Bastwick, Leighton and Burton. Another allusion to this matter is on p. 57, l. 4.

29. *I know not what two thousand guards.* 'I know not what' is the Latin 'nescio quid,' and is used to indicate some vague imaginary idea. On the King's determination to have a guard about his person, see Clarendon v. 140.

PAGE 29.

1. *even to the very skin.* On the way in which the Church and the clergy were dealt with by the puritanical party, see Clarendon, V. 135, 136. Also Evelyn is constant in his lamentations on this subject during the whole time of the Commonwealth. Cf. his entry for March 18, 164⅘: 'Mr Owen a sequestered and learned minister preached in my parlour and gave us the blessed Sacrament, now wholly out of use in the parish Churches, on which the Presbyterians and fanatics had usurped.'

3. *councils of rapine, and courts of murder.* Alluding to such courts as 'the high court of justice' of 1654; of which Clarendon (XIV. 35) says, 'A high court of justice was erected to try criminals, which rarely absolved any man who was brought before them.' A little later on he speaks of it as a tribunal which was 'continued to root out all who had adhered to the King.'

15. *his own general.* General Lambert was second in command, but first in the affections of the army. He aided Cromwell in becoming Protector, but Cromwell afterwards became jealous of him, and turned him out of the army.

24. *as St Paul says.* 1 Cor. viii. 4.

26. *the valley of Hinnom.* A valley on the southern side of Mount Zion, which opens out into the valley of the Kidron. It was the place where sacrifices were offered to Moloch. Hence Cromwell is called in the next line 'his Molochship.' The place is mentioned in Josh. xv. 8, and its Hebrew name 'Ge-Hinnom' has been modified into the Greek γέεννα, which became the type of hell (Matth. v. 22).

27. *bowels of men.* Clarendon, XV. 102, says, 'Colonel Ashton, Stacy and Betteley...were treated with more severity, and were hanged, drawn and quartered, with the utmost rigour, in several great streets in the city, to make the deeper impression upon the people, the two last being citizens. But all men appeared so nauseated with blood, and so tired with those abominable spectacles that Cromwell thought it best to pardon the rest who were condemned, or rather to reprieve them.' These are the circumstances to which Cowley alludes under the figure of the 'valley of Hinnom.'

PAGE 30.

16. *the most antient of the heathen divines.* He thus styles Homer. The quotation which follows is from *Odyss.* XXII. 412.

22. *a person who was proud.* Here his highness, the angel, makes a slip. The words are really addressed to Euryclea, the aged attendant on Penelope, when she was about to indulge in exultation over the slaughter of the suitors.

PAGE 31.

15. *a Lambert.* After Cromwell's death, General Lambert was regarded as likely to make a party in the army which should depend upon him rather than the parliament. It was known that he had aided the late Protector in his advance to power, on the understanding that he should succeed him. It is to the probability of such a future that Cowley here alludes. On the whole of Lambert's actions and aims see Clarendon, XVI. 78, *seqq.*

18. *Syracusians,* i.e. 'Syracusans.' The allusion is to those proceedings which followed the success of Timoleon. When all the tyrants were expelled from Sicily and the free towns had submitted to the Syracusan alliance, the citadel and town of Ortygia were demolished, and every fortress destroyed in which a tyrant

could be likely to defend himself. Commissioners were sent for
from Corinth to revise the ancient laws of the Syracusan constitution, and the new constitution appears to have been reduced to a
very simple form.

'To implead' is 'to bring an action at law', and the Syracusans
thus legally did their best to efface the records of the preceding
tyrannies.

27. *momentany.* We now only use 'momentary' but the form
in the text is in accord with the Latin, which has both 'momen-
tarius' and 'momentaneus.'

32. *Marius or Sylla.* Caius Marius, the celebrated Roman
leader in the war against Jugurtha. His acts of despotic violence
were committed after he with Cinna had blockaded Rome and become masters of it. There was then carried out a general massacre
of the patrician party who had opposed Cinna and Marius. Marius
died in the following year B.C. 86.

Sylla, i.e. Lucius Cornelius Sulla, who for some time was
legate to Marius. The latter was disgusted at the popularity ol
Sulla, and when that commander was entrusted with the leadership
in the Mithridatic war, Marius used every effort to wrest it from him,
and it was in Sulla's absence that the blockade of Rome just mentioned was carried on, after which Marius and Cinna made themselves consuls. On Sulla's return, after having made peace with
Mithridates, his great aim was to annihilate the popular party, which
had supported his adversaries. This he did by wholesale banishment, and heavy fines, and in B.C. 82 he caused himself to be made
dictator. These are the acts for which Cowley mentions him as a
parallel to Cromwell.

PAGE 32.

3. *curst on.* Here *on* denotes continuity. Let him be cursed
without ceasing. Cf. Shakespeare, *Two Gent.* II. 3. 29, 'He
weeps *on.*' *Much Ado,* 'Benedick, love *on.*'

13. *the son of earth,* i.e. the giant Briareus, who in the fable of
the war of the Titans against the Gods is said to have helped the Gods.
The Titans piled the three mountains Pelion, Ossa and Olympus
one upon another, that they might be able to scale heaven, but their
rebellion was defeated by Jove's thunderbolts. The poet's mythology
has ranged Briareus on the wrong side.

24. *a basilisk he grows, if once he gets a crown.* Cf. Shakespeare,
Jul. Cas. II. I. 12:

'He would be crown'd:—
How that might change his nature, there's the question,
It is the bright day that brings forth the adder,
And that craves wary walking.'

PAGE 33.

1. *no guards can oppose assaulting fears.* Cf. Gray, *The
Bard,* l. 5:

'Helm nor hauberk's twisted mail,
  Nor e'en thy virtues, Tyrant, will avail
  To save thy secret soul from nightly fears.'

16. *darkness to be felt.* Alluding to the Egyptian plague,
Exod. x. 21.

19. *croaking sects.* The nasal tones in which the sectaries of the
period gave utterance to their teaching form the subject of much
ridicule in the writings of this period, cf. Butler, *Hudibras*, pt. 1.
canto 1:

'This light inspires and plays upon
  The nose of saint like bagpipe drone.'

PAGE 34.

1. *the eleventh plague.* Egypt felt the terrors of ten, but the
poet invites another, whatever it may be, to clear the land of this
infection. Nothing could be worse than what they now suffer.

4. *God's sword,* i.e. pestilence. This was sent to Israel when
David chose rather to fall into the hand of God, than into the hand
of man. 2 Sam. xxiv. 14.

11. *some denouncing Jonas.* On Jonah's message to Nineveh
and its effect, see Jonah iii. 4—10.

19. *in the enclosures of metre.* Where by reason of the labour
of versifying, you must the sooner be forced to stop. The verse is
enclosed each line by its proper rhyme.

23. *sciomachy.* From the Greek σκιά, a shadow, and μάχομαι,
to fight = a fighting with shadows. The speaker hints that all this
wordy battle has been fought groundlessly, that there was no reason
or warrant for it.

27. *juvans pater* = 'aiding father.' Supposed, as it seems, in
Cowley's day, to be the origin and sense of the name Jupiter.

PAGE 35.

23. *containing themselves* = restraining themselves. Cf. Shakespeare, *Troilus* v. 2. 180: '*O contain yourself,* your passion draws
ears hither.'

PAGE 36.

16. *that patent of their destiny.* The book of fate, in which is
written down what shall befall each man, but which is mercifully
hidden from view.

20. *Lord Strafford.* Made Lord Deputy of Ireland in 1631 and
Lord Lieutenant in 1639. This title had not been used since the time
of Essex. Strafford was beheaded on Tower-Hill 12 May, 1641.

PAGE 37.

5. *the confusions of a civil war.* Which beginning in 1641 had
continued till the execution of Charles I.

29. *Roman virtue.* Used in the original sense of the Latin '*virtus*'='prowess,' 'valour.'

PAGE 38.

19. *banditos.* The Italian form of this word, or something near it, prevailed for a time in English, as it does in the plural *banditti,* still. The word means 'declared (*dictus*) or placed under a *ban.*' Cf. Shakespeare, 2 *Hen. VI.* IV. I,

> 'A Roman sworder and *bandetto* slave
> Murdered sweet Tully.'

PAGE 39.

23. *Did we furnish him etc.* This sentence is not very clear, but to judge by the context the contrast is between 'our enemies' and 'his friends.' The latter is equivalent to 'ourselves.' The previous sentence says 'Are we conquered by him whom we employed to conquer our foes?' This seems to mean 'Did we arm him against our enemies, and has he on the contrary plunged the weapons we gave him into our own bowels?' So that 'and keep them'='and did he keep them?'

PAGE 42.

1. '*and trembled*', i.e. 'and that he trembled.' The sentence is not strictly grammatical, but the sense is clear.

5. *Rode caper vitem.* The quotation is from Ovid, *Fasti* I. 357, and the passage, an address to a goat nibbling at the vines, tells how, for all that, there will be wine enough left to pour over the victim when the goat is sacrificed.

18. *canow.* The spelling of this word varies. We find *canoa, canow,* and *cannowe.* The derivation is said to be from *canna,* a reed. Cf. Browne, *Britannia's Pastorals,* bk. I. st. 2 :

> 'Unto the rougher stream, the cruel swain
> Hurries the shepherdess, where having lain
> Her in a boat like the *cannowes* of Inde,
> Some seely trough of wood, or some tree's rind,
> Puts from the shore.'

30. *foolish daughters in the fable.* The legend in the Greek mythology is that Medea desiring to be avenged on Pelias for the murder of Æson, the father of her husband Jason, persuaded his daughters to cut Pelias their father in pieces, and boil the parts, asserting that thereby they would restore him to youth and vigour, as she had before changed a ram into a lamb by boiling the dissected parts of its body in a cauldron.

PAGE 43.

12. *syllogism.* A syllogism is an argument stated at full length. Thus stated it contains three propositions, the major, the minor, and the conclusion. In the syllogism of the text these would be :

He who has the best parts in a nation ought to be king.
O.C. has the best parts in the nation,
Therefore O.C. ought to be king.

17. *two branches of the same family.* As in the wars of the Roses between the houses of York and Lancaster.

23. i.e. 'By our misery thou art Great.' The words are found in Cicero, *Ad Att.* II. 19. 3, with the whole story of their repetition by the actor in whose part they came.

PAGE 44.

17. *Jack of the clock-house.* A little figure of a man, which is placed outside some public clocks to strike the quarters. One was formerly to be seen on the church of St Dunstan's, Fleet Street. Cf. Cotgrave's Dictionary s.v. *Jaquelet.* See also Shakespeare, *Richd. II.* V. 5. 60:

'My time
Runs posting on in Bolingbroke's proud joy
While I stand fooling here, his *Jack o' the clock.*'

Cf. *Richd. III.* IV. 2.

27. The quotation is from Hor. *Odes,* III. 29. In the original *Cetera* is the reading, not *omnia* in the first line. Francis renders the lines :

'The rest is all beyond our power,
And like the changeful Tiber flows,
Who now beneath his banks subsides,
And peaceful to his native ocean glides.
But when descends a sudden shower,
And wild provokes his silent flood,
The mountains hear the torrent roar,
And echoes shake the neighbouring wood :
Then swoln with rage he sweeps away
Uprooted trees, herds, dwellings to the sea.'

PAGE 45.

12. *a beardless boy.* Caius Octavius, afterwards the emperor Augustus. The allusion in Cowley's text is to the events which immediately followed the murder of Julius Cæsar, by whom Octavius had been adopted. On hearing what had occurred at Rome, he went thither from Illyricum and demanded the property which Cæsar had left him. Antony had in his possession the money and papers of Cæsar and refused to give them up. This was one difficulty, and Dec. Brutus (one of Cæsar's assassins), who was in possession of Cisalpine Gaul, was also an adversary to Octavius and wished to prevent his succeeding to Cæsar's property and influence. Octavius however had the favour of the army, and when Cicero saw the troops largely siding with him he changed from opponent to supporter, believing that Octavius alone could save the republic. By a series of bold strokes Octavius first defeated Antony at Mutina,

then obtained for himself the Consulship, secured Cæsar's property, and made himself popular by distributing the money he had left to the people. Then reconciled to Antony and uniting with Lepidus (Dec. Brutus had already been murdered at Aquileia by order of Antony) the three agreed that Octavius should lay down the Consulship, and that the empire should be divided among them under the title of *triumviri.* At Philippi, B.C. 42, Octavius and Antony defeated M. Junius Brutus and C. Cassius, by whose death two powerful opponents were removed. Subsequently Octavius gained for himself the power assigned to Lepidus, while Antony, through his infatuation for Cleopatra, became regarded by the Romans as an enemy of the republic. War was declared against him and he was defeated at Actium B.C. 31. After this Octavius (named Augustus by the senate and people) was appointed imperator for ever.

13. *a voluptuous madman.* Mark Antony. Octavius because of a dream of his physician quitted his tent where he was sick and so saved his life, and took part in the battle of Philippi, which as is said in the text gained him the empire of the world. The defeat at Philippi, which was followed by the death of Cassius, was owing to a mistake which that general fell into by reason of his shortness of sight. To these matters the allusions in the lines immediately following relate.

22. *Cyrus.* That Persian king, by whom, after his conquest of Babylon, the Jews were sent back to their own land at the end of the 70 years captivity. Babylon was taken by him B.C. 538.

Alexander. Known as 'the Great.' Son of Philip of Macedon, born B.C. 356, died B.C. 323.

23. *Scipio and his contemporaries.* This is Publius Cornelius Scipio Africanus, who was so distinguished in the third Punic war, and by whom Carthage was taken B.C. 146. Among his contemporaries were the aged Cato, Lælius and Polybius.

30. *pleased to call him.* The reference is to Isaiah xliv. 28, 'That saith of Cyrus, He is my shepherd,' and in Isaiah xlv. 1, 'Thus saith the Lord to his anointed, to Cyrus, whose right hand I have holden.' Cf. also 2 Chron. xxxvi. 22 and the identical passage Ezra i. 1.

32. *Massenellos.* Masaniello (a name corruptly formed from Tommaso Aniello) was a young fisherman at Naples towards the middle of the 17th century, by whose efforts the taxes on fruit and vegetables imposed at Naples by the duke d'Arcos were abolished. After the success of his insurrection Masaniello went mad, and was afterwards shot while confined in one of the convents where he had been brought in consequence of the excitement caused by his incoherent harangues.

33. *Johns of Leyden.* John Bockold, known as John of Leyden, was a chief man in the Anabaptist revolution in Westphalia in the earlier half of the sixteenth century. He, with others, was executed and their bodies exposed in iron cages at the summit of one of the church towers in Münster.

PAGE 46.

20. *untempered mortars.* The allusion is to Ezek. xiii. 10. The whole passage is full of scriptural allusion, and the zeal of the Royalist borders somewhat on profanity in the words which he applies to the Restoration of the Royal family.

25. *chargeable,* 'costly, expensive,' cf. Hooker, *Eccl. Pol.* v. 15: 'Suppose we that God himself delighteth to dwell sumptuously or taketh pleasure in *chargeable* pomp?'

PAGE 47.

5. *three millions a year.* Cowley has dwelt before on the greater burden to the nation during the Commonwealth period than at any time during the reign of Charles I. See p. 28.

14. *five children.* The children of Charles I. were (1) Charles II. afterwards king, (2) Mary, who married Prince William of Nassau, and was mother of William III., (3) James II., who also reigned, (4) Henry Duke of Gloucester who died in 1660, (5) Elizabeth, who died in 1649, (6) Henrietta, who married Philip Duke of Orleans. There were therefore *five* living when Cowley wrote.

19. *as great dangers.* The queen of Charles I. and her children also were reduced to great straits during the time of the civil war. On one occasion the queen was compelled to sell her plate to supply her wants, and was obliged to leave the kingdom and take refuge in France.

PAGE 48.

8. *That little in print.* At this time all that could be in print of Cromwell s must have been only the speeches which he had made on various occasions, which had the reputation of being exceedingly prolix.

16. *intellectuals,* i.e. his intellectual powers. The use of the adjective in a plural form instead of a noun remains in 'morals' (see line 17), but 'intellectuals' has become obsolete. Wood (*Ath. Ox.*) says of Philemon Holland, 'His *intellectuals* and his senses remained perfect until the 84th year of his age.' Cf. also Naunton's *Regalia,* pp. 15, 60.

31. *explode.* See above on p. 18, l. 15.

PAGE 49.

31. *Chartreux.* See on p. 7, l. 30.

34. *'larum.* For 'alarum.' A similar aphæresis is seen in 'prentice' for 'apprentice' and in the old form of 'potticary' for 'apothecary.'

PAGE 50.

5. *Faux,* i.e. Guy Fawkes, the well-known conspirator in the reign of James I.

29. *use*, i.e. 'are wont.' Cf. for this sense of the word, Ps. cxix. 132, 'As thou *usest* to do unto those that love thy name.' See also above, p. 26, l. 5, and p. 47, l. 27.

PAGE 51.

3. *Nero to kill his mother.* Agrippina, Nero's mother, through whose instrumentality he had become emperor, was murdered by her son, partly because she made an effort to obtain the management of public affairs, and partly at the instigation of Poppæa, who hoped after Agrippina was removed to become the wife of the emperor.

9. *wanted...that courage.* Nero attempted to commit suicide, and at last was put to death at his own request by one of his attendants.

23. *a sin that is called like it in the Scriptures.* 1 Sam. xv. 23, 'Rebellion is as the sin of witchcraft.'

PAGE 52.

3. *a peace with our brethren of Holland.* It has generally been asserted that Cromwell, in his negotiations with the Dutch, instead of securing for England the commercial advantages, which he was entitled, after Blake's victories, to demand, sacrificed the glories of the navy to an impatience for peace, or to the furtherance of his own views against the Stuarts and the House of Orange.

4. *first...that God chastised.* The Dutch were the first people affected by the legislation of the Parliament in the Act of Navigation (1652), an ordinance which totally suppressed their trade. At that time they were (as the English are now) the carriers for all nations.

6. *abetting our troubles,* i.e. augmenting and making worse.

16. *Beatus pacificus,* i.e. Blessed peace-maker. The words are from the Vulgate, Matth. v. 9.

17. *carrying a war two thousand miles off, westwards.* That is, the expedition to the West Indies under Penn and Venables.

18. *vails.* Money given in consideration of service, presents to servants. Cf. Shakespeare, *Pericles,* II. I. 157, 'There are certain condolements, certain *vails.*' On the *two millions a year* mentioned in this line see above on p. 28, l. 27, and p. 47, l. 5, where Cowley says *three millions.* In this latter sum he must include the *vails.*

23. *Anti-Solomon.* So styled because he did the opposite of Solomon, who made gold as abundant as silver had been in the times before him. See 1 Kings x. 21, 27.

26. *his fantastical Ophir,* i.e. the West Indies, which he fancied would be to him what Ophir was to Solomon. On 'fantastical,' cf. Shak. *Macbeth,* I. 3. 139, 'Whose murder yet is but *fantastical,*' i.e. a matter of imagination and no reality.

28. *the Faustus.* Sylla had a son named Faustus. The name signifies 'prosperous,' 'blessed.' Hence the words of the text.

Sylla. See above on p. 31, l. 32.

PAGE 53.

5. *this ignominy.* At St Domingo the English soldiers and sailors were destroyed by the climate and by the fury of the natives, who concealed themselves in the woods where the European troops could not follow them. See below, line 22.

6. *Jamaica.* Foiled in their attempt on Hispaniola, the commanders directed their course to Jamaica, which surrendered to them without a blow. It is the boasting about such a capture that Cowley here ridicules. In Cowley's time nobody foresaw the importance of Jamaica.

10. *the war with Spain.* The Spaniards declared war because a positive treaty had been broken by the proceedings in the West Indies.

14. *the silver fleet.* These were the treasure ships of Spain that were on their way to Europe. These Blake attacked and captured, and the silver was displayed publicly that the English people might be satisfied with some results of the war, though Penn and Venables had been so little fortunate in the West Indies.

17. *twelve hundred of her ships.* It is said that 1500 merchant vessels of England were captured by the Spaniards, and thus the impolicy of the Protector's conduct made itself severely felt in all the trading towns on the English coast.

21. *Dunkirk.* This town, valuable to the English as a seaport on the French coast, a point for easy communication in peace, and still more convenient if war should break out, was the price for which Cromwell stipulated in helping France against Spain.

34. *a greater kingdom than itself.* Alluding to the conquests made in France in the times of Edward III. and Henry V.

PAGE 54.

17. *decimation.* This was an ordinance published by the Protector in 1665 that all who had ever borne arms for the king should pay *a tenth* part of all the estates they had left to support the charges of the Commonwealth. On the way in which it was carried out by the Major-generals, see Thurloe, vol. IV. *passim.*

24. *a whole book.* This book is probably that which was written at Cologne, perhaps by Sir Edw. Hyde, at the king's command. Clarendon, *Hist. of Rebellion,* XIV. 151 says: 'This declaration [the decimating ordinance] was quickly sent to Cologne, where the king caused such an answer to be made to it...that it obliged all the nation to look upon him [Cromwell] as a detestable enemy, who was to be removed by any way that offered itself: many of which arguments were made use of against him in the next parliament that he called.'

31. *the calling in and establishment of the Jews.* After having been banished from England nearly 4 centuries the Jews were re-admitted by Cromwell in 1652, in virtue of a treaty with Manasseh ben-Israel.

PAGE 55.

2. *he invented*, i.e. had a design. Almost equivalent to *intended*.

3. πονηρὸν and πονηρὸς, i.e. wicked scheme and wicked person.

10. *S. Peter's.* To this Saint the abbey of Westminster is dedicated.

11. *a mosquito.* We have now only the form 'mosque,' for the Turkish place of worship. The form in the text is nearly like the Spanish *mosquita*, which has remained in their language from the Moorish occupation. Donne, *Satire 4*, writes:

'Would not Heraclitus laugh to see Macrine,
    From hat to shoe himself at dore refine,
    As if the presence were a *moschite*?

where the pronunciation must be trisyllabic as in our text.

14. *heathenish way of the Common-prayer-book.* Cf. Twell's *Life of Pocock.* Pocock was Hebrew professor at Oxford, and in the proceedings taken against him it was charged, among other things, 'that he had frequently made use of the idolatrous Common Prayer Book as he performed divine Service.' The 'Directory for Publique Worship' was the book sanctioned by the Assembly of Divines. See on p. 22, l. 25.

21. *moss-troopers.* A name originally given to those banditti who inhabited the marshy country of Liddesdale, and subsisted chiefly by rapine. Fuller says of them, 'they are called *moss-troopers* because dwelling in the *mosses* and riding in *troops* together. They dwell in the bounds or meeting of two kingdoms, but obey the laws of neither.'

25. *Mr Coney.* Of the proceedings here alluded to Clarendon (XV. 150) says: 'When Cromwell had laid some very extraordinary tax upon the city, one Cony, an eminent fanatic...positively refused to pay his part. Cromwell sent for him and cajoled him with the memory of the old kindness and friendship that had been between them. But...this man remembered him how great an enemy he had expressed himself to such grievances, and declared that all who submitted to them were more to blame and greater enemies to their country, than they who imposed them, and that the tyranny of princes could never be grievous but by the tameness and stupidity of the people.' The narrative goes on to say that Cromwell at last committed Mr Coney to prison, and when Maynard, his counsel, demanded his liberty, the Protector's attorney delayed the proceedings and in the meantime Maynard was put in the Tower, and the judges censured for suffering him to question or make doubt of the Protector's authority. It was on this occasion that Cromwell is said to have spoken those words about Magna Charta, alluded to below, p. 57, l. 31.

34. *ship-money.* The tax for providing shipping, levied at first on seaboard counties and afterwards extended to the whole kingdom

by Charles I. Mr Hampden's refusal to pay was one of the first stages of the Rebellion.

16. *the peroration*, i.e. the concluding portion of an address.
26. On Marius and Sylla, see p. 31, l. 32.
the cursed triumvirate. This alludes to the first triumvirate B.C. 60, composed of Julius Cæsar, Crassus and Pompey.
30. *against a Roman.* The declaration 'Civis Romanus sum' availed to save one who could make it from many indignities, such as imprisonment or scourging. We can see this from S. Paul's history. There might be reasons why a Roman citizen should be put to death, but he was deemed exempt from degrading penalties.
33. *deficient to*, i.e. inferior to. We now should say 'deficient *from*,' though that is not a very common form of expression.

4. *two or three ears.* See note above on p. 28, l. 28.
8. *the broyling.* Noticed above on p. 29, l. 26.
11. *Sicilie.* The tyrants of Sicily are celebrated for the cruelties they exercised.
14. *slaves in America.* This refers to the action taken by Cromwell after Penruddock's rebellion in 1655. Penruddock and Grove (the leaders) were beheaded at Exeter, several others were hanged, and the rest of the prisoners were sent to Barbadoes to be sold for slaves. See also 'The humble petition of Marcellis Rivers and Oxenbridge Foyle as well on behalf of themselves as of three score and ten freeborn people of this nation now in slavery.'
31. *words which he spoke.* Of Cromwell's language about the Magna Charta Clarendon gives a specimen in connexion with Mr Coney's case (see on p. 55, l. 25).

8. *The representative*, i.e. the representative assembly, the parliament.
15. *phrensie.* This use of 'ph' where we now write 'f' is frequent in Cowley. It has some warrant in the present word on account of its derivation from the Greek φρήν, but he even writes *prophane* (p. 139, l. 10 &c.) which cannot be so defended.
19. *major-generals.* This was the name Cromwell gave to those officers whom he appointed, after the act of decimation, to be over those military governments into which he portioned out the whole kingdom. They were to raise a militia, collect taxes, suppress all tumults, disarm all Catholics and Cavaliers, and to arrest, bind over and imprison all suspected or dangerous persons.
21. *seventy peers of the land at one clap.* In allusion to Cromwell's attempt to form a House of Lords. He induced a few of the

ancient nobility to accept a place therein, but he included in it also many of the most active friends of the reigning Government. Thus he produced a contemptible medley, and weakened his party in the Commons.

26. *It was antiently said of Fortune.* The allusion is to Juvenal, *Sat.* III. 39, 40.

31. *haut-goust.* The 's' retained in this form points to the derivation of the latter portion from Latin *'gustus'*=taste. In modern French orthography the letter is dropped, but was not so in Cowley's time.

PAGE 59.

8. *concurring to,* i.e. assenting to. The more common expression is 'to concur *with* any thing.'

17. The words written on the wall of Belshazzar's palace (Dan. v. 25).

29. *his son.* Richard Cromwell, whom the Protector appointed to succeed him. This is what Cowley calls 'to entail his own injustice upon his children.' On Richard Cromwell's resignation of his position, see Clarendon, *Hist. Reb.* XVI. 14, 15. See above on p. 27, l. 25.

PAGE 60.

6. *fell a laughing.* The 'a' in forms like this is the preposition 'on'. Thus 'fell on sleep' became 'fell asleep.' See above on p. 21, l. 30.

17. *Cynick.* The Cynic philosophers, whose typical representative is Diogenes, were always represented as morose and ill-tempered. Hence the 'frowardness' spoken of in the text.

Epicurean. The Epicureans, holding that the end of existence was to secure the greatest possible amount of enjoyment, were supposed to avoid every exertion which could be escaped. Hence their name is equivalent to 'lazy,' 'self-indulgent.' Theirs were the 'lethargical morals' alluded to below, l. 32. See on the word p. 113, l. 26.

22. *Platonical statesman.* One who indulges in fanciful plans of government, incapable of realization, like those of Plato in his 'Republic,' which was such a commonwealth as sounded very well in theory, but could never be worked in practice.

23. *Utopian dreamer.* Sir Thos. More in his 'Utopia' describes a fancied state with government and laws approaching very nearly to perfection. Hence 'Utopian' is applied to things 'fanciful,' 'incapable of being carried out.'

26. *Aristotle's politicks.* Which were of a practical character. Taking human nature as it is, the philosopher of Stagira endeavoured to teach how a state can be best organized so as to answer to the requirements of men. The education of the citizens to live a life in harmony with virtue is the great principle on which he makes his system depend.

28. *Machiaval,* i.e. the famous Florentine statesman and

diplomatist, Niccolo Machiavelli. His principles are laid down in two works, *The Prince* and *The Practice of Politics.* He is said to countenance, in these works, the doing of any act whereby ambitious sovereigns and their ministers may accomplish whatever their extravagant desires prompt them to, at the expense either of the peace of their country or the safety of their subjects. Clarendon (*Hist. Reb.* xv. 156) speaks of Machiavelli's method as prescribing 'upon any alteration of a government, as a thing absolutely necessary, to cut off the heads of all those, and extirpate their families, who are friends to the old one.'

PAGE 61.

8. *favourite to.* We now say 'favourite with.'
16. *the first city.* See Genesis iv. 17. Cain's city was called Enoch.
18. *grand-child of the Deity.* Regarding Adam as 'the son of God' (see Luke iii. 38), Cain would thus be 'grand-child.'
25. *Abimelech.* For the history, see Judges ix. 5.
27. *a hecatomb.* This was an offering of 100 victims. Abimelech's brethren were 70 in number.
29. *to make it hold,* i.e. to make it retain its colour. We have the same figure in the expression '*fast* colours.'

PAGE 62.

1. *Athaliah.* On Athaliah's fury, see 2 Kings xi. 1—3.
15. *better got by one.* Joash being the only one of the seed royal that was saved.
19. *Mathusalem.* For 'Methuselah,' whose life extended to 969 years (Gen. v. 27). The orthography, which seems due to a popular acceptance of the termination for the same as that of Jerusalem, was common in Cowley's time (cf. p. 87, l. 18). He also says in *The Mistress*, p. 26,

'So though my life be short yet may I prove
The great *Methusalem* of love.'

29. *you were wont to deliver oracles.* Some of the ancient oracles, which Cowley by implication attributes to the 'kind of angel' seen in his vision, were written in very ambiguous and sometimes limping verse.

PAGE 63.

9. *malignant.* This was a name given by the leaders of faction in these times to all whom they desired to render odious to the people.
12. *you know whither.* Euphemistically alluding to the place of execution.
13. *pounces,* i.e. talons, claws, wherewith the bird pounces, that is, pierces his prey. Cf. Spenser *F. Q.* I. 11,

'As haggard hauke, presuming to contend
  With hardy fowle above his hable might,
His wearie *pounces* all in vain doth spend
  To trusse the pray too heavie for his flight.'

So a '*pouncet*-box' is a box pierced with holes out of which any powder which it contains may be shaken.

25. *a nat'ral crown.* Cowley makes his rescuing angel to come in the likeness of an English king.

33. *the mystic champion's,* i.e. Michael the archangel, who fought with the dragon, i.e. Satan. (Rev. xii. 7).

PAGE 64.

4. *th' English bloody cross.* The significance of the Red Cross is explained by Spenser (*F. Q.* I. 2), in his description of the Red Cross Knight:

'And on his brest a bloodie cross he bore,
The dear remembrance of his dying Lord,
For whose sweet sake that glorious badge he wore
And dead, as living ever, him adored.
Upon his shield the like was also scored
For soveraine hope, which in his helpe he had.'

ESSAYS.

I. OF LIBERTY.

PAGE 66.

6. *Esau.* For the history, see Genesis xxv. 29—34.

8. *Thamer,* i.e. Tamar, see Genesis xxxviii. 18.

14. *Stoical paradox.* The Stoics were fond of maintaining such positions as that 'a wise man is inferior to Jove alone,' and that true philosophy, i.e. Stoicism, made him who followed it superior to all the world beside, alone free, rich, a sovereign in short.

19. *Salust.* The quotation is from the fragments of Sallust, Mattaire's edition, p. 116.

25. *Atalanta.* She was the daughter of Jasus and Clymene. When her father wished her to marry she made it a condition that her suitors should contend with her in a footrace, and she would accept him who conquered her. Meilanion who had obtained from Aphrodite three golden apples, dropped them on the course and Atalanta, captivated with their beauty, tarried to pick them up and so was beaten.

28. *Fertur &c.* i.e. 'the charioteer is borne on by his steed, nor does the team heed the reins.' The line is from Verg. *Georg.* 1. 514.

33. When the Romans were candidates for any office they were willing to submit to anything to gain their end. Tertullian (*de pœnit.* 11) describes them thus : 'Those who go about canvassing for office are neither ashamed nor tired out by any sufferings of mind or body, and not only do they bear sufferings but also every kind of insult for the compassing of their wish. What unseemliness of dress do they assume !'

PAGE 67.

5. *nomenclator*, i.e. a person to announce the names of all whom the candidate met. Cowley in *The Mistress* says :

'Meanwhile I wlll not dare to make a name
        To represent thee by.
Adam (God's *nomenclator*) could not frame
        One that enough should signifie.'

13. 'Lo, Romans the lords of the world.' The allusion is to Verg. *Aen.* I. 282.

19. *the beast with many heads*, i.e. the populace.

Catiline. Lucius Sergius Catilina, notorious for several times stirring up insurrections in Rome. Some of Cicero's most powerful speeches were made against him, and Sallust has left us a history of the man and his doings.

21. *Sylla's.* See on p. 31, l. 32.

28. *Machiavel.* On Niccolo Machiavelli, born 1469, died 1527, see above on p. 60, l. 28.

30. *this man &c.* The passage is translated from Cicero's oration *pro Cælio* v. 12.

PAGE 68.

19. *laveer.* This is a Dutch nautical word, and signifies 'to sail in an oblique direction so as to catch the wind,' and so fitly describes the action of a seeker after popular favour. It is used by Lovelace, *Lucustra* 11. 18,

'Did on the shore himself *laveer.*'

And by Dryden, *Astræa Redux.* 65,

'But those that 'gainst stiff gales *laveering* go
    Must be at once resolved and skilful too.'

33. *an Anti-Paul.* The very contrary of Paul. The Apostle 'became all things to all men' that he might *save* some.

PAGE 69.

8. *Salust.* The passage is from the *Catiline*, chap. x.

20. *Zopyrus.* The history of Zopyrus is narrated in the text. His father Megabyzus was one of the seven chiefs who killed the

false Smerdis. It is said that Darius after Babylon was won used to say he would rather have Zopyrus without his scars than twenty Babylons.

PAGE 70.

15. *painful*, i.e. painstaking. Cf. Gascoigne, *Steele Glass* (Arber's Reprints), p. 43, 'Plato was in his age *painful* to write good precepts of moral phylosophy.' Also Burton's *Anatomy*, p. 208, 'Let there be bountiful patrons, and there will be *painful* scholars in all sciences.'

31. *Seneca.* The words are from the *Liber de Consolatione*, ad Polybium, chap. XXVI. 'Magna servitus est magna fortuna.'

34. *to Atticus.* The passage is in a letter included with the epistles of Cicero to Brutus, I. 16, 4, 'Nimium timemus mortem et exsilium et paupertatem. Hæc mihi videntur Ciceroni ultima esse in malis, et dum habeat a quibus impetret quæ velit, et a quibus colatur et laudetur, servitutem honorificam modo non aspernatur ; si quidquam in extrema ac miserrima contumelia potest honorificum esse?'

PAGE 71.

14. *a groom.* From A. S. *guma* = a man, homo. In general usage however it came to signify 'a serving man.' Cf. Spenser, *Sheph. Cal.* (March) 62,

> 'It was upon a holiday,
>   When shepheard *groomes* han leave to play.'

29. *amatorem &c.* 'Three hundred chains bind the lover Pirithous.' The words are from Horace, *Od.* III. 4. 79.

PAGE 72.

14. *aliena &c.* The words, sufficiently translated in the text, are from Horace, *Satires*, II. 6. 34.

18. *dors.* Cockchafers. Cf. Burton's *Anatomy*, p. 67, 'They shew their wit in censuring others, a company of foolish note-makers, humble-bees, *dors* or beetles.'

26. *table d'host*, i.e. table d'hôte. Cf. above on *haut goust* p. 58, l. 31.

PAGE 73.

8. *as the Scripture speaks.* The allusion is to Ps. lxix. 22.

16. *pan huper sebastos*, i.e. πᾶν ὑπὲρ σεβαστός, 'one altogether superlatively august.'

19. *Leviathans.* The grand people are so styled as being the great fishes of society. Similar is the expression 'This Triton of the minnows,' Shakes. *Cor.* III. 1. 89.

20. *Hitherto &c.* Job xxviii. 11.

21. *Perditur &c.* From Horace, *Sat.* II. 6, 59. The words are translated in the next line.

23. *impertinent.* Aimless, objectless, serving no purpose. See p. 72, l. 17. Cf. Shakespeare, *Tempest*, I. 2. 138,

'Without the which this story were most *impertinent.*'

So Burton, *Anatomy*, p. 22, 'But the story is set down at large by Hippocrates,—which because it is not *impertinent* to this discourse, I will insert verbatim.'

28. *Horace.* The passage translated is from *Sat.* I. 6.

30. *cheapen.* The original sense of the word is 'to buy' or 'to try to buy.' It is connected with *chaffer*, and *couper* in 'horse-couper.' Cf. Shakespeare, *Pericles*, IV. 6. 10, 'She would make a puritan of the devil, if he should *cheapen* a kiss of her.'

Also Earle's *Microcosmographie* (Arber's Reprints), p. 73, 'It is the market of young lecturers whom you may *cheapen* here at all rates and sizes.'

33. *mist*, i.e. missed. See above on 'guest' p. 24, l. 29, and p. 62, l. 27.

PAGE 74.

1. *censure.* The word has not always, as in modern English, the sense of 'blame,' 'rebuke.' Sometimes it means, as here, only 'opinion,' 'judgement.' Cf. Shakespeare, *As You like It* IV. 1. 7, 'How blest am I in my just *censure*, in my true opinion.' So *Hamlet*, I. 3. 69,

'Take each man's *censure*, but reserve thy judgement.'

3. *vexation of spirit.* In allusion to Ecclesiastes i. 14.

10. *care of yours*, i.e. the care for those who are in your service.

15. *fasces*, i.e. his rods, the instruments whereby he asserts his authority. The word is most frequently used in Latin for the rods borne by a Roman lictor, indicating the power of summary punishment. Cowley in his *Sylva*, p. 42 (ed. 1684), uses *fasces* of a schoolmaster's rods, but with a reference to the original meaning,

'I would not be a schoolmaster, though he His rods no less then *fasces* deems to be.'

25. *epidemical*, i.e. of general occurrence. Life is called a disease by reason of the discomforts above enumerated, and as all men share in it, it is called *epidemical*.

30. *masking-habit.* Masks were worn by players to make them look their part. Hence *masking*=playing a part in a masquerade, and the *masking-habit* = the dress suited for a masquerade. Cf. Shakes. *Taming of the Shrew*, IV. 3. 87, 'What *masking* stuff is here?'

32. *a slave in Saturnalibus.* The Saturnalia was a feast in honour of Saturn, beginning on the 17th of December and lasting several days. During this time slaves were allowed abundant license and freedom of speech, so that they could abuse with impunity any whom they disliked, even their masters.

PAGE 75.

3. *He heapeth &c.* From Ps. xxxix. 6.

8. *Unciatim &c.* The quotation, substantially represented in the text, is from Terence, *Phormio*, I. 1. 33.

30. *other.* We should now say 'others.' But the form in the text as a plural was not uncommon. Cf. Ps. lxxiii. 8 (P. Bk. version), 'They corrupt *other*, and speak of wicked blasphemy.'

So Bp. Pilkington (Parker Society), p. 7, 'Phinees turned away God's anger from his people, because he punished that wickedness which *other* winked at.'

31. κακὰ θηρία. The words are quoted from St Paul's Epistle to Titus i. 12.

34. *two directly opposite significations.* ἀργὸς, written exactly in the same form, but no doubt derived from two distinct roots, is applied (1) as in πόδας ἀργοὶ, said of dogs, that are *swift footed*, and (2) to things which do no work, as in the text, = *slow*.

PAGE 76.

3. *Metrodorus.* A Greek philosopher, born according to one authority at Lampsacus, according to others at Athens. His philosophy appears to have been of a more sensual kind than that of Epicurus. The sentiment in the text is alluded to more than once by Cicero, *De nat. deor.* I. 40; *Tusc. disput.* V. 9; *De fin.* II. 28.

5. *Epicurus.* The famous Greek philosopher of Gargettus in Attica. He was the founder of the Epicurean philosophy, which taught that pleasure (rightly understood) was the highest good.

14. *Lepidus.* M. Æmilius Lepidus, one of the second triumvirate with Antony and Octavius. See note on p. 45, l. 12.

16. *Mark Antony*, defeated by Augustus at the battle of Actium.

17. *Quisnam &c.* From Horace, *Sat.* II. 7. 83. 'Who then is free? The wise man, and he who is able to control himself.'

18. *Oenomaus.* King of Pisa, and father of Hippodameia. Not wishing his daughter to marry he always demanded that her suitor should contend with him in a chariot-race. Having a famous charioteer and using other arts he contrived to conquer many, but at last was overcome by Pelops.

27. *masking.* See above on p. 74, l. 30.

PAGE 77.

4. *King James.* In the edition of King James's works (1616) I have not found this saying, though there are words of a somewhat similar import, e.g. (*True Law of Free Monarchies*, p. 209), 'The highest bench is the sliddriest to sit upon.' From the way in which Cowley speaks here it may be that the expression was only a saying of the king's and not included in any published work.

17. *pour faire bonne bouche*, i.e. the verses from Martial &c. are 'to serve as a tit-bit' after his own verses, and what he chooses to call a tedious discourse.

PAGE 78.

7. *guilded.* The spelling of this word is very interesting. The word *guild*, a fraternity formed for mutual aid, and the members of which *paid* a contribution at set periods, is connected with *gold* (geld A.S.=money), and Cowley's orthography shews how the feeling was preserved in his day that the two words were akin.

25. *weathers.* The plural form is not very common. But cf. Shakes. *Winter's Tale*, v. 1. 195,

'Whose honesty endured all *weathers*.'

There however the word is used metaphorically.

30. *the Persian king.* The line in Martial says 'the Parthian king.' But in classic literature the luxurious living of the Persians is much more dwelt on than that of the Parthians (cf. Hor. *Od.* 1. 38. 1). Hence Cowley has substituted the one name for the other.

PAGE 79.

8. *the freeman's hat.* Among the Romans it was the custom to give a slave, on his enfranchisement, a tight-fitting felt cap, called *pileus*, to be worn as a sign of his liberty. By giving up all those things, which others seek so zealously, the freedom of which this is the sign (says the poet) may be procured.

19. *those*, i.e. the poor. They have the laborious task to win their bread. *These* (in line 22) refers, of course, to the rich.

20. *Bridewel.* A house of correction for culprits. The name comes from St Bride's well in London, near which was a building used for this purpose.

PAGE 81.

17. *heroick race.* So Cowley calls the birds because they keep their freedom. Hence are their 'ways and walks the nearest heaven.'

27. *degenerous.* Ignoble, base. The word is uncommon in English. It represents the Latin *degener*.

unbirdly. This is also an unusual word, formed after the analogy of *unmanly*.

PAGE 82.

10. *Cornish mount.* St Michael's Mount. See above p. 20, l. 10.

18. *Rhodian Colossus.* This was a celebrated statue at Rhodes, which stood 70 cubits high and was dedicated to the sun.

29. *The bondman of the cloister*, i.e. the monk, who has bound himself by a vow of poverty. All that he receives is not his own, nor at his own disposal. He goes to his work at the sound of a bell, and only the last sound thereof, which announces his release by death, can be a happy one.

PAGE 83.

7. *hits the white.* The white was the centre of the target, and to hit it was the best shot possible.
Cf. *Lust's Dominion*, III. 5, 9 (Dodsley XIV. 144),
'Which of the two shall be thy *white?*'
i.e. which of the two will you aim at specially?
Also *The True Trojans*, I. 2, 20 (Dodsley XII. 454),
'I'll *hit the white.*'

10. *Pindaric way.* The odes of Pindar are written in very irregular metre. Cowley in some of his poems has imitated this, and called this portion 'the Pindaric Odes.' The allusion is explained by the next line.

19. *transitions,* i.e. right and orderly methods of passing from one subject to another. It shall be fitful and erratic, not a slave to rules.

21. *thorough.* For *through.* Cf. Shakes. *Pericles*, IV. 3. 35, 'It pierced me *thorough.*' Also 2 *Hen. IV.* I. 3. 59, 'Who half *thorough* gives o'er.'
a compass take, i.e. 'go a roundabout road.' 'To fetch a compass' is found 2 Sam. v. 23; Acts xxviii. 13, for 'to go by a roundabout tack' in marching an army or sailing a vessel.

II. OF SOLITUDE.

PAGE 84.

1. *Nunquam &c.*, 'I am never less alone than when alone.' The passage is in Cicero, *Republ.* I. 17. 27. Cf. also Cato apud Prisc. p. 694.

13. *retired himself.* This verb is not now often used as a reflexive. But cf. Shakes. *Winter's Tale*, IV. 4. 663, 'You must *retire yourself* into some covert.'

15. *Linternum.* Also written *Liternum.* It was a city of Campania near to which Scipio Africanus had an estate. Livy XXXVIII. 53.

16. *Seneca.* See Seneca, *Ep.* 86.

23. *Hannibal.* The celebrated son of Hamilcar, who led the Carthaginians in the second Punic war.

PAGE 85.

1. *Scipio,* i.e. Scipio Africanus, alluded to on the previous page.

3. *colourably,* i.e. speciously, plausibly. Cf. Bp. Coverdale p. 92, 'He can give but a counterfeit medicine, as the surgeon doth which *colourably* healeth.'

4. *Montaigne.* Essays, lib. I. 38. The words are 'Respondons

à l'ambition, que c'est elle mesme qui donne goust de la solitude. Car que ne fuit-elle tant que la societé?' On Montaigne, see below p. 131, l. 2.

19. *Tecum &c.* 'With thee I should love to live, with thee I would gladly die,' Horace, *Od.* III. 9. 24.

21. *Sic ego &c.* Tibullus IV. 13. 9.

31. *Catullus.* The quotation below is from 'de Amore suo' 83.

PAGE 86.

22. *parricides.* At first the law prescribed that such a criminal should be sewn up in a sack and thrown into a river. But in the time of Pompey, the punishment was appointed, that he should first be whipped till he bled, then sewn up in a sack with a dog, a cock, a viper and an ape and be cast into the sea.

PAGE 87.

8. *O vita.* The sentence is from Publius Syrus. *Sententiæ,* 202.

24. *arrive.* Seems here equivalent to *arise.* I have not found another example of such use.

PAGE 88.

8. *O qui me &c.* Vergil, *Georg.* II. 489. 'O that some one would set me down in the cool valleys of Hæmus and shield with a mighty shade of boughs.'

PAGE 89.

19. *number's tree.* The whole series of numbers is regarded as having its starting point in the first number, *viz.* one. Hence that is the stem and all the rest are called its branches. Cowley has another form of the same concert in the first book of the Davideis:

'Numbers which still increase more high and wide,
From one, the root of their turned pyramide.'

PAGE 90.

7. *monster London.* The city of London was considered of great extent in Cowley's time. What would he say of it were he writing now, when Islington is no longer a village, but absorbed, and many another village like it, into the huge compass of the metropolis?

14. *village less than Islington.* In Cowley's day London had not absorbed all the villages around it as it has now done, and between London and Islington there was a stretch of open country. A report published about 1714 (nearly half a century after Cowley's death) describes the roads and highways in Islington as 'very ruinous and almost impassable for the space of 5 months in the year.' In 1793 the population of Islington was 6,600.

III. OF OBSCURITY.

PAGE 91.

1. *Nam neque &c.* The passage is from Horace, *Ep.* I. 17. 9.
14. *Secretum &c.* Horace, *Ep.* I. 18. 103.
17. *Mr Broom.* This was Alexander Broom (or Brome) born 1620, died 1666. In connexion with Ben Jonson, Cowley, Hawkins, Fanshaw and Holliday, he translated Horace, his portion being the Odes and Epodes. He is said to have by his songs largely aided the Restoration of Charles II.
22. *same author.* The words are in Horace, *Sat.* II. 7. 114.

PAGE 92.

2. *Quintilian.* *Declam.* XIII. *Apes Pauperis.*
6. *Bene qui &c.* Ovid, *Trist.* III. 4. 25.
16. *the case of Æneas &c.* The passage is from Verg. *Aen.* I. 415.
21. *Demosthenes' confession.* The story is told in Cicero, *Tusc.* V. 103.
22. *tanker-woman,* i.e. tankard-woman, a water-carrier. Cf. Sir T. Harington, *On Playe,* I. 227. 'God send me quickly a fatherless sonne, if I had not rather one of my sonnes were a *tanker-bearer,* that wears sometimes his silk sleeves at the church on Sunday, than a cozener that weares his satten hose at an ordinary on Fridaie.'
The allusion in this passage is to apprentices, who in old times had to carry the water for their masters' houses.
28. *sight-shot.* A word modelled after the fashion of 'ear-shot,' which we still keep in use.
Democritus. The famous philosopher of Abdera, the originator of the atomic theory.
29. *commodity.* Advantage, gain, profit. Cf. Shakes. *King John,* II. I, 573.

> 'That smooth-faced gentleman, tickling *commodity,*
> *Commodity,* the bias of the world.'

and compare the whole speech, which concludes,

> 'Gain, be my lord, for I will worship thee.'

31. *Epicurus.* See above p. 76, l. 5.
33. *Metrodorus.* See above p. 76, l. 3.

PAGE 93.

4. *most talk'd-of and talking country.* One cannot but recall St Paul's account of the Athenians (Acts xvii. 21), 'They spent

their time in nothing else but either to tell or to hear some new thing.'

9. *engage into.* We now say 'engage in.'

11. *quotidian ague,* i.e. a daily shivering fit. Because the intrusions and encroachments on our time will make us shudder.

19. *Bucephalus.* The name of the horse of Alexander the Great.
Incitatus. The horse of Domitian the Roman emperor was so called. Domitian is said to have had it elected to the consulship. This is the allusion in line 24 below.

29. *S. Peter.* The reference is to Acts v. 15, 'They brought forth the sick into the streets...that at least the shadow of Peter passing by might overshadow some of them.'

31. *Cato,* i.e. Marcus Porcius Cato, known as Cato the Censor. He died about 150 B.C. He was so distinguished that Cicero tells us (*de Amic.* 2) that the word 'Sapiens,' wise, became a quasi-cognomen of his.

32. *Aristides.* An Athenian statesman and general, who flourished about 490 B.C. He was celebrated as the best and justest of his countrymen. He was banished from Athens through the influence of Themistocles.

33. *whilest.* The word 'while' (A.S. *hwil*) was originally a noun, meaning *time.* The genitive 'whiles' became used in an adverbial sense = 'at a time,' and the form was afterwards enlarged to 'whilest,' which now is usually written 'whilst'. We can trace the tendency to make such an addition in some dialects of English where *once* is pronounced as 'wunst.'

PAGE 94.

6. *commerce,* i.e. intercourse, without any idea of trade or barter, which now alone is the sense of the word. Cf. Shakes. *Hamlet,* III. 1. 10:

'Could beauty have better *commerce* than with honesty?'

13. *muta persona.* A character on the stage, who appears, but has no speech to make.

15. *Augustus.* The emperor of Rome. See above on p. 45, l. 12.

16. *askt with his last breath.* Suet. *Aug.* 99, 'Ecquid iis videretur mimum vitæ commode transegisse.'

21. *guilded.* Cf. on p. 78, l. 7.

29. *long ruins.* So styled, because being high when they were standing, they stretch far when they fall; hence the prayer to be 'at a good distance' from them.

PAGE 95.

6. *scutcheon.* A shield ornamented with armorial bearings. Cf. Shakes. *Antony and Cleopatra,* V. 2. 135,

'And we
Your *scutcheons* and your signs of conquest shall
Hang in what place you please.'

6. *elogie.* See above p. 8, l. 11.

8. *then.* When death has laid them low. Cf. Shirley, *Contention of Ajax and Ulysses*, Sc. iii.

> 'Sceptre and crown must tumble down,
> And in the dust be equal made
> With the poor crooked scythe and spade.'

IV. OF AGRICULTURE.

PAGE 96.

6. *as he did with Solomon.* See the history, in 1 Kings iii. 11—14.

13. *O fortunatus &c.* O too fortunate man and who knew his blessings. An adaptation of Verg. *Georg.* II. 458.

PAGE 97.

1. *Columella.* The quotation is from *De re rustica*, I. 1.

3. *Varro says.* *De re rustica*, I. 4, 'Ejus principia sunt eadem quæ mundi esse Ennius scribit aqua terra anima et sol.'

8. *Cicero says.* *De Senectute*, XV. 51.

21. *as they were in Rome.* Alluding to the well-known stories of Cincinnatus and M. Curius. See Cicero *de Senect.* XVI. 56.

28. *parcel,* i.e. portion, of ground. Cf. St John iv. 5, 'the *parcel* of ground that Jacob gave to his son Joseph.'

PAGE 98.

20. *tropes,* i.e. metaphorical forms of expression. The word is from the Gk. τρόπος = *a turn,* and is used of language in which the words are *turned* in their application to something to which they did not originally refer.

21. *Many nations have lived &c.* Cf. the account of the Israelites when they went down into Egypt. Gen. xlvii. 3, 'Thy servants are shepherds, both we and also our fathers.' The nomad races of the East are still instances of what is stated in the text.

24. *beholding.* We now use 'beholden.' But the form in the text was common. Cf. Naunton's *Fragmenta Regalia* (Arber's Reprints), p. 56, 'He held the staffe of the Treasury fast in his hand, which once in the year made them all *beholding* to him.' And again p. 59, 'For his person he was not much *beholding* to nature.'

PAGE 99.

8. *all other trades...set forth whole troops.* The City companies have always been forward, when need was, to furnish volunteer companies. The draper John Gilpin was a train-band captain.

13. *twenty years' ruine.* Speaking in round numbers the years between 1640 and 1660.

31. *expenceful.* Now obsolete or nearly so. But cf. Beaumont and Fletcher, *Pilgrim,* I. 1 :

> 'Who will have me?
> Who will be troubled with a pettish girl?
> It may be proud, and to that vice *expenceful.*'

32. *instance in.* In modern English the preposition is omitted, and we should say 'I shall instance one delight more.' But cf. Sir W. Temple, *Letter to Lord Arlington,* July 1669 :
'The Dutch desired the particular instances of what they had felt or thought they had occasion to fear : our merchants *instanced in* Cochin and Cananor.'

PAGE 100.

8. *Hinc atque hinc &c.* Verg. *Æn.* I. 502.

14. *murtherer.* Cain, after Abel's murder, built the city Enoch (Gen. iv. 17). The interchange of *th* and *d* was not uncommon, as in the forms *burthen* and *burden.*

17. *Ecclesiasticus.* Chap. vii. 15.

27. *fields d'or or d'argent.* The heraldic language common in describing coats of arms. The *field* is the tincture, or combination of tinctures, forming the ground on which the device is delineated. These are of three descriptions, metals, colours, furs. The metals are *or*=gold, and *argent*=silver.

31. *complaint of Columella.* Columella's words are in the prologue to the *De re rustica.* ' Adhuc enim scholas rhetorum et (ut dixi) geometrarum musicorumque, vel quod magis mirandum est contemptissimorum vitiorum officinas guliosius condiendi cibos, et luxuriosius fercula struendi, capitumque et capillorum concinnatores non solum esse audivi sed et ipse vidi : agricolationis neque doctores qui se profiterentur neque discipulos cognovi.'

PAGE 101.

15. *dancing.* Lucian says dancing was invented by the goddess Rhea, and by her communicated to her priests in Phrygia and Crete. Of its use in worship we have an instance in Exod. xv. 20.

PAGE 102.

3. *as they call him there.* In Oxford the name given to the head of a Hall is 'Principal.'

9. *villaticas pastiones.* Varro, *R. R.* 3. 2. 13. The expression is also used by Columella, *De re rustica,* VII. 13. 3.

27. *Mr Hartlib.* Samuel Hartlib was a friend of Mede and Milton. He was of Polish extraction, but settled in England and interested himself in education and agriculture. He edited a treatise on Flemish Agriculture. He received from Cromwell a pension of

£300 a year, which ceased at the Restoration. Milton dedicated to him his Tractate on Education.

33. *Poetry was born among the shepherds.* See below on p. 103, l. 23, *seqq.*

PAGE 103.

1. *Nescio qua &c.* Ovid. *Pont.* I. 3. 35.

19. *pariter &c.* Ovid. *Fasti* I. 300. The sense is sufficiently expressed in the previous line.

27. *he has contributed (says Columella).* *De re rustica,* I. I, 'Celeberrimus vates non minimum professioni nostræ contulit Hesiodus Bœotius.' Hesiod's contribution is the *Works and Days,* i.e. the works to be done in agriculture and the most favourable days for undertaking them.

33. πλέον, κ.τ.λ. Hesiod, *Works and Days,* 40.

PAGE 104.

25. *his father Laertes.* See Hom. *Odyss.* XXIV. 226—231.

30. *Eumæus.* Cf. Hom. *Odyss.* XV. 301, and often.

32. *ha'* for *have.* A frequent dialectic abbreviation, but not found often in good prose. See above, line 9, *ha'n't*=have not.

33. *Menelaus or Agamemnon.* The two Greek commanders in the Trojan war, and so the greatest personages in Homer's poem.

Theocritus. The passage alluded to is in Theocr. *Id.* XXV. 51.

PAGE 105.

5. *civil,* i.e. courteous, polished.

8. *Virgil.* The poet Vergil enjoyed much favour at court, but took no advantage of it. His poems on agricultural and pastoral subjects are the *Eclogues* and the *Georgics.*

15. *describing Evander.* The description is in Verg. *Æn.* VIII. 365.

19. *eves,* i.e. eaves.

24. *Escurial.* A village six leagues from Madrid, made famous by a palace of the King of Spain.

Louvre. The palace of the kings of France in Paris.

25. *Whitehal.* One of the palaces of the English king in the days of Cowley. It is now transformed into a Royal chapel.

31. *Alcides.* Hercules, who was the grandson of Alceus.

PAGE 106.

6. *ut nos &c.* 'that he may help us in writing letters.'

8. *Sabin, or Tiburtin mannor.* Horace was presented by Mæcenas with a small Sabine farm (2 *Sat.* VI. I) situate at the village of Mandela, not far from the river Digentia. He afterwards bought or hired a house at Tibur (the modern *Tivoli*).

21. *Qui, quid &c.* 'Who tells us more plainly and better than Chrysippus and Crantor (professors of philosophy) what is beauteous, what is base, what useful and what not so.' The words are from Horace, *Epist.* I. 2. 4.

28. *in Martial's.* Such are the Epigrams, bk. III. 58, '*Ad Bassum,*' bk. IV. 89, '*De Rusticatione*' and many others.

PAGE 107.

14. *poison of Assyrian pride.* *Assyrian* is probably intended for *Syrian* here. The dyes meant would be those of Sidon and Tyre in Phœnicia. On the frequency of the confusion between the two names cf. Drackenb. *ad Sil. It.* ii. 40.

PAGE 108.

3. *Astræa.* A fabled daughter of Jupiter and Themis. She came to dwell among men in the golden age as the goddess of Justice, but their crimes drove her back again to heaven. Cowley in his poem on the king's return out of Scotland (*Sylva*, p. 40) says with the somewhat gross flattery of the times :

'Yet while our Charles with equal balance reigns
'Twixt Mercy and *Astræa*, and maintains
A noble peace, 'tis he, 'tis only he
Who is most near, most like the deity.'

24. *Tempe.* A valley of Thessaly, lying between Mt. Ossa and Mt. Olympus. The river Peneus flowed through it, and its exquisite beauty and the peaceful character of the whole vale are much celebrated by the classic poets.

PAGE 109.

7. *gowned war.* The law-courts are spoken of as scenes of 'gowned war', because the gown is a part of the barrister's dress when pleading.

18. *Tyrian beds.* The luxury of Tyre, and especially the splendour of the robes and furniture of Tyrians, are well known. Cf. *Tyrii amictus*, Ov. *A. A.* II. 297. *Tyrio murice* saturata palla, Ov. *Met.* II. 166. *Tyria purpura*, Cic. *Contra Verrem*, V. 56. Also Tertullian *De habitu mulieb.* chap. I.

drink in gold. We much more frequently now say 'drink out of gold', from golden cups. But cf. Shakes. 2 *Hen. VI.* Act 4. 10, where speaking of a 'sallet' or helmet Cade says, 'Many a time when I have been dry and bravely marching, it has served me instead of a quart pot to *drink in.*'

PAGE 110.

12. *Amidst his equal friends,* i.e. friends of the same age. A common sense of the Latin *æqualis.* Cf. Gal. i. 14, 'And I profited in the Jews' religion above many my *equals* in mine own nation.'

19. *old Hetrurian virtue.* Etruria (called also *Tuscia*) was celebrated in early times for its forwardness in culture. Actors

were brought from Etruria to Rome (Livy VII. 2), also the Romans were taught Tuscan literature (Livy IX. 36).

20. *Sabins.* The Sabines are a type of hardiness and simplicity in all the Roman authors. Livy I. 18, talks of 'disciplina tetrica ac tristis veterum Sabinorum.'

21. *Remus, and the god, his brother.* Romulus the founder of Rome and the brother of Remus is said to have been carried away from the earth in a storm of thunder and lightning, and was worshipped afterwards under the name of Quirinus.

22. *grew the world's head,* i.e. 'grew to be the head of the world.' Cf. Shakes. *Cor.* IV. 4. 21,

'So fellest foes...shall *grow* dear friends.'

24. *poor Saturn's golden days.* So called because in the golden age when Saturn reigned poverty was the rule among men and virtue with it.

PAGE III.

9. *marriageable vine.* So styled because it must be attached to some other tree as its prop.

16. *agin.* *Agin* and *Agen* are not infrequent forms in earlier English for *again.* So (*Sylva*, p. 41) 'Great Charles is come agen.' It is also found in the earlier editions of Dryden, but the printers have in later times changed the spelling.

19. *use,* i.e. the interest, return, produce on his labours. Cf. Selden, *Table Talk, usury,* 'The Jews were forbidden to take *use* one of another.' See also Cowley, *Miscellanies,* p. 7:

'Thus he in arts so vast a treasure gain'd
Whilest still the *use* came in, and stock remained.'

PAGE 112.

17. *sunburnt Sabins.* See above p. 110, l. 20.

18. *Apulia.* Horace could speak with authority of the frugal life of Apulia, his birthplace being Venusia, a border town between Lucania and Apulia.

22. *to pin the sheepfold.* We use now the form 'pen.'

23. *against,* i.e. in expectation of the time when (he will come). Cf. Shakes. *Mids. Nt.'s Dream,* III. 2, 99,

'I'll charm his eyes *against* she do appear.'

29. *lustful shell-fish.* 'Lustful' seems here to be used in the sense of 'ministering to appetite.' There is no adjective in the Latin. Juvenal tells (IV. 140) how the epicure of his day could distinguish at the first mouthful where an oyster had been reared.

31. *ortolans nor godwits. Ortolan.* Said to be derived from L. *hortulanus,* and to signify a bird which frequents *garden hedges.* The *godwit,* another bird, is said to derive its name from its *good flavour.*

PAGE 113.

1. The Version begins from line 79 of the Satire of Horace.

5. *careful of the main.* Lat. *attentus quæsitis,* i.e. careful of what he had stored; looking after the main chance.

10. *belighted,* i.e. 'alighted.'

15. *fitches,* i.e. vetches. So in the Bible we find 'fats' for 'vats.'

peason, i.e. peas. The 'on' is the old plural termination and is still heard in some English counties. Cf. also, Puttenham's *Arte of Poesie* (Arber), p. 125:

'All is but a jest, all dust, all not worth two *peason,*
For why, in man's matters is neither rime nor reason.'

18. *haut goust.* For 'haut gout.' See above p. 58, l. 31.

19. *the swerd of bacon.* 'Swerd' with the variants 'sword' and 'swarth' is applied to the outer skin of swine, and to the grass-covered surface of the ground. It is the A. S. *sweard.* For its use cf. Brewer, *Lingua,* Act II. Sc. 1.

'They would use no other bucklers in war, but shields of brawn, brandish no swords but *swords* of bacon.'

PAGE 114.

24. *Phœbus into Thetis' bosome fell.* A poetic figure for sunset. Phœbus is the sun-god, Thetis a sea-nymph, here named to represent the ocean.

27. *troth.* Another orthography of 'truth,' which by its form keeps in mind the derivation from the verb 'to trow.'

PAGE 115.

2. *Mortlacke's noble loom.* In the reign of King James I. the manufacture of tapestry was set up at Mortlake in Surrey, and the king is said to have given two thousand pounds towards the undertaking. (Cf. Rymer's *Fœdera,* XVIII. p. 66.) The works at Mortlake, which at first followed the old patterns of the Nether-lands, were afterwards supplied by Francis Cleyn with fresh designs, both historical and grotesque, and the manufacture was brought to great perfection.

5. *pale meridies of the night.* 'Meridies,' properly 'mid-day', is here used for the middle time of night. Cynthia, i.e. the moon, had passed through half her nightly course.

17. *th' industrious peasant.* The country mouse has brought with him the diligence of his previous life, and employs it well.

19. *well-fraighted.* We write now 'freighted.'

PAGE 116.

11. *priest's service.* In which, as the priest had for his share much of the honied cakes of the offerings, the diet of the servant would be largely made up of such food.

16. *chuse,* i.e. choose. Written in the usual form p. 117, l. 13.

20. 'The mad celestial dog' is Sirius the dog-star, which is in the ascendant when the hot weather called the dog-days prevails. 'The lyon' in the same way refers to the constellation 'Leo.'

PAGE 117.

8. *right gems.* Of a perfect quality and purity. Cf. Shakes. *As You like It*, III. 2. 127, 'That's the *right* virtue of the medlar.'

PAGE 118.

7. *it burns*, i.e. causes inflammation. It is a literal translation of the Latin 'urit.'

17. *Blest be the man &c.* These lines are a translation from Cowley's own Latin at the beginning of Bk. IV. of his *Sex Libri Plantarum.* As a specimen of his Latinity, the text is given :

> Felix, quem misera procul ambitione remotum,
>   Parvus ager placide parvus et hortus alit.
> Præbet ager quicquid frugi Natura requirit,
>   Hortus habet quicquid luxuriosa petit.
> Cætera sollicitæ speciosa incommoda vitæ
>   Permittit stultis quærere, habere malis.
> Talis erat magni memoratu digna Maronis
>   Corycii quondam vita beata senis.
> Talis (crediderim) tam lætus et impiger hortis
>   Dives in exiguis Abdalonimus erat.
> Illum damnosas runcantem gnaviter herbas
>   Ecce ab Alexandro rege satelles adit.
> Accipe Sidonii, vir magne, insignia regni
>   Sceptrum, ait, et mitram, Sidoniamque togam.
> Missus in imperium tantum (quis credat?) amabam
>   Dicitur invitus deseruisse casam.
> Respicit ille gemens hortum : Meliora relinquo,
>   Heu, ait, infelix deteriora sequor.
> Talis erat generi humano vix nomine notus
>   Aglaus in parvo Dis bene notus agro.
> Namque Gyges Lydas, regum ditissimus olim,
>   Impius et scelerum prosperitate tumens.
> Ecquis, ait, toto me fortunatior orbe est?
>   Hic Clarium est ausus voce rogare deum.
> Numen adulari nescit ; felicior, inquit
>   Aglaus.   Ille furens, Aglaus iste quis est?
> An sit eo quisquam rex nomine quærit? At illo
>   Rex certe dictus nomine nullus erat.
> An sit eo quisquam dux belli nomine clarus,
>   Aut superis tracta nobilitate potens?
> Anne aliquis prædives opum nulloque periclo
>   Inter inexhaustas luxuriosus opes?
> Nullus erat talis generis splendore, vel armis,
>   Divitiisve potens ; Aglaus iste quis est?
> At tandem Arcadiæ vix nota in valle repertus,
>   (Arcadas alta quies umbraque densa tegit.)
> Strenuus exigui cultor prope Psophida fundi
>   (Psophida sed tantum viderat ille semel.)
> Invidia regum dignissimus ille repertus,
>   Teste deo felix, Aglaus ille fuit.
> Talis, magne deus, (si te mihi dicere fas sit
>   Ridiculorum inter nomina vana deûm)
> Talis, vere deus, nunc inclinantibus annis
>   Sit, precor, ætatis scena suprema meæ,

Finis inutilium mihi sit, precor, illa laborum
Jactatæ statio firma sit illa rati.
Sic mea cælestem prægustet vita quietem,
Dormiat et montem discat amare suum.

28. *the old Corycian yeoman.* The allusion is to Vergil *Georg.*
IV. 127 and following lines. *Corycus* was a town in Cilicia.

PAGE 119.

1. *Abdolonymus.* A gardener (mentioned by Quintus Curtius
IV. 1. 19 and by Justin XI. 10. 8) who was of royal descent, though
he lived in retirement. The 'great emperour' was Alexander the
Great, who made him king of Sidon.

11. Aglaus, a poor man of Psophis in Arcadia. Gyges was
king of Lydia. The story, which is found in Pliny *H. N.* VII. 47
and in Valerius Maximus VII. 1. 2, is told in the text.

14. *consign'd.* The verb 'consign' is now most commonly
used in a *bad* sense, e.g. 'consigned to perdition.' But cf. Jer.
Taylor, *Great Exemplar*, pt. I. 6, 'By baptism we are *consigned* to
the mercies of God.'

34. *Sopho*, i.e. Psophis.

PAGE 120.

6. *foolish gods.* The heathen divinities, of which mention is
made in the stories just narrated.

11. *earnest.* A pledge in the present of something to happen
in the future. Thus a quiet life here is to be the pledge of heavenly
rest hereafter. See also p. 122, l. 30, and cf. Shakes. *Macb.* I. 3. 104,

'And for an *earnest* of a greater honour
He bade me call thee thane of Cawdor.'

V. THE GARDEN.

PAGE 121.

13. *studiis &c.* 'To flourish in pursuits of inglorious ease.'
From Verg. *Georg.* IV. 564.

This essay is addressed to Mr John Evelyn, the author of the
famous diary, to which reference has been already made, p. 20, l. 1.
He had published in 1664 his *Kalendarium Hortense*, to which he
prefixed a letter to Cowley, alluded to p. 122, l. 17—19. The
present essay is Cowley's acknowledgement.

20. *inn.* A hired house is so called by Cowley, because he
cannot treat it and its surroundings as if they were his own.

PAGE 122.

5. The quotation is from Genesis xix. 20, and the allusions are
to the history of Lot's flight from Sodom.

9. *Pindarical.* In the style of Pindar. Highflown and fanciful.

11. *like a chymist.* In the infancy of chemistry many of the experiments were probably failures, and the alchemist never found his great end, the philosopher's stone.

19. *as long as months and years.* Being a calendar, and guiding the works of the garden, which were unchanging.

26. *to the main.* To have the chief part of the estate, i.e. to be specially distinguished above the rest of your literary progeny.

29. *that book, which you are pleased to promise.* The allusion is to the 'Compleat Gardener,' which, however, Evelyn did not give to the world for nearly 30 years, *viz.* in 1693.

PAGE 124.

8. *a Louvre or Escurial.* See above p. 105, l. 24.

10. *Babel.* 'Whose top may reach unto heaven,' Gen. xi. 4.

20. *the first city Cain.* Gen. iv. 17. Cowley is never weary of repeating this. See above p. 61, l. 16.

24. *lion-star.* The constellation Leo. See p. 116, l. 20, and also on the dog-star, mentioned in the next line.

PAGE 125.

9. *poets live without reward or thanks.* Cowley's own case was an instance in point, and the words are no doubt written with that feeling.

13. *base.* We now write 'bass,' but thereby obscure the meaning and connexion of the word, as the *foundation* part of the entire harmony.

16. *theorbo.* A kind of musical shell fitted with strings, from the Fr. *théorbe.* Cf. Drayton, *Polyolbion* 4 :

'Some that delight to touch the sterner wiry chord
    The cythern, the pandore, and the *theorbo* strike.'

See also Evelyn's Diary, 11 July, 1654, 'At All Souls where we had music, voices and *theorbos* performed by some ingenious scholars.'

27. See Verg. *Æn.* I. 691—694.

PAGE 126.

8. *female men.* Alluding to effeminate, scented dandies.

10. *Epicurus.* See above p. 76, l. 5. Cowley hints in the words which follow that Epicurus' meaning, when he called pleasure the chief good, ought to be interpreted by his definition of what pleasure is.

17. *Vitellius his table.* On this manner of forming a possessive case, see above p. 16, l. 7.

Aulus Vitellius, a Roman officer during the reigns of Tiberius, Caligula, Claudius and Nero. His great talent was eating and drinking, and he spent enormous sums of money on the pleasures of the table. Hence his table is called 'fiscal' partly because of its costliness, and partly because it taxed largely the resources of the whole empire for its supply.

28. *listed*, enlisted, included in a list.

30. *the third story high.* Because the dessert, consisting of fruits, formed the third course at dinner in Cowley's day.

<h2 align="center">PAGE 127.</h2>

3. *the great Hebrew king*, i.e. Solomon. The allusions which follow are to his entertainment of the Queen of Sheba. Sheba was probably part of Arabia, hence it lay south of Judæa. On the history, see 1 Kings x. Assyria and Babylonia were wealthy nations in Solomon's day, and he drew much of his gold and precious stones from Ophir.

13. *Hiram's princely dy.* Hiram, king of Tyre, was a great friend of Solomon, and helped him both in building the Temple and his own dwelling, as well as in fitting out a fleet to go to Ophir. The Tyrians were famous for their skill in dyeing, Tyrian purple being celebrated in all lands.

23. *one, that would not be so rich.* The allusion is to Christ's words in the Sermon on the Mount (S. Matth. vi. 29), 'Even Solomon in all his glory was not arrayed like one of these (lilies of the field).'

<h2 align="center">PAGE 128.</h2>

1. The *arbor vitæ*, which Cowley assumes to have been the tree which was in Paradise.

21. *staff and shield.* The corn from which bread, the staff of life, is made, and the simples, herbs, which cure, as Cowley says, nearly every kind of disease.

27. *the third day's volume of the book.* The book of creation (Gen. i.) tells how on the third day, grass, herbs and fruit-trees were created.

28. *intend.* 'to stretch,' 'strain,' 'exert to the full.' Hence a person earnestly gazing is said to be 'intent' upon something.

<h2 align="center">PAGE 129.</h2>

1. *the flowers of heaven.* The stars. It was held that the stars influenced the destiny of men, and that according to the ascendency of certain planets at their birth, such would men's fortune in life be. Hence arose what was known as judicial astrology, and the fortune-telling after this sort has not entirely died out. Cowley with his love for plants, and a knowledge of their medicinal properties, suggests that these 'stars of earth' have more to do with the welfare of mankind than the stars in heaven.

27. The allusion is to the sportive nymph, Galatea, described in Verg. *Georg.* III. 64—72.

PAGE 130.

1. *Daphne's coyness.* In the mythological story, Daphne, the daughter of the river-god Peneus, was changed into a laurel-tree to escape from Apollo (Ovid, *Met.* I. 452). Cowley uses her name to designate the laurel.

7. *Dioclesian.* The Emperor of Rome, A.D. 284. The early part of his reign was signalized by much severity. He resigned the imperial power in A.D. 305, and lived in retirement at Salona in Dalmatia, near which place he had been born. Aurelius Victor (*de Cæs.* 39 *Epit.* 39) has preserved the story of his being urged to resume his throne once more. To this request he answered, 'If you could see the vegetables planted by my own hands at Salona, you would never think of urging such a petition.'

20. *rod,* i.e. rode.

VI. OF GREATNESS.

PAGE 131.

2. *Sieur de Montagne.* Michael Eyquem de Montaigne, born 1533, was a famous French moral philosopher. His most famous work is his 'Essays'. He died in 1592. His Essays are greatly characterised by the tone of jesting manifest in the sentence which Cowley quotes. Montaigne's words are (Bk. III. chap. 7), 'puisque nous ne la pouvons atteindre, vengeons nous à en mesdire.'

10. *convinced,* i.e. convicted, proved guilty. Cf. St John viii. 46, 'Which of you *convinceth me of sin?*' Also St James ii. 9, 'Ye commit sin, and are *convinced* of the law as transgressors.'

PAGE 132.

3. *Di bene fecerunt &c.* Horace *Sat.* I. 4. 17, 'The gods have acted kindly in making me of a poor and lowly mind.'

12. *bona roba.* A term in the mouths of swaggerers to signify a grandly handsome woman. Cf. Shakes. 2 *Hen. IV.* III. 2. 26,

'We knew where the *bona robas* were.'

Florio's Dictionary. *Buona robba,* as we say 'good stuff,' i.e. a good wholesome plump-cheeked wench.

15. *Parvula &c.* Lucr. IV. 1158,

'A tiny, a fairy, one of the Graces, all pure sparkling wit.'

18. *Seneca the elder,* i.e. Marcus Annæus Seneca, father of the more famous Seneca, the tutor of Nero. Seneca the elder was born at Corduba in Spain, and was famous as a rhetorician in the times of Augustus and Tiberius. The writings of Seneca have come down

to us only in fragments. The account of Senecio which Cowley repeats is found in the *Suasoriarum Liber* Suas. II.

30. *horse-plums.* The prefix 'horse' is added to various terms to indicate unusual size, as 'horse-radish,' 'horse-chestnut,' 'horse-laugh.' Similar use was made of βοῦς, =ox, in Greek. Cf. βουλιμία, βούπαις, βουφάγος. So 'pound-pears' are named because of their unusual weight of a pound each.

32. *chiopins.* From the Italian *cioppini.* A kind of high shoe worn by ladies. Spelt also 'chopine' and 'chippine.' Cf. Shakes. *Ham.* II. 2. 447, 'Your ladyship is nearer to heaven than when I saw you last, by the altitude of a *chopine.*'

So Ben Jonson, *Cynthia's Revels,* II. 2, 'I do wish myself one of my mistresse's *cioppini.*'

And Fuller's Worthies, *Wales generally,* 'After she has put off her lofty attire, and high *chippines,* she almost pares away herself to nothing.'

PAGE 133.

1. *cognomentum.* Using a longer word, instead of a short one, after the fashion of Senecio's mania.

PAGE 134.

2. *the keeping of little singing birds.* The allusion is to one of the amusements of Louis XIII. of France.

7. *gods too.* Because they were each at death styled *divus.* See also below on l. 31 and p. 135, l. 9, 14.

10. *in catching of flies.* This is said (Sueton. *Domitian* 3) to have been the frequent occupation of the Emperor Domitian. So that it was wittily remarked by Vibius Crispus, when the inquiry was made whether any one was in the emperor's room, 'Not even a fly.'

12. *Beelzebub.* The name signifies 'lord of flies.'

22. *divine voice.* Vox cælestis was the language which the imperial flatterers applied to Nero's singing. See Tac. *Ann.* XVI. 22; XIV. 15; Suet. *Nero,* 21.

26. *the Cæsarian race of deities.* Nero was the last of the emperors sprung from the family of Cæsar. Their names were Julius, Augustus, Tiberius, Caius (Caligula), Claudius, Nero.

28. *Alas &c.* 'Qualis artifex pereo!' (Suet. *Nero,* 49).

31. *madnesses of Caligula's delight.* The disorder of Caligula's brain was shewn by his appearance in public in the garb of a god, as Bacchus, Apollo, Jupiter, or even Venus and Diana. He placed himself between the statues of Castor and Pollux and commanded people to worship him. His madness also manifested itself in his extravagant expenditure.

32. *sordidness of Tiberius.* Cowley here alludes to the life of Tiberius in his retirement at Capreæ. He was surrounded by a troop of Chaldæan soothsayers in whom he put great confidence, and gave himself up to unnatural excesses. Cf. Suet. *Tib.* 42—45.

PAGE 135.

3. *bounding-stones,* i.e. stones which could be tossed about and made to rebound. Suetonius in his life of Augustus, (98), says that apples, cakes, and other things were thrown about in this imperial hilarity.

19. *cates,* dainties, delicious food. Cf. Shakes. *Com. of Errors,* III. 1. 28, 'Though my *cates* be mean, take them in good part.'

34. *wanscot.* We now write *wainscot.*

PAGE 136.

18. *sed quantum &c.* Verg. *Georg.* II. 291.

27. *cousenage.* We write now *cozenage.*

29. *Mancipiis &c.* Horace *Epist.* I. 6. 39. The line is substantially translated below.

PAGE 137.

15. *Says Solomon.* Eccl. v. 11, 'When goods increase, they are increased that eat them.'

17. *like Ocnus in the fable.* The reference is to an allegorical picture by Polygnotus, mentioned by Pausanias X. 29. 2, and by Pliny, *Hist. Nat.* XXXV. 31 (11).

25. *Pic of Tenariff.* The French form of the word *Pic* had not in Cowley's time given place to the English *Peak.*

31. *Ossa upon Olympus.* See above on p. 32, l. 14.

PAGE 138.

3. *the late gyant of our nation.* The allusion is to Oliver Cromwell, on whose career, and Cowley's opinion thereon, see above, 'Discourse by way of vision' with the notes.

20. *an idol is nothing in the world.* 1 Cor. viii. 4.

PAGE 140.

7. *Damocles.* A flatterer of the elder Dionysius the tyrant of Syracuse. On one occasion Damocles had been praising the felicity of Dionysius, whereupon the latter invited him to a magnificent banquet, but in the midst of the entertainment Damocles discovered a naked sword suspended above his head by a single hair. Thus did the tyrant forcibly demonstrate the real character of the happiness which had been so much lauded.

13. *over-noise.* Be noisy enough to drive away your fears. The word is an unusual one.

3. *Let Mars and Saturn...conjoyn.* An allusion to the supposed influence of the stars on the fortunes of mankind. The Martial and Saturnine conjunction in the sky might portend war and trouble, but the Jovial influence within the man's heart is superior to all external powers and nothing can disturb him.

VII. OF AVARICE.

4. *refunding.* In the literal sense of the Lat. *refundere*, 'to pour back again.'

12. *excern.* To separate, to draw away. So Bacon, *On Learning*, bk. IV. c. 3, 'The body of a living creature assimilates that which is good, for it *excerneth* what is unprofitable.' Also Ray, *On the Creation*, pt. 2, speaks of 'humours *excerned* by sweat.' Here Cowley means that the covetous man derives from his wealth something which he thinks satisfactory.

7. *Desunt &c.* Cowley is mistaken in assigning these words to Ovid. They are found in the *Controversiæ* of the elder Seneca, VII. 3. (Basil, 1557, p. 609).

12. *Somebody says.* St Paul, 2 Cor. vi. 10.

13. *antipode.* In the sense of 'opposite,' 'contrary.' I have not met with the singular anywhere else.

18. *The rich poor man &c.* With the exception of a transposition of the two adjectives, we have the line (in the same sense) p. 146, l. 27.

2. Horace's first satire. The passage translated is I. i. 1—79.

5. *pismire.* The ant or emmet. So called in line 15 below.

8. *strait.* Straightway, at once.

20. *almighty-ship.* A word apparently coined by Cowley, in the sense of 'omnipotence.'

3. *The prudent Macedonian king.* Philip of Macedon, father of Alexander the Great. His boast was that no town was impreg-

nable into which an ass laden with gold could be introduced. Cicero gives the story, *ad Atticum* I. 16. 12.

5. *petar.* We now write 'petard.' The Italian is *petardo.* It was an engine, charged with explosives, and used for bursting open strong gates. So Drayton, *Battle of Agincourt,*

'The engineer providing the *petard*
To break the strong portcullice.'

Also Shakes. *Hamlet,* III. 4. 207,

'To have the engineer hoist with his own *petar.*'

10. *creature,* i.e. subject, owning it for a master. Cf. Shakes. *Tim.* I. 1. 116, 'This fellow here, lord Timon, this thy *creature* by night frequents my house.'

21. *The vast Xerxean army.* Cowley compares towns and courts, with their crowds, to the army which Xerxes led to Thermopylæ, and which is said to have numbered 5,283,220. These were resisted and defeated in the pass of Thermopylæ by Leonidas, king of Sparta, and the Laconian troops, numbering about 5,000, of whom 300 were from Sparta. These the poet compares to the poor who 'hold the *streights* of poverty.'

24. *Sellers,* i.e. cellars.

27. See above on p. 143, l. 18.

VIII. The Dangers of an Honest Man in much Company.

Page 150.

5. *cap a pe,* i.e. *cap a pie,* from head to foot.

11. *campagne.* The level plain country. It. *campagna.* Other forms of the word are 'champain,' 'champaign.'

Page 151.

13. *Toupinambaltians.* A people formerly dwelling in Central America, near Brazil. Their name is variously written, *Tupinimbæ, Tupinambæ, Tovopinambautii, Toropinambuti,* and *Toupinambous.* See Moreri's *Lexicon,* under the last form.

Page 152.

1. *topick.* A general idea. The word comes from the Gk. τόποι, which Cicero (*Top.* II. 8) translates by 'loci' and defines thus, 'loci, e quibus argumenta promuntur,' also as 'argumenti sedes.'

9. *Go to &c.* Gen. xi. 4.

13. *a concourse of thieves.* Romulus offered an asylum to all those who from other places chose to take refuge with him. The other allusions in the sentence are to the birds seen by Romulus and

Remus when they were looking for omens at the foundation of the city, and to the slaying of Remus by his brother.

17. *first town.* See on p. 61, l. 16.

30. *at all pieces.* We now more usually say 'at all points.'

PAGE 153.

13. *Quid Romæ &c.* 'What can I do at Rome? I don't know how to lie.' From Juv. *Sat.* III. 41.

22. *Honest and poor &c.* Martial, *Epig.* IV. 5, 'Vir bonus et pauper &c.'

PAGE 154.

3. *Lucretius.* The allusion is to Lucr. II. 1.

'Suave mari magno turbantibus æquora ventis
E terra magnum alterius spectare laborem.'

6. *Democritus.* The philosopher of Abdera. He flourished about 430 B.C. He was famed among other things for looking ever at the cheerful or comical side of affairs.

10. *Bedlam*, i.e. Bethlehem hospital, for the insane. See above p. 23, l. 10.

28. *ut nec facta &c.* A quotation from Cicero *ad Atticum*, XV. 11. 3.

33. *qua terra patet &c.* Ovid, *Met.* I. 241.

PAGE 155.

3. *As the Scripture speaks.* See 1 Kings xxi. 20; 2 Kings xvii. 17; Rom. vii. 14.

10. *Sir Philip Sydney.* The famous Elizabethan soldier and writer, a friend and contemporary of Spenser, who dedicated more than one of his works to him. *The Countess of Pembroke's Arcadia* is the pastoral romance alluded to by Cowley, in which rural life is painted as of unbroken felicity.

11. *Monsieur d'Urfe.* Honoré d'Urfe, count of Chateauneuf, born 1572, wrote a romance called *Astræa*, something in the same style as Sydney's *Arcadia.* The scene is laid on the river Lignon, a tributary of the Loire in La Forrest.

14. *Chertsea.* Now written *Chertsey.* It is a small town in Surrey, on the Thames, where Cowley retired towards the close of his life.

19. *in the Court &c.* i.e. among courtiers or merchants, or the legal crowd that throng Westminster-hall.

24. *St Paul's advice.* 1 Cor. vii. 29.

28. *mundum ducere.* Here Cowley alludes to a Latin mode of expression. When a man marries he is said uxorem *ducere*, i.e. 'to lead' (as if he were the head) his wife; whereas the woman was said marito *nubere*, 'to veil or cover herself' for her husband, and thus admit his superiority. Thus Cowley says men must bear themselves to the world. They must lead not follow.

PAGE 156.

1. The passage is from Claudii Claudiani *Epigrammata* II.

26. *Benacus.* A lake in Gallia Transpadana, not far from Verona. But near though it be the old man has not seen it, any more than the Red Sea.

27. *a third age.* That is, he lives to be known among his grandchildren.

IX. THE SHORTNESS OF LIFE AND UNCERTAINTY OF RICHES.

PAGE 157.

14. *Pas de Vie.* The strait (narrow term) of life, as the narrow strip of water at the Straits of Dover is named the *Pas de Calais.* More force still is given to the remark when it is remembered that *pas* = a step.

16. Pindar. *Pythian* VIII. 135.

17. *Our Saviour bounds our desires.* By teaching us to pray only for *daily* bread. Also (Matth. vi. 34) 'Take no (undue) thought for the morrow.'

PAGE 158.

2. *tam brevi &c.* Adapted from Horace, *Odes* II. 16. 17.

4. *Millenaries.* The Millenarians, or Chiliasts, believed that Christ would come to reign with His saints a thousand years upon earth. This was to take place before the general resurrection, though there must be a resurrection of the saints preceding it. Their notion was founded upon the 20th chapter of the Apocalypse.

5. *the patriarchs.* Their lives were very long. The longest is that of Methuselah (Gen. v. 27), which was 969 years.

21. *As we are taught.* Psalm xc. 12.

27. *Spatio brevi &c.* The passage, which is translated in the next line, is from Horace *Odes* I. 11. 6.

33. *Vitæ summa &c.* From Horace, *Odes* I. 4. 16.

34. *O! quanta &c.* 'Oh, how great is the madness of those who lay the foundation of long hopes.'

PAGE 159.

2. *Senecio,* see above p. 132, l. 19.

11. *Insere &c.* Verg. *Ecl.* I. 73.

13. *graff.* We now write 'graft.' For the older form cf. Rom. xi. 23, 'God is able to *graff* them in.' Cf. also 'engraff' below p. 160, l. 23.

17. *poor rich man in St Luke.* Luke xii. 16—20.

PAGE 161.

2. *husband.* A thrifty person, an economist. Cf. Shakes. *Taming of the Shrew* V. I. 71, 'While I play the good *husband* at home, my son and my servant spend all.'

11. *travail,* i.e. travel.

X. THE DANGER OF PROCRASTINATION.

PAGE 163.

7. *ærugo mera,* i.e. 'nought but rust.'

14. *cum dignitate otium.* 'Ease with dignity.'

15. *Joshua.* Alluding to Josh. x. 12.

19. *two sixes.* The highest throw of the dice, and so making a man a winner.

PAGE 164.

4. *Idomeneus.* He was of Lampsacus, and was a disciple and friend of Epicurus. (See Diog. Laert. X. 23. 25.)

27. *utere velis.* Juvenal I. 149.

30. *beaten up,* i.e. attacked, broken into.

31. *band.* A neckcloth and collar.

PAGE 165.

1. *Festina lente,* i.e. hasten slowly.

7. *sapere aude.* Horace, *Epist.* I. 2. 40. The whole passage is translated l. 17 etc.

11. *portam &c.* From Varro, *De re rustica,* I. 2. 2.

PAGE 166.

3. *Jam cras &c.* Persius *Sat.* v. 68.

14. *Triarii.* Soldiers in a Roman army, who formed the third rank from the front, and so did not come into the conflict so soon as those of the two foremost ranks. Hence the remark in the text.

PAGE 167.

5. *preposterous.* According to the literal meaning of the Lat. *præposterus:* reversing the order of things, putting the last first.

XI. OF MYSELF.

PAGE 169.

10. *An ode.* The quotation below is from Cowley's *Sylva,* and is entitled 'A Vote' by which the author means 'a wish' or 'a prayer.'

PAGE 170.

2. *Sabine.* See above p. 110, l. 20.
12. *out of Horace.* Hor. *Od.* III. 29. 41—48.

PAGE 171.

5. *violent public storm.* It was in 1643, or perhaps the year before, in the midst of the civil war, that Cowley was obliged to leave Cambridge.
10. *one of the best persons.* Lord Jermyn, afterwards earl of St Albans. (See Introduction.)
11. *one of the best princesses.* Queen Henrietta Maria.
27. *rid,* i.e. rode. In a previous passage, p. 130, l. 20, Cowley wrote *rod.*

PAGE 172.

3. *Well then.* This poem is from Cowley's *Mistress,* and is entitled 'The Wish.'

PAGE 173.

20. Apollo was the god of poetry and music, as well as of prophecy.
22. *Thou neither great.* The extract is from the poem on 'Destinie' in the *Pindarick Odes* of Cowley.

PAGE 174.

15. *Ben.* That is, Ben Jonson, a later contemporary of Shakespeare, and author of many dramas, the best known of which is 'Every Man in his humour.' Jonson died in 1637.
17. *acquit,* i.e. accomplish, effect. The verb in this sense is not often found.
25. *Non ego &c.* Hor. *Od.* II. 17. 10.

PAGE 175.

13. *quantum sufficit,* i.e. just sufficient.
19. *a vestal flame.* A repetition of the idea 'Let constant fires' in the previous line. The fire on the altar of Vesta was kept ever-burning.
27. *ana.* A term in use in medical prescriptions to signify 'equal quantities' of any ingredients.

PAGE 176.

30. *the other three,* i.e. the elements of air, earth and water.

PAGE 177.

3. *score.* Count up and make into a total. The word in modern days is largely confined to the game of cricket. Cf. Shakes. *Othello* IV. 1. 130. Have you *scored* me? (i.e. made up my reckoning.)

NOTES. 243

PREFACE TO 'CUTTER OF COLEMAN STREET.'

PAGE 178.

1. *a comedy call'd the Guardian.* This was acted in Trinity College before Prince Charles, in March 164½, the prince being then rather less than twelve years old.

4. *the troubles.* Euphemistic for 'the civil war and the Commonwealth times.'

10. *this new name.* Cutter of Coleman Street. Cutter is one of the characters in the play, described in the list of *dramatis personæ* as "a merry, sharking fellow about the town, pretending to have been a Colonel in the King's army." He has a comrade of the same kidney, called Worm.

PAGE 179.

5. *twenty years.* On Cowley's service to the Royal cause during all the troubles, see 'Introduction.'

17. *continu'd,* i.e. unbroken, uniform.

PAGE 180.

6. *Deacon Soaker.* He is one of the characters in the play, and described as 'a little fuddling deacon.'

12. *two sharks.* These are Cutter and Worm.

16. *at London.* The preposition sounds strange in our ears. We should say 'in London.'

19. *cavaliers.* The name given to the adherents of the Royal party in the civil wars.

33. *will take no colour,* i.e. cannot be made to wear any semblance of truth. Cf. above p. 142, l. 18.

PAGE 181.

1. *a true gentleman.* This character in the play is Colonel Jolly, a gentleman whose estate was confiscated in the late troubles. Mrs Lucia is his niece, left under his guardianship, and the circumstances alluded to in the preface are those in which the Colonel is tempted to take advantage of his authority as guardian to help himself out of difficulties by means of her fortune.

19. *allay.* We now write 'alloy,' but this is not the older spelling; cf. Ben Jonson, *On Vulcan*:

> 'But thou'lt say,
> There were some pieces of as base *allay*
> And as false stamp there, parcels of a play
> Fitter to see the firelight than the day;
> Adulterate moneys, such as would not go.'

31. *the lees of Romulus.* 'fæx Romuli' is found in Cicero *ad Att.* II. I. 8.

PAGE 182.

2. *Sed &c.* 'But now was no place for these things.' From Horace *Ars Poetica* 19.

8. *whose skulls are not yet bare.* In allusion to the custom of placing the heads of great offenders on London Bridge, Temple Bar, or elsewhere, and leaving them to be worn bare by the ravages of birds and the action of the weather.

14. *Harrison's return.* The reference is to one of Cutter's speeches, in which he is professing to be one of the strictest of the Puritans, and uttering prophecies after the fashion of some of them. 'I say again, I am to return, and to return upon a purple dromedary, which signifies Magistracy, with an axe in my hand that is call'd Reformation, and I am to strike with that axe upon the gate of Westminster Hall, and cry, Down Babylon, and the building call'd Westminster Hall is to run away, and cast itself into the river, and then Major General Harrison is to come in green sleeves from the North upon a sky-coloured Mule, which signifies heavenly instruction.'

26. *wretchless,* i.e. reckless. Cf. Hooker, *Sermon* (ii. 23) *on Jude:* 'It is want of faith in ourselves, which makes us *wretchless* in building others.'

Also Article xvii. in the Book of Common Prayer, '*wretchlessness* of most unclean living.'

29. *plant it almost wholly with divinity.* He alludes no doubt to the largest of his poems, the Davideis, a sacred poem of the troubles of David. No one can read these essays without being struck with the amount of Scriptural allusion and reference which they contain. We need go no farther for an illustration than lines 9 and 10 of the next page.

PAGE 183.

13. *piece.* Not unfrequently used for some work of art, a picture or a statue. Cf. Shakes. *Winter's Tale,* v. 2. 104, 'Her mother's statue...a *piece* many years in doing and now newly performed by that rare Italian master Julio Romano.'

So *Timon of Athens,* I. 1. 255 (of a picture) 'When dinner's done, shew me this *piece.*'

29. *reparations.* 'Cutter of Coleman Street' was the result of a remodelling of the former play 'The Guardian.'

34. *Tully says.* Cicero's words are (*Pis.* 2.) 'fors domina campi.'

PAGE 184.

9. *brutals,* i.e. brutish persons. An instance of an adjective used as a noun, which has fallen out of the language. Cf. p. 48, l. 16 above on '*intellectuals.*'

16. *the strictest conjurations of a paternal blessing.* Meaning 'I would conjure him, if he desired my blessing, to have done with this folly of poetry.'

33. *Qui multis &c.* The line, which is at once translated, is from Lucretius, *de Rer. Nat.* III. 1038.

PAGE 185.

INDEX TO THE NOTES.

CAMBRIDGE: PRINTED BY C. J. CLAY, M.A. AND SONS, AT THE UNIVERSITY PRESS.

THE PITT PRESS SERIES.

I. GREEK.

Platonis Apologia Socratis. With Introduction, Notes and Appendices by J. ADAM, B.A., Fellow and Classical Lecturer of Emmanuel College. *Price 3s. 6d.*

Herodotus, Book VIII., Chaps. 1—90. Edited with Notes and Introduction by E. S. SHUCKBURGH, M.A., late Fellow of Emmanuel College. *[Nearly ready.*

Sophocles.—Oedipus Tyrannus. School Edition, with Introduction and Commentary by R. C. JEBB, Litt.D., LL.D. Professor of Greek in the University of Glasgow. *Price 4s. 6d.*

Xenophon—Anabasis. With Introduction, Map and English Notes, by A. PRETOR, M.A. Two vols. *Price 7s. 6d.*

—— **Books I. III. IV. and V.** By the same Editor. *Price 2s.* each. **Books II. VI. and VII.** *Price 2s. 6d.* each.

Xenophon—Cyropaedeia. Books I. II. With Introduction and Notes by Rev. H. A. HOLDEN, M.A., LL.D. *Price 6s.*

Xenophon—Agesilaus. By H. HAILSTONE, M.A., late Scholar of Peterhouse, Cambridge. *Price 2s. 6d.*

Luciani Somnium Charon Piscator et De Luctu. By W. E. HEITLAND, M.A., Fellow of St John's College, Cambridge. *3s.6d.*

Aristophanes—Ranae. By W. C. GREEN, M.A., late Assistant Master at Rugby School. *Price 3s. 6d.*

Aristophanes—Aves. By the same. New Edition. *3s. 6d.*

Aristophanes—Plutus. By the same Editor. *Price 3s. 6d.*

Euripides. Hercules Furens. With Introduction, Notes and Analysis. By A. GRAY, M.A., and J. T. HUTCHINSON, M.A. New Edition with additions. *Price 2s.*

Euripides. Heracleidæ. With Introduction and Critical Notes by E. A. BECK, M.A., Fellow of Trinity Hall. *Price 3s. 6d.*

Plutarch's Lives of the Gracchi. With Introduction, Notes and Lexicon by Rev. H. A. HOLDEN, M.A., LL.D., Examiner in Greek to the University of London. *Price 6s.*

Plutarch's Life of Sulla. With Introduction, Notes, and Lexicon. By the Rev. H. A. HOLDEN, M.A., LL.D. *Price 6s.*

London: Cambridge Warehouse, Ave Maria Lane.

II. LATIN.

P. Vergili Maronis Aeneidos Libri I.—XII. Edited with Notes by A. Sidgwick, M.A., Tutor of Corpus Christi College, Oxford. *Price 1s. 6d.* each.

P. Vergili Maronis Georgicon Libri I. II. By the same Editor. *Price 2s.* **Libri III. IV.** By the same Editor. *Price 2s.*

Gai Iuli Caesaris de Bello Gallico Comment. I. II. III. With Maps and Notes by A. G. Peskett, M.A. Fellow of Magdalene College, Cambridge. *Price 3s.*

—— **Comment. IV. V., and Comment. VII.** *Price 2s.* each.

—— **Comment. VI. and Comment. VIII.** By the same Editor. *Price 1s. 6d.* each.

M. Tulli Ciceronis Oratio Philippica Secunda. With Introduction and Notes by A. G. Peskett, M.A. *Price 3s. 6d.*

M. T. Ciceronis de Amicitia. Edited by J. S. Reid, Litt. D., Fellow of Gonville and Caius College. Revised edition. *3s. 6d.*

M. T. Ciceronis de Senectute. By the same Editor. *3s. 6d.*

M. T. Ciceronis Oratio pro Archia Poeta. By the same Editor. Revised edition. *Price 2s.*

M. T. Ciceronis pro L. Cornelio Balbo Oratio. By the same Editor. *Price 1s. 6d.*

M. T. Ciceronis pro P. Cornelio Sulla Oratio. By the same Editor. *Price 3s. 6d.*

M. T. Ciceronis in Q. Caecilium Divinatio et in C. Verrem Actio. With Notes by W. E. Heitland, M.A., and H. Cowie, M.A., Fellows of St John's College, Cambridge. *Price 3s.*

M. T. Ciceronis in Gaium Verrem Actio Prima. With Notes by H. Cowie, M.A., Fellow of St John's Coll. *Price 1s. 6d.*

M. T. Ciceronis Oratio pro L. Murena, with English Introduction and Notes. By W. E. Heitland, M.A. *Price 3s.*

M. T. Ciceronis Oratio pro Tito Annio Milone, with English Notes, &c., by John Smyth Purton, B.D. *Price 2s. 6d.*

M. T. Ciceronis pro Cn. Plancio Oratio, by H. A. Holden, LL.D. Second Edition. *Price 4s. 6d.*

M. T. Ciceronis Somnium Scipionis. With Introduction and Notes. Edited by W. D. Pearman, M.A. *Price 2s.*

Quintus Curtius. A Portion of the History (Alexander in India). By W. E. Heitland, M.A. and T. E. Raven, B.A. With Two Maps. *Price 3s. 6d.*

M. Annaei Lucani Pharsaliae Liber Primus, with English
Introduction and Notes by W. E. HEITLAND, M.A., and C. E.
HASKINS, M.A., Fellows of St John's Coll., Cambridge. 1s. 6d.

P. Ovidii Nasonis Fastorum Liber VI. With Notes by A.
SIDGWICK, M.A., Tutor of Corpus Christi Coll., Oxford. 1s. 6d.

Beda's Ecclesiastical History, Books III., IV. Edited, with
a life, Notes, Glossary, Onomasticon and Index, by J. E. B.
MAYOR, M.A., and J. R. LUMBY, D.D. Revised Edition. 7s. 6d.

III. FRENCH.

La Canne de Jonc. By A. DE VIGNY. Edited with Notes by
Rev. H. A. BULL, M.A., late Master at Wellington College. *Price 2s.*

Bataille de Dames. By A. E. SCRIBE. Edited by Rev.
H. A. BULL, M.A. *Price 2s.*

Jeanne D'Arc. By A. DE LAMARTINE. Edited with a Map
and Notes Historical and Philological, and a Vocabulary, by Rev.
A. C. CLAPIN, M.A., St John's College, Cambridge. *Price 2s.*

Le Bourgeois Gentilhomme, Comédie-Ballet en Cinq Actes.
Par J.-B. Poquelin de Molière (1670). By the same Editor. 1s. 6d.

La Picciola. By X. B. SAINTINE. The Text, with Introduction, Notes and Map. By the same Editor. *Price 2s.*

La Guerre. By MM. ERCKMANN-CHATRIAN. With Map,
Introduction and Commentary by the same Editor. *Price 3s.*

Le Directoire. (Considérations sur la Révolution Française.
Troisième et quatrième parties.) Revised and enlarged. With
Notes by G. MASSON, B.A. and G. W. PROTHERO, M.A. *Price 2s.*

Lettres sur l'histoire de France (XIII—XXIV). Par AU-
GUSTIN THIERRY. By GUSTAVE MASSON, B.A. and G. W.
PROTHERO, M.A. *Price 2s. 6d.*

Dix Années d'Exil. Livre II. Chapitres 1—8. Par MADAME
LA BARONNE DE STAËL-HOLSTEIN. By G. MASSON, B.A. and
G. W. PROTHERO, M.A. New Edition, enlarged. *Price 2s.*

Histoire du Siècle de Louis XIV. par Voltaire. Chaps. I.—
XIII. Edited with Notes by GUSTAVE MASSON, B.A. and G. W.
PROTHERO, M.A. *Price 2s. 6d.*

—— **Part II. Chaps. XIV.—XXIV.** By the same. With
Three Maps. *Price 2s. 6d.*

—— **Part III. Chaps. XXV. to end.** By the same. 2s. 6d.

Lazare Hoche—Par ÉMILE DE BONNECHOSE. With Three
Maps, Introduction and Commentary, by C. COLBECK, M.A. 2s.

London: Cambridge Warehouse, Ave Maria Lane.

Le Verre D'Eau. A Comedy, by SCRIBE. Edited by C. COLBECK, M.A. *Price 2s.*

M. Daru, par M. C. A. SAINTE-BEUVE (Causeries du Lundi, Vol. IX.). By G. MASSON, B.A. Univ. Gallic. *Price 2s.*

La Suite du Menteur. A Comedy by P. CORNEILLE. With Notes Philological and Historical, by the same. *Price 2s.*

La Jeune Sibérienne. Le Lépreux de la Cité D'Aoste. Tales by COUNT XAVIER DE MAISTRE. By the same. *Price 2s.*

Fredégonde et Brunehaut. A Tragedy in Five Acts, by N. LEMERCIER. By GUSTAVE MASSON, B.A. *Price 2s.*

Le Vieux Célibataire. A Comedy, by COLLIN D'HARLEVILLE. With Notes, by the same. *Price 2s.*

La Métromanie. A Comedy, by PIRON, with Notes, by the same. *Price 2s.*

Lascaris ou Les Grecs du XVᴱ Siècle, Nouvelle Historique, par A. F. VILLEMAIN. By the same. *Price 2s.*

IV. GERMAN.

Selected Fables. Lessing and Gellert. Edited with Notes by KARL HERMANN BREUL, M.A., Lecturer in German at the University of Cambridge. *Price 3s.*

Zopf und Schwert. Lustspiel in fünf Aufzügen von KARL GUTZKOW. By H. J. WOLSTENHOLME, B.A (Lond.). *Price 3s. 6d.*

Die Karavane, von WILHELM HAUFF. Edited with Notes by A. SCHLOTTMANN, PH. D. *Price 3s. 6d.*

Hauff, Das Wirthshaus im Spessart. By A. SCHLOTTMANN, Ph.D., late Assistant Master at Uppingham School. *Price 3s. 6d.*

Culturgeschichtliche Novellen, von W. H. RIEHL. Edited by H. J. WOLSTENHOLME, B.A. (Lond.). *Price 4s. 6d.*

Uhland. Ernst, Herzog von Schwaben. With Introduction and Notes. By the same Editor. *Price 3s. 6d.*

Goethe's Knabenjahre. (1749 — 1759.) **Goethe's Boyhood.** Arranged and Annotated by W. WAGNER, Ph. D. *Price 2s.*

Goethe's Hermann and Dorothea. By W. WAGNER, Ph. D. Revised edition by J. W. CARTMELL. *Price 3s. 6d.*

Der Oberhof. A Tale of Westphalian Life, by KARL IMMERMANN. By WILHELM WAGNER, Ph.D. *Price 3s.*

Der erste Kreuzzug (1095—1099) nach FRIEDRICH VON RAUMER. THE FIRST CRUSADE. By W. WAGNER, Ph. D. *Price 2s.*

London: Cambridge Warehouse, Ave Maria Lane.

A Book of German Dactylic Poetry. Arranged and Annotated by WILHELM WAGNER, Ph.D. *Price 3s.*

A Book of Ballads on German History. Arranged and Annotated by WILHELM WAGNER, PH. D. *Price 2s.*

Der Staat Friedrichs des Grossen. By G. FREYTAG. With Notes. By WILHELM WAGNER, PH. D. *Price 2s.*

Das Jahr 1813 (THE YEAR 1813), by F. KOHLRAUSCH. With English Notes by the same Editor. *Price 2s.*

V. ENGLISH.

Theory and Practice of Teaching. By the Rev. E. THRING, M.A., Head Master of Uppingham School. New edition. *4s. 6d.*

John Amos Comenius, Bishop of the Moravians. His Life and Educational Works, by S. S. LAURIE, A.M., F.R.S.E. Second Edition, Revised. *Price 3s. 6d.*

Outlines of the Philosophy of Aristotle. Compiled by EDWIN WALLACE, M.A., LL.D. Third Edition, Enlarged. *4s. 6d.*

The Two Noble Kinsmen, edited with Introduction and Notes by the Rev. Professor SKEAT, Litt.D. *Price 3s. 6d.*

Bacon's History of the Reign of King Henry VII. With Notes by the Rev. Professor LUMBY, D.D. *Price 3s.*

Sir Thomas More's Utopia. With Notes by the Rev. Professor LUMBY, D.D. *Price 3s. 6d.*

More's History of King Richard III. Edited with Notes, Glossary, Index of Names. By J. RAWSON LUMBY, D.D. *3s. 6d.*

Cowley's Essays. With Introduction and Notes, by the Rev. Professor LUMBY, D.D. *Price 4s.*

Locke on Education. With Introduction and Notes by the Rev. R. H. QUICK, M.A. *Price 3s. 6d.*

A Sketch of Ancient Philosophy from Thales to Cicero, by JOSEPH B. MAYOR, M.A. *Price 3s. 6d.*

Three Lectures on the Practice of Education. Delivered under the direction of the Teachers' Training Syndicate. *Price 2s.*

General aims of the Teacher, and Form Management. Two Lectures delivered in the University of Cambridge in the Lent Term, 1883, by F. W. FARRAR, D.D. and R. B. POOLE, B.D. *Price 1s. 6d.*

Milton's Tractate on Education. A facsimile reprint from the Edition of 1673. Edited, with Introduction and Notes, by OSCAR BROWNING, M.A. *Price 2s.*

Other Volumes are in preparation.

London: Cambridge Warehouse, Ave Maria Lane.

𝕮𝖍𝖊 𝕮𝖆𝖒𝖇𝖗𝖎𝖉𝖌𝖊 𝕭𝖎𝖇𝖑𝖊 𝖋𝖔𝖗 𝕾𝖈𝖍𝖔𝖔𝖑𝖘 𝖆𝖓𝖉 𝕮𝖔𝖑𝖑𝖊𝖌𝖊𝖘.

GENERAL EDITOR: J. J. S. PEROWNE, D.D.,
DEAN OF PETERBOROUGH.

"It is difficult to commend too highly this excellent series, the volumes of which are now becoming numerous."—*Guardian.*

"The modesty of the general title of this series has, we believe, led many to misunderstand its character and underrate its value. The books are well suited for study in the upper forms of our best schools, but not the less are they adapted to the wants of all Bible students who are not specialists. We doubt, indeed, whether any of the numerous popular commentaries recently issued in this country will be found more serviceable for general use."—*Academy.*

"Of great value. The whole series of comments for schools is highly esteemed by students capable of forming a judgment. The books are scholarly without being pretentious: information is so given as to be easily understood."—*Sword and Trowel.*

Now Ready. Cloth, Extra Fcap. 8vo.

Book of Joshua. By Rev. G. F. MACLEAR, D.D. With Maps. *2s. 6d.*

Book of Judges. By Rev. J. J. LIAS, M.A. *3s. 6d.*

First Book of Samuel. By Rev. Prof. KIRKPATRICK, M.A. With Map. *3s. 6d.*

Second Book of Samuel. By Rev. Prof. KIRKPATRICK, M.A. With 2 Maps. *3s. 6d.*

First Book of Kings. By Rev. Prof. LUMBY, D.D. *3s. 6d.*

Book of Job. By Rev. A. B. DAVIDSON, D.D. *5s.*

Book of Ecclesiastes. By Very Rev. E. H. PLUMPTRE, D.D., Dean of Wells. *5s.*

Book of Jeremiah. By Rev. A. W. STREANE, M.A. *4s. 6d.*

Book of Hosea. By Rev. T. K. CHEYNE, M.A., D.D. *3s.*

Books of Obadiah and Jonah. By Arch. PEROWNE. *2s. 6d.*

Book of Micah. Rev. T. K. CHEYNE, M.A., D.D. *1s. 6d.*

Books of Haggai and Zechariah. By Arch. PEROWNE. *3s.*

Gospel according to St Matthew. By Rev. A. CARR, M.A. With 2 Maps. *2s. 6d.*

London: Cambridge Warehouse, Ave Maria Lane.

Gospel according to St Mark. By Rev. G. F. MACLEAR, D.D. With 4 Maps. 2s. 6d.

Gospel according to St Luke. By Archdeacon FARRAR. With 4 Maps. 4s. 6d.

Gospel according to St John. By Rev. A. PLUMMER, M.A., D.D. With 4 Maps. 4s. 6d.

Acts of the Apostles. By Rev. Professor LUMBY, D.D. With 4 Maps. 4s. 6d.

Epistle to the Romans. Rev. H. C. G. MOULE, M.A. 3s. 6d.

First Corinthians. By Rev. J. J. LIAS, M.A. With Map. 2s.

Second Corinthians. By Rev. J. J. LIAS, M.A. With Map. 2s.

Epistle to the Ephesians. By Rev. H. C. G. MOULE, M.A. 2s. 6d.

Epistle to the Hebrews. By Arch. FARRAR, D.D. 3s. 6d.

General Epistle of St James. By Very Rev. E. H. PLUMPTRE, D.D. 1s. 6d.

Epistles of St Peter and St Jude. By Very Rev. E. H. PLUMPTRE, D.D. 2s. 6d.

Epistles of St John. By Rev. A. PLUMMER, M.A., D.D. 3s. 6d.

Preparing.

Book of Genesis. By Very Rev. the Dean of Peterborough.

Books of Exodus, Numbers and Deuteronomy. By Rev. C. D. GINSBURG, LL.D.

Second Book of Kings. By Prof. LUMBY, D.D.

Book of Psalms. By Rev. Prof. KIRKPATRICK, M.A.

Book of Isaiah. By W. ROBERTSON SMITH, M.A.

Book of Ezekiel. By Rev. A. B. DAVIDSON, D.D.

Epistle to the Galatians. By Rev. E. H. PEROWNE, D.D.

Epistles to the Philippians, Colossians and Philemon. By Rev. H. C. G. MOULE, M.A.

Epistles to the Thessalonians. By Rev. W. F. MOULTON, D.D.

Book of Revelation. By Rev. W. H. SIMCOX, M.A.

The Cambridge Greek Testament for Schools and Colleges,

with a Revised Text, based on the most recent critical authorities, and English Notes, prepared under the direction of the General Editor,

J. J. S. PEROWNE, D.D., DEAN OF PETERBOROUGH.

Gospel according to St Matthew. By Rev. A. CARR, M.A.
With 4 Maps. 4s. 6d.

Gospel according to St Mark. By Rev. G. F. MACLEAR, D.D.
With 3 Maps. 4s. 6d.

Gospel according to St Luke. By Archdeacon FARRAR.
With 4 Maps. 6s.

Gospel according to St John. By Rev. A. PLUMMER, M.A.
With 4 Maps. 6s.

Acts of the Apostles. By Rev. Professor LUMBY, D.D.
With 4 Maps. 6s.

First Epistle to the Corinthians. By Rev. J. J. LIAS, M.A. 3s.

Epistle to the Hebrews. By Archdeacon FARRAR, D.D.
[*In the Press.*

Epistle of St James. By Very Rev. E. H. PLUMPTRE, D.D.
[*Preparing.*

Epistles of St John. By Rev. A. PLUMMER, M.A., D.D. 4s.

London: C. J. CLAY AND SONS,
CAMBRIDGE WAREHOUSE, AVE MARIA LANE.
Glasgow: 263, ARGYLE STREET.
Cambridge: DEIGHTON, BELL AND CO.
Leipzig: F. A. BROCKHAUS.

CAMBRIDGE: PRINTED BY C. J. CLAY, M.A. & SONS, AT THE UNIVERSITY PRESS.

www.ingramcontent.com/pod-product-compliance
Lightning Source LLC
Chambersburg PA
CBHW030730280326
41926CB00086B/1036